PHARMACEUTICAL ANALYSIS

Theory, Methodology and Drug Assay

PHARMACEUTICAL ANALYSIS
Theory, Methodology and Drug Assay

Volume I

Ashutosh Kar

Professor & Head of Pharmacy,
Shri RNS College of Pharmacy, Gormi, Bhind (MP)

Formerly

Professor, School of Pharmacy, Addis Ababa University,
Addis Ababa (Ethiopia)

Dean, Chairman & Professor, Faculty of Pharmaceutical Sciences,
Guru Jambheshwar University, Hisar (India)

Professor, School of Pharmacy, Al Arab Medical University,
Benghazi (Libya)

Professor, College of Pharmacy (University of Delhi), Delhi (India)

Professor & Head, Department of Pharmaceutical Chemistry,
Faculty of Pharmaceutical Sciences, University of Nigeria,
Nsukka (Nigeria)

CBSPD

CBS Publishers & Distributors Pvt Ltd

New Delhi • Bengaluru • Chennai • Kochi • Kolkata • Lucknow • Mumbai
Hyderabad • Jharkhand • Nagpur • Patna • Pune • Uttarakhand

PHARMACEUTICAL ANALYSIS
Vol I

ISBN: 978-81-239-1477-0

First Edition: 2007
Reprint: 2010, 2015, 2017, 2018, 2020, 2023, **2025**

Published by **Satish Kumar Jain** and produced by **Varun Jain** for

CBS Publishers & Distributors Pvt Ltd

4819/XI Prahlad Street, 24 Ansari Road, Daryaganj, New Delhi 110 002, India.
Ph: 011-23266838, 23289259   Website: www.cbspd.com
                                    e-mail: delhi@cbspd.com

Corporate Office: 204 FIE, Industrial Area, Patparganj, Delhi 110 092
Ph: 011-4934 4934   Fax: 011-4934 4935
                           e-mail: publishing@cbspd.com; publicity@cbspd.com

Branches

- **Bengaluru:** Seema House 2975, 17th Cross, KR Road, Banasankari 2nd Stage, Bengaluru 560 070, Karnataka, India
  Ph: +91-80-26771678/79   Fax: +91-80-26771680   e-mail: bangalore@cbspd.com
- **Chennai:** 7, Subbaraya Street, Shenoy Nagar, Chennai 600 030, Tamil Nadu, India
  Ph: +91-44-26680620, 26681266   Fax: +91-44-42032115   e-mail: chennai@cbspd.com
- **Kochi:** 42/1325, 1326, Power House Road, Opp KSEB, Power House, Ernakulum Kochi 682 018, Kerala, India
  Ph: +91-484-4059061-65,67   Fax: +91-484-4059065   e-mail: kochi@cbspd.com
- **Kolkata:** 147, Hind Ceramics Compound, 1st Floor, Nilgunj Road, Belghoria, Kolkata-700056, West Bengal, India
  Ph: +033-25633055, 033-25633056   e-mail: kolkata@cbspd.com
- **Lucknow:** Basement, Khushnuma Complex, 7 Meerabai Marg (Behind Jawahar Bhawan), Lucknow-226001, UP, India
  Ph: +0522-4000032   e-mail: tiwari.lucknow@cbspd.com
- **Mumbai:** PWD Shed, Gala no 25/26, Ramchandra Bhatt Marg, Next to JJ Hospital Gate no. 2, Opp. Union Bank of India, Noorbaug, Mumbai-400009, Maharashtra, India
  Ph: 022-66661880/89   e-mail: mumbai@cbspd.com

Representatives

• Hyderabad	0-9885175004	• Jharkhand	0-9811541605	• Nagpur	0-8692091830
• Patna	0-9334159340	• Pune	0-9664372571	• Uttarakhand	0-9716462459

Printed at Neekunj Print Process, Haryana, India

Dedication

The present book is humbly dedicated to the following Scientists and Researchers who have immensely contributed to the vast domain of Pharmaceutical Analysis:

- Arrhenius
- Bronsted
- Fajan
- Franklin
- Gay-Lussac
- Goldberg
- Hober
- Handerson
- Hastings
- Hasselbalch
- Klemensiewics
- Lewis
- Lowry
- Mohr
- Nernst
- Ostwald
- Sendroy
- Volhard
- Waage
- Walker

It's not that I'm so smart, it's just that I stay with problems longer.

—Albert Einstein

Ability is what you are capable of doing.
Motivation determines what you do.
Attitude determines how well you do it.

—Napoleon Hill

Preface

Latest emerging trends in **Pharmaceutical Analysis**, in its own right, amply demonstrates that it essentially and predominantly encompasses almost any kind of **Quantitative Determination** that provides information with respect to the **chemical composition of an analyte.**

In a broader perspective such nagging, uncertain, ambiguous, unreliable, and non-reproducible results have been profusely replaced by distinctly quantified, most trustworthy, accurately repeatable, duly validated, and widely accepted ultimate results. In fact, the scope for chemical interferrents, lower limit of detection, poor data, non-replicable measurements, and lengthy-tedious assay procedures have been virtually reduced to a bear minimum level.

Nevertheless, the utmost objective of the **pharmaceutical analysis** is to practise, perform, and participate in the quantitative estimation of life-saving **drugs** in its *purest form* as well as *dosage form* from **mg** (milligramme) to **pg** (picogramme) levels. Therefore, the unique judicious blend of skill, wisdom, passion, talent, and dogged determination is indeed a prime requirement to accomplish perfect and precise results.

The present text exclusively deals with *five* important chapters, namely: (a) *Theoretical Aspects of Quantitative Analysis*; (b) *Acid-Base (Neutralization) Titrations*; (c) *Oxidation-Reduction Titrations*; (d) *Precipitation Titrations*, and (e) *Gravimetric Analysis*, which have been duly elaborated as per the AICTE stipulated norms (2000) meant for **Bachelor of Pharmacy (B. Pharm.) Programmes** throughout the Indian universities, and also covering similar degree programmes in the pharmacy schools abroad.

The principal features and cardinal structure of the textbook solely revolve around the basic theoretical concepts and ideas; extensively elabroated treatment of the subject matter in the most lucid, crisp, and simple language; adequately illustrated diagramatic sketches and graphics; studded with appropriate and exhaustive examples; *Probable Questions* at the end of each chapter; and above all an up-to-date *Further Readings* as well as well-documented *Foot Note References* wherever required throughout the entire text material.

It is earnestly believed that the excellent and dedicated faculty members in all the **Pharmacy Degree Institutions** across India, the African continent, South-East Asia, the Indian continent and the

Arab countries will certainly find the present textbook highly subjective, informative and educative in acquiring the latest knowledge in **Pharmaceutical Analysis**. It is earnestly expected that the text will also grossly benefit to brilliant students embarking on **Research Careers through Ph.D.**, or allied **Research Degree Programmes** who might really seek an honest elabororative introduction to various latest emerging techniques in the better familiarization with **Pharmaceutical Analysis**.

The author is pleased to place on record the excellent cooperation due to Shri S.K. Jain, MD, CBS Publishers & Distributors, and to Shri B.R. Sharma and his superb production team in bringing out this book in a record time frame.

Gurgaon (India)   **Ashutosh Kar**
January, 2007

B. Pharm. Syllabus as per A.I.C.T.E. 2000

PHARMACEUTICAL ANALYSIS - I

1. **Theoretical Aspects of Quantitative Analysis:** Significance of quantitative analysis in quality control. Different techniques of analysis. Preliminaries and definitions. Significant figures. Rules for retaining significant digits. Types of errors. Mean deviation. Standard deviation. Statistical treatment of small data sets. Selection of sample. Precision and accuracy. Fundamentals of volumetric analysis. Methods of expressing concentration. Primary and secondary standards.

2. **Acid-Base Titrations:** Acid-base concepts. Role of solvent. Relative strengths of acids and bases. Ionization. Law of mass action. Common ion effect. Ionic product of water. pH. Hydrolysis of salts. Henderson-Hesselbalch equation. Buffer solutions. Neutralization curves. Acid-base indicators. Polyprotic system. Polyamine and amino acid systems. Amino acid titration. Applications in assay of H_3PO_4, NaOH, $CaCO_3$ etc.

3. **Oxidation-Reduction Titrations:** Concepts of oxidation and reduction. Redox reactions. Strengths and equivalent weights of oxidizing and reducing agents. Theory of redox titrations. Redox indicators. Cell representations. Measurement of electrode potential. Oxidation-reduction curves. Iodimetry and iodometry. Titrations involving ceric sulphate, potassium iodate, potassium bromate, potassium permanganate, titanous chloride and sodium 2,6-dichlorophenol indophenol.

4. **Precipitation Titrations:** Precipitation reactions. Solubility products. Effect of acids, temperature and solvent upon the solubility of a precipitate. Argentometric titrations and titrations involving ammonium or potassium thiocyanate, mercuric nitrate, and barium sulphate. Indicators. Gay-Lussac method. Mohr's method. Volhard's method and Fajan's method.

5. **Gravimetric Analysis:** Precipitation techniques. Solubility products. The colloidal state. Supersaturation co-precipitation. Post-precipitation. Digestional washing of the precipitate. Filtration. Filter papers and crucibles. Ignition. Thermogravimetric curves. Specific examples like barium sulphate, aluminium as aluminium oxide, calcium as calcium oxalate and magnesium as magnesium pyrophosphate. Organic precipitants.

Contents

3. Oxidation-Reduction Titrations   78–121

PHARMACEUTICAL ANALYSIS
Volume I

Contains

1

Theoretical Aspects of Quantitative Analysis

1.1 INTRODUCTION

In a broader sense **the theoretical aspects of quantitative analysis** or **pharmaceutical analysis** or **drug assay** still very much retains a strategical place, status, and recognition in the Diploma as well as Degree Curriculum in most of the Indian Universities imparting Pharmacy programmes. It is, however, pertinent to state here that there are two reasonably vital and important aspects of 'pharmaceutical analysis' to a **professional pharmacist**, namely:

(*a*) As an expert on drugs a pharmacist's knowledge is judiciously exploited not only in the development, production, and distribution of drugs, but also in the appropriate usage of drugs in their respective analysis, and

(*b*) A good component of the '**pharmaceutical analysis**' related information is found to be critically fundamental to various analytical techniques; besides, the results that are directly involved in certain other specified allied fields, for instance: **pharmaceutics**, **medicinal chemistry**, **biotechnology**, **biochemistry**, **phytochemistry** and the like.

Nevertheless, another school of thought advocates that a comprehensive analytical data essentially deals with **bulk drugs**, **dosage forms** (or **secondary pharmaceutical products**); and more recently and abundantly a full range of biological samples *viz.*, *blood, urine, serum, cerebriospinal fluid* (**CSF**), *sputum*, very much in support of a plethora of such extensive and intensive investigative studies *as:* **bioavailability**, **biopharmaceuticals**, and **pharmacokinetics**.

The main objective and aim of **quantitative analysis** is to carry out the determination of the quantitative contents of the individual compounds or elements present in a **drug substance**.

Example: SHELCAL-500 [Calcium and Vitamin D Tablets]*; It contains 1.25 g of **Calcium Carbonate**, derived from an '**organic source**' (**Oyster Shell**) equivalent to 500 mg of the '**elemental calcium**'.

In such typical instances, the analytical results are invariably expressed in terms of the **percentages.** In the analysis of calcium carbonate [$CaCO_3$] one may actually observe what percentages

---

* Manufactured by: Elder Pharmaceuticals Ltd., Mumbai (India)

Ca (Calcium), C (Carbon), and O (Oxygen) are present actually. Bearing in mind the fact that $CaCO_3$ (Calcium Carbonate) may be considered as a combination of CaO (Calcium Oxide) together with CO_2 (Carbonic Anhydride), the ultimate composition of this particular salt (*i.e.*, $CaCO_3$) is also frequently expressed in terms of the corresponding percentages of the *two* **oxides** CaO and CO_2 respectively.

1.2 IMPORTANCE OF QUANTITATIVE ANALYSIS IN QUALITY CONTROL

Quantitative **pharmaceutical analysis** is of enormous importance and relevance not only confined to the ever expanding knowledge in various disciplines of science, but also in industry, particularly the pharmaceutical industry for the critical analysis of raw materials, intermediates, and final dosage forms (*i.e.,* the secondary pharmaceutical products).

Salient Features

The various salient features with respect to the **quantitative analysis in quality control** are as enumerated under:

1. **Chemical Formula of an Unknown Substance:** The chemical formula of an 'unknown substance' either synthesized in the laboratory or isolated from naturally occurring plant sources is invariably determined and established from the percentage contents of its constituents found by actual analysis.

2. In fact, the '**chemical analysis**' represents the backbone of a plethora of most important method of investigation; and, therefore,employed extensively and profusely in practically all branches of science that are intimately associated to chemistry.

   Examples: It finds its abundant utility in pharmaceutical analysis of both inorganic and organic chemical substances, microbiology, biochemistry, biotechnology, pharmaceutical technology, besides, certain highly specific disciplines *e.g.,* physiology, geology, minerology, medical, and agricultural sciences.

3. The '**chemical analysis**' possesses an enormous potential in a **pharmaceutical industry** in particular, and other **allied industries** in general. On a rather more specific note—a '**pharmacist**' should be fully aware at each and every step of the adopted **production process** the **qualitative** as well as the **quantitative** chemical composition of the materials (substances) that have undergone expected and desired **conversion** (or modification).

   Example: **Thermogravimetric Analysis (TGA) of Calcium Oxalate Monohydrate:** It has been duly observed that a large number of chemical substances usually get decomposed upon heating. In fact, this very idea and concept of heating a particular given sample to observe carefully the ensuing weight variations is the underlying principle of thermogravimetric analysis (TGA). Interestingly, the TGA of Ca-oxalate monohydrate represents the '**dynamic thermogravimetric analysis**' wherein the said sample is specifically subjected to conditions of predetermined and controlled continuous increase in temperature which is mostly observed to be '**linear with time**'.

Method

The '**thermogram**' for calcium oxalate monohydrate $[CaC_2O_4.H_2O]$ is duly represented in Figure 1.1. One may, however, distinctly observe the **successive plateaus,** namely:

(*i*) Correspond to the **anhydrous oxalate** (100-250°C),

(*ii*) Correspond to the **anhydrous calcium carbonate** (400-500°C), and

(*iii*) Correspond to the **calcium oxide** (700-850°C).

In other words, the *three* observed plateaus (in Fig. 1.1) clearly designate the following vital aspects of the decomposition curve, namely:

(*a*) clear indication of **constant weight**, and

(*b*) stable phases encountered within a specified temperature interval.

The various distinct **chemical reactions** that are actually involved may be summarized as follows:

$$CaC_2O_4 \cdot H_2O \xrightleftharpoons[\textbf{STAGE-1}]{100\text{-}250°C} CaC_2O_4 \; [+H_2O\uparrow] \xrightleftharpoons[\textbf{STAGE-2}]{400\text{-}500°C} CaCo_3 \; [+CO\uparrow] \xrightleftharpoons[\textbf{STAGE-3}]{700\text{-}850°C} CaO \; [+CO^2\uparrow]$$

Calcium oxalate monohydrate   Calcium oxalate   Calcium carbonate   Calcium oxide

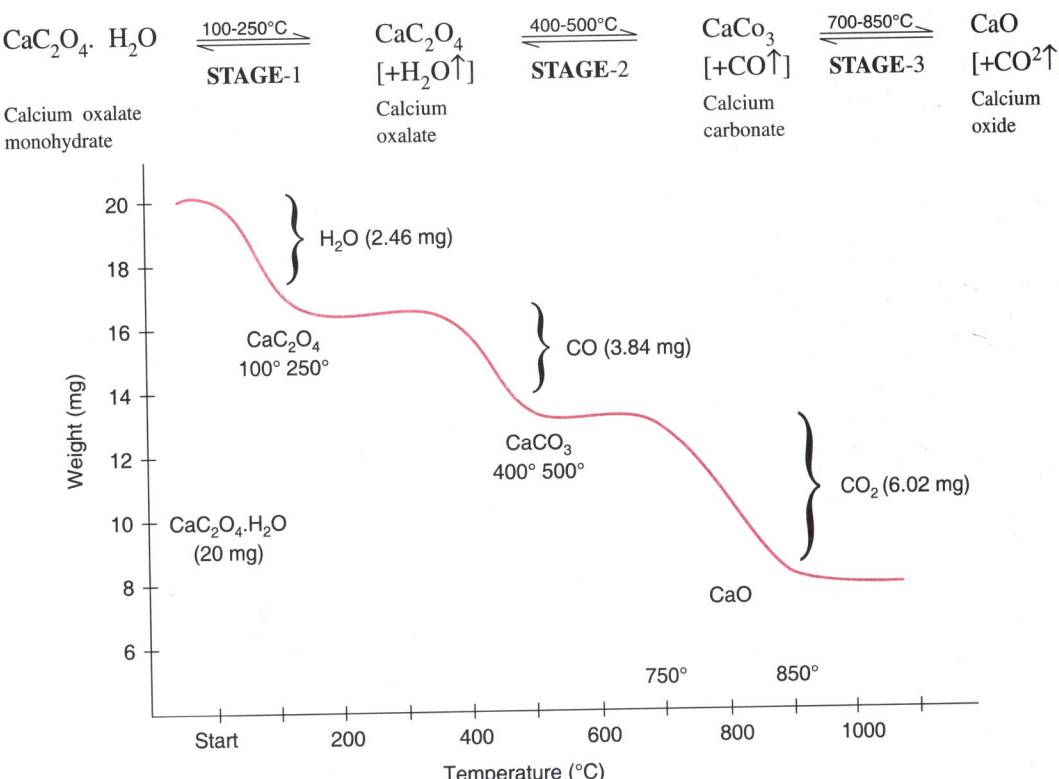

Fig. 1.1 Thermogravimetric Analysis (TGA) of Calcium Oxalate Monohydrate at the Rate of 6°C per Minute.

Explanations

The adequate explanations of the *three* cardinal stages intimately encountered in Fig. 1.1 are as given below:

STAGE-1

The inherent water of crystallization (or hydration) from calcium oxalate monohydrate is virtually lost that corresponds to 2.46 mg (12.3%) equivalent to 1 mole of water (H_2O) between the temperature range 100-250°C.

In actual practice, the 12.3% weight loss that usually occur between 100-250°C must correspond to 12.3% of the original formula weight for $CaCo_3.H_2O$ (FW = 146). Therefore, the product which gets lost eventually has a formula weight (FW) of 0.123 × 146 = 17.958 ($\simeq$ 18.0), and it definitely corresponds to H_2O **(water)**.

STAGE-2

One mole of carbon monoxide (CO) gets evolved from calcium oxalate $[CaC_2O_4]$, corresponding to 3.84 mg (19.2%) between the temperature varying from 400-500°C.

In fact, the 19.2% weight loss which took place between 400-500°C must actually correspond to 19.2% of the original formula weight of 146. Hence, the resulting product being produced bears a formula weight of 0.192 × 146 = 28.0, which corresponds to **CO (carbon monoxide)**.

STAGE-3

At this **'final stage'** one mole of CO_2 (carbon dioxide) gets evolved from one mole of $CaCO_3$ (calcium carbonate) which eventually corresponds to 6.02 mg (3.01%) in the temperature range varying between 700-850°C.

Interestingly, the weight loss corresponding to 3.01% which occurred in the temperature range between 700-850°C should be equivalent to 3.01% of the original formula weight (FW) of 146. Hence, the generated product bears a formula weight of 0.301 × 146 = 43.946 ($\simeq$ 44), and it corresponds to CO_2 **(carbon dioxide)**.

4. As to date, this is a widely accepted common practice that no **'drug substance'** is either taken into the production zone of released for actual consumption without proper quality control screening that essentially characterize its overall quality, stability, and suitability for various purposes. Importantly, these **ultimate results** serve *two* major objectives, namely:

   (a) to form the fundamental basis of **all the processing calculations, and**

   (b) to determine precisely the **'naked costs'** of the various **material inputs** that predominantly serve as the core basis of **all financial estimates.**

5. In a broader perspective, the utmost importance of adequate and proper control of production is quite evident. Hence, it is absolutely necessary that each and every **pharmaceutical industry** should essentially have an **well-equipped analytical laboratory** under the command of a qualified, experienced, and highly motivated pharmaceutical-analysis personnels. The latest trend is to name such laboratories as: **Quality Assurance Laboratory:** and **Quality Control Laboratory** (a rather older nomenclature), for the chemical control, physical parameters, and microbiological screening of raw materials, intermediates, and finished products.

6. In actuall practice, however, the pharmaceutical analyst's major problem is most commonly simplified to a great extent significantly, by virtue of the fact that the **'qualitative composition'** of majority of the investigated products *viz.,* raw materials, pure drug substances, chemical additives, pharmaceutical adjuvants, intermediates, and finished dosage forms is well-known (as described in the **'official compendia'** *e.g.,* IP, BP, USP, Eur. P., Int. P etc.). Furthermore, the approximate contents of the individual elements are obviously known quite frequently.

Evidently, in such particular instances the usual preliminary qualitative analysis becomes more or less unnecessary absolutely, thereby rendering the proper selection of the most appropriate technique of the **'quantitative analysis'** becomes much more easier and meaningful.

1.3 DIFFERENT TECHNIQUES OF PHARMACEUTICAL ANALYSIS

Over the years, the domain of **'Pharmaceutical Analysis'** have witnessed the emergence of a host of vital and important different techniques that have been used predominantly in the analysis of raw materials, intermediates, and finished dosage forms (*i.e.*, secondary pharmaceutical products). Each individual technique of **'Pharmaceutical Analysis'** is essentially governed by an underlying principle which caters to the dependable and reproducible assay of several **'official drug substances'**, pharmaceutical adjuncts, chemical additives, and preservatives as well.

A few typical variant technique frequently, and abundantly employed in **'Pharmaceutical Analysis'** are as enumerated under:

(*i*) Volumetric Analysis,

(*ii*) Gravimetric Analysis,

(*iii*) Biomedical Analysis,

(*iv*) Aqueous Titrations,

(*v*) Non-Aqueous Titrations,

(*vi*) Redox Titrations,

(*vii*) Iodometry,

(*viii*) Bromometry,

(*ix*) Argentometric Techniques,

(*x*) Complexometric Analysis,

(*xi*) Thermoanalytical Analysis,

(*xii*) Diazotization Method, and

(*xiii*) Tetrazolium Assay of Steroids.

The various **pharmaceutical analytical methods** described from (*i*) through (*xiii*) shall now be treated individually with a few typical examples.

1.3.1 Volumetric Analysis

In general, the **Volumetric Analysis** exhibits an enormous advantage *vis-a-vis* the **gravimetric method** by virtue of the significantly rapid speed of the former. The actual assays are distimctly more rapid due to the fact that instead of weighing the **'reaction product'** (as in **Gravimetric Method**) the actual volume of a reagent solution consumed for the reaction is being measured carefully. Thus, the **Concentration** (termed as the **'titre value'**) of the solution under investigation is determined accurately and precisely.

Titre value

The titre of a solution is normally regarded as the mean number of grammes of substance per 1 ml of solutions.

Example: The titre of the H_2SO_4 solution is found to be 0.0049 g. mL^{-1} (Mol. wt. of H_2SO_4 is 49), which signifies that 1 mL of this H_2SO_4 solution contains 0.0049 g H_2SO_4. Thus, in the present instance:

$$T_{H_2SO_4} = 0.0049 \text{ g.mL}^{-1}$$

where, T = Titre value (with the formula of the actual substance *i.e.*, H_2SO_4 in question)

Standard Solution: A solution for which the **titre value** is known precisely is usually termed as a **Standard Solution.**

Comparison of Volumetric Analysis Vs Gravimetric Analysis

Following are some of the vital points of difference between the **Volumetric Analysis** and the **Gravimetric Analysis:**

Volumetric Analysis	Gravimetric Analysis
1. It is a much more rapid method of estimation that involves only one operation *i.e.*, titration, which normally takes only a few minutes with practice.	1. It is a rather lengthy and tedious method which involves a series of vital steps *viz*, precipitation, ripening of precipitate, filtration, washing, ignition of the empty crucible, and the crucible with the precipitate.
2. It is a somewhat less precise method of estimation.	2. It is a more precise method of '**assay**', because weighing on an '**analytical balance**' is regarded to be rather more percise in comparison to the volume determination using a buretle.*
3. It is regarded to be more versatile and a more specific method based on certain chemical reactions involved in the assay.	3. It is not so broad-based because of its prime requirement that the '**analyte**'** has got to be precipitated in one form or the other.

*However, with proper precautions and expert working mode the actual difference is found to be so small that it may be disregarded in most instances.

** **Analyte:** The chemical entity (or substance) which requires to be determined precisely by any one of the approved methods of assay.

1.4 COMPUTATION OF ANALYTICAL RESULTS

The accumulation of copius volumes of the **analytical results** has critically necessitated their **computation** with respect to the following aspects, such as:

(*a*) Addition and Subtraction,

(*b*) Multiplication and Division,

(*c*) Rounding Numbers, and

(*d*) Retention of as Many Significant Figures.

The aforesaid different aspects of **computation of analytical results,** otherwise known as **'Computation Rules',** shall now be treated individually with appropriate example in the sections that follows:

1.4.1 Addition and Subtraction

In this particular instance, retain only as many decimal places as do they appear in the number that has the fewest decimals.

Example: Add algebraically the numbers given: 18.46+8.375–4.5450+116.9.

Following *three* steps need to be carried out sequentially:

(*i*) All numbers are required to be rounded up first and foremost in to *two* **decimal places.**

(*ii*) Add the rounded numbers, and

(*iii*) Final result is then rounded to **one decimal place.**

$$
\begin{array}{rr}
+ \ 18.46 & + \ 18.46 \\
+ \ 8.375 & + \ 8.38 \\
- \ 4.5450 & - \ 4.55 \\
+ \ 116.9 & + \ 116.9 \\
\hline
& \textbf{148.29}
\end{array}
$$

Final rounding gives: **148.3**

Note: **This specific method tends to eliminate the accumulation of rounding errors in the final result.**

1.4.2 Multiplication and Division

In multiplication or division, retain in each term one more significant figure than is contained in the term with the largest uncertainty. Nevertheless, the percentage precision of product cannot be greater than the percentage precision of the least precise term entering the calculation. Therefore, the **multiplication:** $3.64 \times 2.127 \times 0.9524 \times 34.9453$ must be achieved employing the values:

$$3.64 \times 2.127 \times 0.952 \times 34.95$$

which is equal to 257.6042. Hence, the result thus obtained may be expressed to **five significant figures** as **257.60.**

1.4.3 Rounding Numbers

In an attempt to **rounding numbers,** always drop the last digit in case it happens to be less than 5, *viz.,* 7.63 shall turn out to be 7.6. In case, the last digit is more than 5, always enhance the preceding digit by one *viz.,* 8.38 shall become 8.4. In the event, the digit to be dropped is 5, always round up the preceding digit to the **nearest even number** *i.e.,* 7.75 shall become 7.8; and 9.65 will become 9.6. Obviously, this particular method avoids a tendency to round up numbers in one direction only.

Importantly, while rounding off quantities to the nearest correct number of significant figures, add one to the last figure retained provided the following figure is either 5 or more than 5. Hence, the average of 0.6526, 0.6521, and 6.6524 is 0.6525 (0.65237).

1.4.4 Retention of as many Significant Figures

In actual practice, always **retain as many significant figures** in a result as will yield **only one uncertain figure.**

Example: A weight, to the nearest 0.1 mg is duly recorded as 2.4500 g; and it should not be written as either 2.450 g or 2.45 g, because in the **latter instance** and accuracy of a **centigram** is categorically emphasized, whereas in the **former instance** a **milligram.**

1.5 PRELIMINARIES AND DEFINITIONS

In actual practice, one may invariably come across a plethora of **Preliminaries and Definitions** that are specifically used in the present context of **Pharmaceutical Analysis.** An attempt has been made to look into some of these aspects briefly, such as:

(*i*) Statistical Validation,	(*ii*) Validation of a Method,
(*iii*) Titrimetric (Volumetric) Analysis,	(*iv*) Instrumental Analysis,
(*v*) Sources of Errors in Weighing,	(*vi*) Protein-Free Filtrates,
(*vii*) Quality Control Chart,	(*viii*) True Value,
(*ix*) Sample Size,	(*x*) Minimum Number of Samples,
(*xi*) Precision,	(*xii*) Sensitivity,
(*xiii*) Range,	(*xiv*) Limit of Detection,
(*xv*) Precision of a Result, and	(*xvi*) Limit of Quantitation.

1.5.1 Statistical Validation

After having carried out the thorough investigation of different aspects of possible '**determinate errors**', and having applied the relevant corrections, one may observe that the '**analytical data**' thus generated invariably show **apparent fluctuations** that are observed to be absolutely **random in nature.** The powerful, magical, and effective **technique of statistics** may ultimately turn such results, which usually scatter in a random manner, into a better form which could be used intelligently and judiciously. Evidently, the particular desired **statistical treatment of the calibration data,** duly helped by **preprogrammable calculators** and **micro-computers,** frequently gives rise to a fairly accurate and more presentable determination of the '**graphs**' plotted between **absorbance** and **concentration** in comparison to those obtained manually.

In fact, the **statistical validation** of analytical results has the following *six* aspects, which may be employed both extensively and intensively to accomplish clear-cut acceptable results:

(*a*) Statistical treatment of '**Finite Samples**',

(*b*) Distribution of '**Random Errors**',

(*c*) **Significant Errors,**

(*d*) **Composition of Results,**

(*e*) Method of '**Least Squares**', and

(*f*) Criteria for '**Rejection of an Observation**'.

1.5.2 Validation of a Method

In actual practice, a great care should be taken that accurate and precise results are duly accomplished in a **pharmaceutical analysis.** It is, however, pertinent to mention here that the best way and means to **validate a method (technique)** is to analyze a **standard reference substance (material)*** of known composition.

One may critically observe that each and every measurement essentially possesses some sort of imprecision associated with it, that predominantly gives rise to **certain array of random distribution of results,** such as:

(*a*) **Gaussian Distribution:** The number of individual sample increments needed to accomplish a given level of confidence in the **'analytical results'** is usually estimated by the following expression:

$$n = \frac{t^2 S^2{}_s}{r^2 x^{-2}}$$

...(*i*)

where, t = Student t value for the desired confidence level,

$S^2{}_s$ = Sampling variance,

r = **Acceptable** relative standard deviation of the average of the analytical results, $\overline{x}$;

S_s = **Absolute** standard deviation, in the same unit as $\overline{x}$; and hence, x is unitless.

S_s and $\overline{x}$ = Values are invariably obtained from the **preliminary measurements** or from the **prior knowledge.**

Equation (*i*) actually holds good for a **Gaussian Distribution** of analyte concentrations very much with in the bulk material, *i.e.,* it would be centered around x having **68%** of the values falling within **one standard deviation** or even upto **95%** very much within **two standard deviations.**

Therefore, the experiment may be carefully planned and designed in such a fashion so as to narrow its range, but it cannot be eliminated completely.

(*b*) **Systematic Error:** A **systematic error** refers to one that specifically **biases a result consistently in one direction.**

(*c*) **Sample Matrix:** The **sample matrix** (*i.e.,* and environment in which a sample gets developed) may usually suppress the signal emanated by an instrument.

(*d*) The **weight of an analytical balance** may be in error, made biased either high or low.

(*e*) The sample may not be dried sufficiently.

***BPCRS:** British Pharmacopoea Chemical Reference Substance;

EPCRS: Europeon Pharmacopoea Chemical Reference Substance;

Salient Features

The various **salient features** of **validation of a method** are as enumerated under:

1. Proper calibration of an 'analytical instruments' is regarded to be the very first step in assuring utmost accuracy.

2. While 'developing a new method', the samples must be 'spiked' adequately with known exact quantum of the 'analyte'(*i.e.,*both above and beyond what is already present in the sample).

3. The exact quantum as determined by the proposed analysis procedure* must fall very much within the accuracy required necessarily in the analysis.

4. However, a **New Method** may be validated legitimately by comparing the sample results with those obtained with another **accepted method** *viz.,* 'official method' (as in IP, BP, USP, EurP., and Int. P.,).

5. **Certified standards (or Reference Materials)**: There exist various sources of **Certified standards** or **reference materials** which could be analyzed to standards for pure drug substances in dosage forms.

6. **National Institute of Standards and Technology (NIST)** provides the **Standard Reference Materials (SRMs)** having various matrix compositions (*e.g.,* ground leaves, roots, seeds, barks, stems, fruits etc.) which has been **duly certified** for the exact and precise content of the **particular analytes,** by meticulous and careful estimation by **at least two independent methods.**

7. The determined 'assay values' are adequately assigned with **statistical ranges.**

8. In the present globalization scenario one may avail the involvement of 'different testing agencies' and the 'commercial concerns' across the world that may provide adequate samples for **Round-Robin** or **Blind Tests** wherein the so-called 'control samples' are duly submitted to the participating laboratories for **carrying out the desired analysis at random.****

9. The 'standards' (*viz.,* BPCRS, EPCRS) must be run intermitently with the 'samples'.

10. **Quality Control Chart:** A **control sample** must be run atleast every day; and the **results** thus obtained be **plotted as a function of time** to produce a **quality control chart,** which is subsequently compared with the **known standard deviation of the method.**

11. **Relationship with Gaussian Distribution:** In reality, the measured amount (quantity) is **perceptually assumed to be constant with time** *vis-a-vis* a **Gaussian Distribution,** and thus *two* distinct situations arise, namely:

    (*a*) when there exists a **1 in 20 chance** the **observed values** will very much **fall outside two standard deviations from the known value,** and

    (*b*) when there exists a **1 in 100 chance** the **observed values** shall distinctly fall **2.5 standard deviations away.*****

---

  * After due subtraction of the amount apparently present in the sample as estimated by the same methodology.

 ** The laboratory is not aware of the 'control value prior to analysis'.

*** The **numbers** exceeding these limits usually suggest **uncompromised errors,** *viz,* **improper callibration, reagent spoilage,** and **instruments malfunction**.

12. **Good Laboratory Practice (GLP) Validation: GLP validation** is of great utility and importance because it is emphatically required to assure accuracy of analyses.

In actual practice, the **Government Regulations** duly promulgated essentially demand and very much require the carefully proven and established **protocol and validation of methods and analyses** when implied exclusively for absolutely **official** and critically **legal** purposes. For the benefit of all, the **World Health Organization (WHO)** has documented well defined **GLP-Guidelines** in order to assure adequate **validation of analysis.**

1.5.3 Titrimetric (Volumetric) Analysis

The **titrimetric (volumetric) analysis,** in a broader perspective, comprises of the most accurate and reasonably precise measurement of the interacting solutions or reagents.

It essentially makes usage of a good number of certified ('A'-Class) graduated glass apparatus, for instance: burettes, pipettes, volumetric flasks, and measuring cylinders of different capacities (volumes).

In reality, the method based on accurate measurement of the volume of a **reagent solution of accurately known concentration** (*i.e.,* **standard solution**), used up for a specific chemical reaction is termed as **volumetric (titrimetric) analysis.**

It is, however., pertinent to state here that in the volumetric determinations it is quite obvious and necessary to establish precisely and exactly the end point of the on-going reaction, and this is not possible always. Besides, the ensuing interactive reaction itself should invariably satisfy a number of experimental parameters. Therefore, the applicability of the **volumetric analysis** is evidently for more restricted in comparison to that of the **gravimetric analysis.**

Advantage

An important and vital advantage of the titrimetric (volumetric) method is its greater fast speed, which being extremely critical and advantageous in actual practice, such as: quick and precise control and management of **chemical on-going processes.**

Emphatically, the specific **chemical reactions** that are solely associated with **typical colour changes** are invariably utilized in quantitative determinations for instance:

Fe^{3+} ions are swiftly detected by the aid of either KCNS (potassium thiocyanate) or NH_4CNS (ammonium thiocyanate), to give rise to the production of soluble ferrous thiocyanate [Fe $(CNS)_2$] which has a deep red colouration according to the following reaction:

$$FeCl_3 \quad + \quad 2NH_4CNs \quad \longrightarrow \quad Fe\ (CNS)_2 \quad + \quad 3NH_4Cl$$

| Ferrie chloride | | Ammonium thiocyanate | | Ferrous thiocyanate | |

Formation of Sparingly Soluble Reaction Products

Besides, the aforesaid distinct and apparent colour changes, certain specific reactions followed immediately by the **formation of sparingly soluble reaction products** are occasionally employed for estimation. In actual practice, the exact quantum of a given element in solution is duly detemined from the ensuing **'degree of turbidity'** of the solution produced by certain reagent or other, when compared with the turbidity of a corresponding standard solution. And the underlying techniques that are based on this particular principle are known as **naphelometric assays.**

1.5.4 Instrumental Analysis

In general, the instruments are much **more selective** and **significantly sensitive** in comparison to the **titrimetric (volumetric)** and the **gravimetric methods of assay.**

Precisely, the **instrument techniques** are employed both extensively and intensively for several critical analyses and hence constitute the ever-expanding discipline of **instrumental analysis.** Consequently, these highly sophisticated methods of analyses are entirely based upon the specific measurements caused by a certain physical characteristic feature of the sample under investigation *viz.,* **electrical property, applied magnetic field, electron bombardment, or absorption of electromagnetic radiation, chromatography, X-ray spectroscopy.**

Examples: The various typical examples of the **instrumental analysis** are as given under:

(*a*) **Electroanalytical chemistry** *e.g.,* potentiometric, electrolytic, voltammetric.

(*b*) **Applied Magnetic Field** *e.g.,* nuclear magnetic resonance (NMR) spectroscopy.

(*c*) **Electron Bombardment** *e.g.,* mass spectroscopy.

(*d*) **Absorption of Electromagnetic Radiation** *e.g.;* infrared (IR), ultraviolet (UV) or visible spectrophotometry

(*e*) **Chromatography** *e.g.,* gas chromatography (GC), high performance liquid chromatography (HPLC), and high performance thin-layer chromatography (HPTLC).

(*f*) **X-Ray Spectroscopy** *e.g.,* absorption spectroscopy and fluorescence spectroscopy.

Salient Features

The **salient features** of **instrumental analysis** are as described under:

1. Generally, the **instrumental techniques** are relatively more selective and sensitive in comparison to the **classical techniques** but are definitely less precise, on the order of 1 to 5% or so.

2. Most of these **analytical instrumental techniques** happen to be appreciably much more expensive, capitalwise. However, based on the actual number of analyses being performed per 8-hour shift they may prove to be much less expensive when one takes into consideration the **exhorbitant personnel costs.**

3. In fact, most of these **instrumental techniques** are invariably much more rapid, fast, less time consuming, may be automated and fully computerized, and are certainly capable of measuring more than one '**analyte**' at a given time frame.

4. The **hi-tech chromatographic methodologies** (*viz,* GC, HPLC, and HPTLC) are proved to be specifically powerful for **analyzing complex mixtures** of synthetic drug substances as well as various major classes of naturally occurring plant materials. These techniques usually carry out the desired separation and articulated measurement step(s) simultaneously. The various chemical entities (constituents) are duly separated as they are eluted sequentially from a column of suitable adsorbent that particularly interacts with the, '**analytes**' to varying extents; and, therefore, the '**analytes**' are sensed meticulously with an appropriate detector

(*viz.*, UV-detector, Fluorescence detector, Refractive-Index detector, Multipurpose detector, and Electrochemical detectors)*—as they emerge from the column, to produce a transient-peak signal, which being, directly proportional to the exact quantum of '**analyte**' present in the complex mixture.

Table 1.1 records the comparative characteristic features of various analytical techniques, for instance: range, mole per litre (mol. L^{-1}), percentage precision, speed, selectivity, cost-factor, and major applications.

Table 1.1 Comparative Characteristic Features of Various Analytical Techniques						
Analytical Technique	**Approx. Range [mol. L^{-1}]**	**Speed**	**Selectivity**	**Cost Factor**	**Approx. Precision**	**Major Applications**
1 **Titrimetry (Volumetry)**	10^{-1} to 10^{-4}	Moderate	Poor/ Moderate	Low	0.1 to 1	Inorganic; Organic
2 **Gravimetry**	10^{-1} to 10^{-2}	Slow	–do–	–do–	0.1	Inorganic
3 **Potentiometry**	10^{-1} to 10^{-6}	Fast	Good	–do–	2	Inorganic
4 **Voltammetry**	10^{-3} to 10^{-10}	Moderate	–do–	Moderate	2 to 5	Inorganic; Organic
5 **Spectro-photometer**	10^{-3} to 10^{-6}	Fast, Moderate	Good, Moderate	Low, Moderate	2	Inorganic, Organic
6 **Fluorometry**	10^{-6} to 10^{-9}	Moderate	Moderate	Moderate,	2 to 5	Organic
7 **Atomic Spectroscopy**	10^{-3} to 10^{-9}	Fast	Good	Moderate High	2 to 10	Multielement inorganic
8 **Chromato-graphy [GC, HPLC]**	10^{-3} to 10^{-9}	Fast, Moderate	Good	Moderate High	2 to 5	Multicompo-nent; Organic

1.5.5 Sources of Errors in Weighing

A plethora of possible sources of error have been duly cited in the literature, but some of them intimately associated with '**weighing**' area as enumerated below:

(*i*) zero-point drift,

(*ii*) the weights,

(*iii*) buoyancy,

(*iv*) alteration in ambient temperature or temperatures of the object being weighed*,

(*v*) hot or cold objects require to be essentially brought to ambient temperature before actually being weighed, and

(*vi*) hygroscopic samples do have a tendency to retain moisture, specifically on being exposed to high-humidity environment both prior to and during actual weighing, which should be minimized to a great extent.

---

* Variation in ambient temperature is perhaps the greatest source of error, thereby critically causing a drift either in the '**zero**' or '**rest point**' due to air-current convections.

1.5.6 Protein-Free Filtrates

It has been observed that the proteins present in the **biological fluids**, such as: blood, serum, urine, cerebrospinal fluid etc. particularly interfere with a good number analyses; and, hence, should be eliminated non-destructively. In actual practice, one may make use of several highly specific reagents that would categorically **coagulate (precipitate)** the proteins, such as:

(*a*) Trichloroacetic acid (TCA),

(*b*) Tungstic acid (Sodium tungstate + sulphuric acid), and

(*c*) Barium hydroxide + zinc sulphate (a neutral mixture).

Methodology

A known measured volume of sample (*e.g.,* **serum**) is normally treated with a measured volume of reagent. The precipitate of the respective protein (obtained nearly within a span of 10 minutes) is either centrifuged or filtered through a dry filter paper without washing. An **aliquot** of the **protein-free filtrate (PFF)** is subsequently subjected to routine specified analysis.

1.5.7 Quality Control Chart (QCC)

Definition

The **quality control chart (QCC)** may be defined as – **'a time plot of a measured quantity which is assumed to be constant (with a Gaussian Distribution) for the purpose of ascertaining that the actual measurement very much remains within an acceptable range statistically'.**

In usual practice, a control chart is invariably constructed by periodically running a **'known'** control sample simultaneously.

Salient Features of QCC

These are as stated below:

1. QCC comprises of a **'central line'** representing either the assumed or known value of the control; besides, either one or two pairs of **'limit lines'** *viz.,* the **inner** and **outer control limits.**

2. Invariably the **standard deviation** of the entire procedure is known, and this is overwhelmingly employed to determine and establish the **control limits.**

Figure 1.2, represents the illustration of a **'control chart'** showing distinctly the following two aspects, namely:

(*a*) A plot of the every-day results of the analysis pertaining to a **pooled serum calcium,** and

(*b*) A **control sample** which is assayed either **blindly** or **randomly** together with the **'samples'** everyday.

Observations: From Fig. 1.2, one may infer the following vital and important **observations**, such as:

1. A useful **inner control limit** has essentially **two standard deviations** because there exists only 1 in 20 chance which an individual measurement may exceed this limit by chance exclusively. Ultimately, it could signify predominantly a **'warning limit'**.

2. However, the **outer control limit** could be either 2.5 or 3 ∞, in such a situation there exists only 1 in 100 chance or 1 in 500 chance, thereby a specific measurement shall certainly fall very much outside this particular range in the absence of **systematic error**.

3. In usual practice, only **one control** is run along with each batch of samples *viz.* 25 samples, which may eventually give rise to a plethora of **control points** everyday. Subsequently, one may plot the mean of these ensuing values each day.

4. **Random scatter** of the resulting values obtained in (3) above may be expected to be smaller by $\sqrt{N}$ compared to the individual points.

5. Specific attention must be given to the prevailing trends in one particular direction *i.e.*, the points mostly lie on one side of the **central line**, thereby critically suggesting that either there exists a **systematic error** or the **very control is in error** in the **entire measurement**.

6. An observed tendency for the points to fall outside the **control limits** may strongly indicate the presence of either one or more occurrence of the **determinate error** in the entire determination; and, therefore, the **analyst** should critically check the following aspects meticulously:

(*a*) Instrument malfunction,

(*b*) Deterioration of reagents, and

(*c*) Environmental and other effects.

Calcium Quality Control Chart (QCC) for January–2005

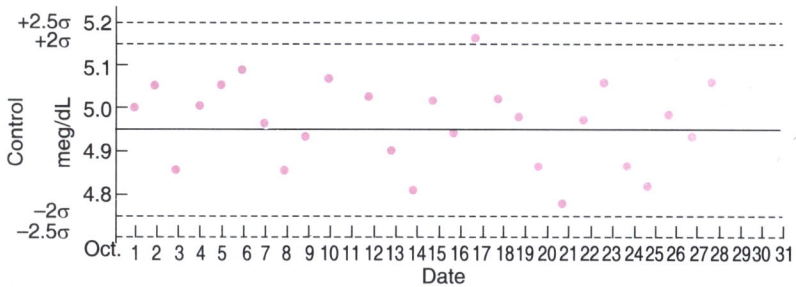

Fig. 1.2 Diagramatic Representation of a Typical **Quality Control Chart (QCC)**

1.5.8 True Value

The range wherein the **true value** falls precisely for the specific 'analyte content' in a bulk material may be determined conveniently from the *t* test at a **given confidence level** according to the following expression:

$$\mu = \bar{x} \pm \frac{ts}{\sqrt{N}}$$

where, μ = True value,

$\bar{x}$ = Values obtained from the preliminary measurements*,

---

* The average of the analytical results for the particular material analyzed.

t = Student t value for the desired confidence level,

s = Sampling variance,* and

N = Degree of freedom.

1.5.9 Sample Size

Evidently, one encounters a major problem intimately linked with the **'sampling process'** is concerned to the sample size. In actual practice, however, the **'sample size'** carefully taken from a heterogeneous material is guided exclusively by *two* cardinal factors, such as:

(*i*) Variation in particle size, and

(*ii*) Precision required in the analytical results.

The **sampling variance** V, is given by the expression:

$$V = \frac{k}{n}$$

where, k = Constant solely dependent on the size of the increment and variation very much within the bulk material, and

n = Actual number of sampling increments.

In other words, the sampling variance is inversely proportional to the actual number of the sampling increments.

It is, however, pertinent to state here that one may consider the following aspects with respect to **'sampling'**, namely:

(*i*) A major source of error in **sampling** may be introduced from the actual process of taking increments from the bulk material,

(*ii*) The accuracy of the **sample** is determined by its total size (which is solely based upon the **Random Sampling Theory**), and

(*iii*) The number of increments affected will influence directly the **sampling accuracy** only if the bulk material essentially comprises of varying **particle sizes**.

1.5.10 Minimum Number of Samples

It has been duly observed that the actual number of individual sample increments required to accomplish a **given level of confidence in the analytical results** is determined by the following expression:

$$n = \frac{t^2 S_s^2}{r^2 \bar{x}^2} \qquad \qquad \dots(a)$$

where, t = Student t value for desired confidence level,

S_s^2 = Sampling variance,

---

* The **standard deviation** which is obtained previously from analysis of identical material samples or from the current analysis provided there are sufficient samples.

r = **Acceptable relative standard deviation** of the average analytical results $(\bar{x})$,

$\bar{x}$ = Average of the analytical results,

s = Absolute standard deviation

Since, r is equivalent to $S_x/\bar{x}$, we may rewrite Eqn. (a) as under:

$$n = \frac{t^2 S_s^2}{S_x^2} \qquad ...(b)$$

In eqn. (b) S_s and S_x may be expressed either in **absolute** or **relative standard deviations** as long as they are both expressed the same.

Besides, **'n'** is not known initially, hence the **'t value'** for the **given confidence level** is determined first and foremost; and thereafter, an **interactive procedure** is usually employed to calculate **'n'**.

1.5.11 Precision

Precision may be defined as—'**the degree of agreement between the replicate measurements of the same quantity**'.

In other words, **precision** may also be referred to as the **repeatability of a result**. Thus, one may express **'precision'** as stated under:

(a) Standard deviation,

(b) Coefficient of variation,

(c) Range of the data,

(d) Confidence interval (viz., 95%), and

(e) Mean value.

It is pertinent to emphasize at this point in time that – '**good precision does not either guarantee or assure good accuracy**.

The said statement only holds good if:

• a **systematic error** in the analysis, and

• a **'weight'** employed to weigh each of the samples may be **in error.***

In general, **all real analyses** are **'unknown',** which implies mostly that **higher the degree of precision**, the **greater would be the chance of accomplishing the true value**.

Another school of thought may logically expatiate **'precision'** as—"**the agreement amongst a cluster of experimental results; however, it does not imply anything with regard to their relation to the 'true value'.**"

1.5.12 Sensitivity

The **sensitivity** may be defined as—'**the ability to distinguish clearly and distinctly two different concentrations, and is determined aptly by the slope of the calibration curve.**'

---

* This specific error fails to affect the **'precision'**, whereas it does affect the precision.'

Interestingly, one may conveniently measure either the **slope** of the calibration curve or precisely measure a variety of such samples that essentially possess narrowly related concentrations at *three* levels *viz.,* **low, intermediate, and high concentrations.**

It has been established beyond any reasonable doubt that both **sensitivity** and **precision** may govern how many significant figures must be aptly reported in a measurement.

However, the degree of sensitivity as stipulated in a **'Limit Test'** varies widely according to the standard laid down by **'official compendia'** *viz.,* IP, BP, USP, Eur. P., and Int. P.

Importantly, the **sensitivity** is predominantly modulated by a good number of **variable factors** with a common aim and objective to **produce reproducible results**, such as:

(*a*) **Gravimetric Analysis:** In 'gravimetric analysis' the extent of precipitation is modulated by the concentration of the **solute** and also of the **precipitating reagent, reaction time, reaction temperature,** and **nature/quantum** of other ingredients present in solution, and

(*b*) **Colour Tests:** The emergence of distinct and visible colouration may be accomplished by ascertaining the requisite quantities of **reagents, reactants, time period,** and stability of colour so produced.

1.5.13 Range (R)

With reference to a small set of measurements the **range (R)** proves to be highly efficient for describing the **actual spread of results in an elaborated manner**. In other words, the range really designates as good a measure with regard to the **spread of results** as in the **'standard deviation'** for either four or less measurements.

In a broader perspective, this high relative efficiency comes into being based on the fact that the **standard deviation** designates a rather poor estimate of the **'spread of results'** very much confined to a small number of observations, though one may still regard it to be the best known and best expressed real estimate for a given set of data. Therefore, in order to convert the **range*** to a measure of **'spread of results'** which is absolutely independent of the number of observations, it should be duly multiplied by the **deviation factor K**. In fact, this **'factor'** significantly adjusts the **range (R)** so that on an average it critically reflects the **'standard deviation'** of the population, which may be represented by s_r as given under:

$$s_r = RK_R$$

1.5.14 Limit of Detection

The **limit of detection** may be defined as – **'the lowest concentration level that can be estimated to be different statistically with respect to an analyte blank'.**

In actual practice, the specific concentration which critically gives rise to a signal almost **three folds the standard deviation** of the background is invariably regarded as the **limit of detection (or detection limit).**

---

* The working range of a method is the concentration range over which acceptable accuracy and precision are obtained adequately.

However, one may determine the **limit of detection** by spiking a matrix together with the analyte very close to the detection limit, such as: to accomplish a 10 fold **standard deviation signal** above the **blank mean signal.**

1.5.15 Precision of a Result

It has been proved and established as well that the **accuracy** and **precision** of an analysis is particularly limited by the **sampling procedure** rather than the **measurement procedure** adopted. In actual practice, the overall observed variance of an analysis is adequately represented by the sum of the sampling variance together with the rest of the analytical operations, which may be given by the following expression:

$$S_0^2 = S_s^2 + S_a^2$$

In case, the **actual variance on account of sampling is known***, one may gain very little by carrying out the **reduction of S_a to less than 1/3 S_s.** In other words, almost little is gained by improving the **analytical variance (S_a)** to less than one third the **sampling variance (S_s).** Therefore, in such a situation it is always better to analyze definitely more number of samples by employing a rather **'faster analytical technique'**, even with **less precise results.**

Example: Assuming that the **absolute standard deviation** for sampling is 4.0%, and that of the corresponding analysis is 1.0%, we may have:

$$S_0^2 = (1.0)^2 + (4.0)^2 = 17$$

or $\qquad\qquad S_0 = 4.123$

or $\qquad\qquad S_0 = 4.1\%$

Here, 92% of the observed imprecision is an account of the **sampling procedure,** and the remaining 8% is solely due to the **actual measurement.**** Therefore, to circumvent such anomalies in the **observed sampling imprecision**, which happens to be appreciably large, it is invariably advisable and better to make use of an exceptionally fast and rapid analytical procedure even with a **lower degree of precision**, but **instead to analyze more number of samples positively.**

1.5.16 Limit of Quantitation

The **limit of quantitation** may be referred to as – **'the lowest concentration of an analyte which can be measured in the sample matrix at a reasonably acceptable level of accuracy and precision'.**

However, one may accomplish an acceptable precision critically ranging between 10 to 20% of the **relative standard deviation** that depends exclusively upon the actual concentration levels measured.

---

* By having carried out **multiple sampling** of the substance of interest and analyzing it by employing a **precise measurement method.**

** Here, S_0 is enhanced from 4.0 to 4.1% , so 0.1% is caused due to the measurement.

1.6 SIGNIFICANT FIGURES

In general, **significant figures** may be defined as—**'the number of digits necessary to express the results of a measurement consistent with the measured precision.'**

Thus, one may observe critically that the apparent **weak link in the sequence of any analysis** is the critical and meticulous measurement which may be accomplished with the least accuracy. It is, however, pertinent to state here that it is more or less absolutely useless to extend an effort to render the other measurements of the analysis realistically more accurate in comparison to this particular **limiting measurement.**

Importantly, as there exists predominantly an element of uncertainly **(or imprecision)** in any measurement of at least **± 1 in the last significant figure,** hence the actual number of **significant figures** essentially comprises of **all the digits that are known** together with the very **first uncertain one.** In fact, each and every digit distinctly designates the actual quantum it specifies predominantly. Each and every digit duly designates the actual quantum it specifies particularly.

Example: In the number 467, one may have 4 hundreds, 6 tens, and 7 units.

Salient Features

The **salient features** of the **significant figures** are as enumerated under:

1. Digit zero (0) may be either significant component of a measurement, or it may be employed simply to place the decimal point.

2. The exact number of **significant figures** in a measurement is absolutely independent of the placement of the decimal point.

Example: Let us take into consideration the number 82,047. The said number has **four significant figures** irrespective of the strategical place where the decimal is located actually, *viz.* **82,047, μm; 8.2047 cm; 0.82047 dm; and 0.082047 m**—all of them do possess the **same number of significant figures,** besides the following criteria, namely:

- Simply signify different ways and means (*i.e.,* **units**) of expressing one specific measurement.
- Location of **'zero'** existing between **the decimal point** and **the digit 8** in the above **'last number'** is usually employed to place the **'decimal point'** exclusively.

Alternatively, one would state the *two* criteria, namely:

(*a*) proper number of **significant figures,** and

(*b*) point out which **'zeros'** deem to be **significant**, in the following **four** numbers:
0.715; 87.6; 600.0; 0.0780; as given below:

        0.715   : **three significant figures;**

        87.6   : **three significant figures; zero is also significant**

        600.0   : **four significant figures; all zeros are significant;**

        0.0780   : **three significant figures; only the last zero is significant.**

1.7 TYPES OF ERROR, *VIS-A-VIS* CONCEPT OF ERROR

Skilful quantitative determinations of various **'drug substances'** and **'secondary pharmaceutical products'** (*i.e.,* dosage forms of drugs) invariably give rise to copius volumes of results which are duly obtained as a **set of numbers** adequately symbolizing '**replicate estimations**' carried out under similar experimental parameters. Obviously, these **set of numbers** normally correspond to such characteristic informative properties (or features) as: **normality, molarity, weight of compound, percentage purity,** and the like.

However, the possible interpretation(s) of these raw data emphatically poses *two* extremely important and vital questions, such as:

(*a*) **Best estimate** pertaining to the '**true value**' of the exact quantum under determination, and

(*b*) Reliability of the '**number**' as a correct estimator of the '**true value**'.

Statistics—the highly specialized branch of mathematics, adequately and reasonably justifies the above *two* cited question. In other words, the statistical treatment of the analytical results (data) would go a long way for their critical and valid interpretations.

1.7.1 Types of Errors

An **error** usually refers to an inadvertent mistake which is intimately associated with each measurement. Although a large and appreciable segment of the so called '**obvious errors**' encountered frequently in **analytical methods** or **critical** calculations are duly eliminated, yet errors do remain and persist. Therefore, it is absolutely necessary for a '**pharmaceutical analyst**' to minimize the volume as well as the magnitude of the error to a reasonably acceptable limit and level obviously it may never be eliminated completely.

Importantly, one may usually encounter *two* different types of errors, such as: (*a*) Determinate (Systematic) Errors; and (*b*) Interminate (Random) Errors, which shall now be discussed briefly in the sections that follows:

1.7.1.1 Determinate (Systematic) Errors

The **determinate (systematic) errors** are those which are evidently incorporated by one of the following discrepancies, for instance:

(*a*) Inadequacy in the analytical technique adopted,

(*b*) Poor judgment in the analytical procedure, and

(*c*) Unconscious bias by an analyst.

Following are some of the glaring examples that would expatiate the **determinate errors** to a great extent, namely:

(*i*) **Incomplete Reaction** *i.e.,* such reaction usually caused by an **inadvertent and unavoidable equilibrium** that may incorporate an obvious error into the results based on the calculation of **complete reaction,**

(*ii*) **Stray light** *i.e.,* incorrectly seated **spectrophotometer-cell compartment cover** which evidently gives passage to **stray light,**

(*iii*) **Improper Calibration** *i.e.,* improperly calibrated analytical weight, glasswares (*viz.,* burettes, pipettes, volumetric flasks etc),

(*iv*) **Colour Blindness** *i.e.,* poorly ascertained visual end points in **volumetric (titrimetric analysis,** and (*v*) **Temperature Effect on Kw** *i.e.*, the obvious gross neglect of the temperature effect on Kw may give rise to erroneous results.

Estimation of Systematic Error

In actual practice, the **estimation of systematic error** happens to be intimately associated, with the intricate problem(s) of accuracy that need to be teken care of meticulously.

Based on the assumption that a 'true value' pertaining to the quantity under scrutiny and measurement does exit, we may take into consideration the under mentioned cardinal aspects, such as:

(*a*) **Absolute Error (E):** In fact, the **absolute error** of a measurement refers to the difference between the **observed value (O)** and the **true value (T)**; and thus we have:

$$E = O - T$$

(*b*) **Relative Error (E/T):** The **relative error** designates the ratio of **absolute error** and **true value** *i.e.,* E/T; as it is a **ratio** it bears no unit.

(*c*) **Additive Error:** It has been duly observed that quite a few 'systematic errors' are either **additive** or **proportional** in character.

An **additive error** invariably refers to the one whose **quantum as well as magnitude** certainly fulfils the following *two* important criteria, namely:

   (*i*) Remains **absolutely independent** of the ensuing 'sample size', and

   (*ii*) Causes **effectively constant absolute error** involved in a sequence of estimations with **enhancing (incremental) sample weights.**

   Example: Partial (proportional) loss of a determinant precipitate by means of **'dissolution'**; and, therefore, when the **solvent volume remains more or less identical** in a particular series of analyses, an **identical weight of the precipitate** would eventually get lost in every experiment performed sequentially.

(*d*) **Proportional Error:** One may, however, observe that a **proportional error** predominantly **increases** with the consistent **increment in sample size,** which may ultimately produce a constant relative error.

Salient Features

The various **salient features of** proportional error are as enumerated under:

   1. Incorrectly and improperly '**standardized titrant solution**' shall duly lead to a **proportional error** particularly in the titration of a series of samples with increasing weight, and

   2. In the course of either developmental or testing stages of an altogether '**new assay methodology**', different quantum of a **known sample** must be estimated carefully so as to locate strategically the following *two* aspects, namely:

   (*a*) **Systematic error,** and

   (*b*) Ascertain and determine if the **error** is **proportional** or **additive.**

Note: The said information is extremely important and may aid in the detection and elimination of the precise and exact source of error.

1.7.1.2 Indeterminate (Random) Errors

The **indeterminate (random) errors** represent distinctly the **remnant ones** *i.e.,* when most of the 'systematic errors' have been eliminated completely. However, one may observe abundantly that the estimations carried out in 'duplicate' for a **specific amount** never produced the **same number** even after employing the **maximum sensitivity of the measuring technique.**

> **Note: This observed changeability is caused predominantly by the ensuing manifestation of the random errors.**

Salient Features

The **salient features** of the **indeterminate (random) errors** are as stated under:

1. They are significantly caused by the particular limitations that are found to be inherent in the **observational technique.**

2. The **random errors** may be reduced to an appreciable extent, but never eliminated altogether.

3. **Random errors** emphatically induct a certain degree of uncertainty which is invariably associated with each and every measurement.

> **Note: The statistical methods exclusively evaluate the prevailing element of uncertainty to a reasonable extent.**

4. From the **ultimate numerical results** one may introduce the **'random errors'** at various stages, such as: **sampling, manipulation,** and **observation.**

   Example: **Titrimetric Analysis of Analgin Tablets:** In this instance the targetted manipulation might include such vital and important steps as: **weighing, preparation/standardization of solution(s), removal of aliquots by pipette,** and **titration.** Besides, the **observational component** stated above is the **exact burette reading.**

1.8 MEAN (AVERAGE) DEVIATION

It designates the average of the differences between the individual results and the mean. It is considered as a measure of variability. However, it has been duly observed that in the case of a small number of actual results the **mean deviation** is found to be not significant statistically. One may calculate the **mean (average) deviation** by adopting the following steps in a sequential manner:

(a) Find the differences between the individual results and the mean, without taking into consideration either the +ve or the –ve sign,

(b) Add all these individual deviations, and

(c) Divide by the actual number of results (*i.e.,* n).

Therefore, a **mean (average) deviation** $\bar{d}$ may be expressed as:

$$\bar{d} = \frac{\sum\limits_{i=1}^{i=n}[x_i - \bar{x}]}{n}$$

or

$$\bar{d} = \frac{\sum[x_i - \bar{x}]}{(n-1)}$$

1.9 STANDARD DEVIATION

The **standard deviation** may be defined as—'**the distance from the mean to the point of inflexion of the normal distribution curve**'.

In comparison to the **average (mean) deviation,** the **standard deviation** is invariably found to be much more meaningful and useful statistically. In actual practice, a finite number of values it is usually symbolized as 'S'; and may, therefore, be expressed as stated under:

$$S = \sqrt{\frac{\sum\limits_{i=1}^{i=n}(i-\overline{x})^2}{n-1}}$$

In case, 'n' is fairly large, say to the extent of 50 or more, it hardly matters whether the denominator in the aforesaid expression is either $n - 1$ or n; however, the former (viz., $n - 1$) is regarded to be **strictly correct.**

A graphic representation of the **normal curve** is illustrated in Figure 1.3. Hence, graphically the **standard deviation** may be showm as the **horizontal distance** from the **mean** to either **point of inflexion** of the curve as displayed in Fig. 1.3. From this figure one may notice distinctly that nearly 68% of the area within the **normal curve** (*i.e,* 68% of the entire population) lie very much within '1' **standard deviation** of the mean *viz.,* falling within the range $\mu \pm \sigma$. Besides, 95% of the entire population are observed to be included in the range $\mu \pm 2\sigma$, and more than 90% in the range $\mu \pm 3\sigma$.

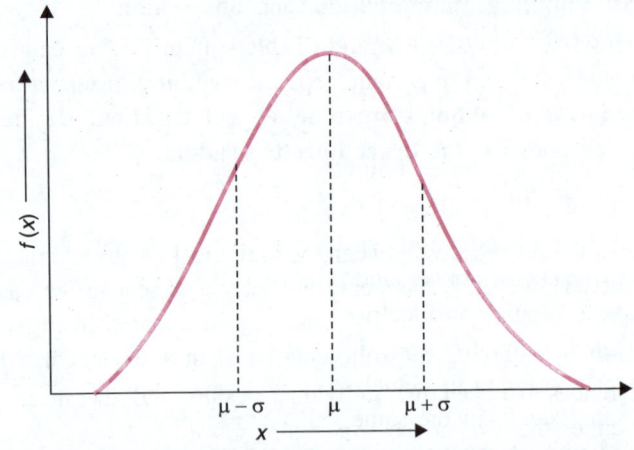

Fig. 1.3 Normal error curve with mean μ and standard deviation σ

1.10 STATISTICAL TREATMENT OF SMALL DATA SETS

It has been amply observed that there are certain specific **statistical values** which are confined strictly for a relatively **large population,** such as:

Central value (**mean** $\overline{x}$),

Spread of results (**standard deviation, x**), and

Confidence limits (*t*-test).

It is, however, pertinent to state at this point in time that in '**pharmaceutical analysis**', one specifically and typically deals with invariably less than 10 results; and virtually for a given analysis may be 2, or 3. In true sense, such **small data sets,** there are certain other estimates that may definitely prove to be much more appropriate.

Therefore, in order to afford the **statistical treatment of small data sets,** we may satisfactorily engage the **Q-test** (*i.e.,* the **rejection of a result**).

In actual practice, the **Q-test** is usually employed to estimate appropriately if an '**outlier**' is on account of a **determinate (systematic) error** (see section 7.1.1). In case, it is not, it falls eventually very much within the desired and expected **indeterminate (random) error;** and hence must be retained gracefully as expressed below:

$$Q = \frac{a}{w}$$

In other words, **Q-test** is, amongst the many proposed tests, in fact, one of the utmost statistically correct test usually performed for a relatively small number of observations; and, therefore, is overwhelmingly recommended as and when a '**test**' is an absolute necessity.

In short, the **ratio Q** is evidently calculated by carefully arranging the data in a **descending order of numbers.** The prevailing difference between the **suspect number** and its closest neighbour (**a**) is articulately divided by the range (**w**)*.

1.11 CALIBRATION OF ANALYTICAL INSTRUMENTS, APPARATUS AND APPLYING NECESSARY CORRECTIONS

Systematic (determinate) errors can be minimized appreciably and significantly by following any one of the following methods stringently and methodically, for instance:

(*a*) **Calibration of Instruments and Apparatus:** A plethora of commonly and extensively employed analytical instruments and apparatus, namely: UV-Spectrophotometer, FTIR-Spectrophotometer, Single-Pan Electric Balance, pH-Meter, Turbidimeter and Nephelometer, Flame Photometer, Refractrometer, Polarimeter, Potentiometer, and the like should be calibrated properly, prior to its actual usage in order to eliminate all possible errors to the maximum extent. Exactly in the same vein all glass/measuring apparatus essentially need to be calibrated duly *viz.,* burettes pipettes, volumetric flasks, thermometers, and analytical weight etc.; and thus, the necessary required corrections must be duly incorporated into the observed measurements.

However, in certain highly specific cases wherein the '**inherent error**' cannot simply be avoided for one reason of the other, it would be quite easy and convenient to implement a suitable correction for the '**actual error**' which it causes finally.

---

* *w*: The differences between the **highest** and the **lowest** number.

Example: The presence of the **inherent impurity** duly present in a **weighed precipitate** may be adequately determined first, and subsequently removed from its observed weight duly.

Calibration of Glassware (Apparatus): The **Calibration of glassware** to accomplish the **ultimate, superb, and excellent uncompromised accuracy** *via* the following ways and means are known widely, such as:

1. To correct duly the buoyancy of the **'water'** employed for calibration.*
2. To divide the weight of the water in vacuum by its density at a given specified temperature shall convert it (weight) to the corresponding desired volume.
3. To correct buoyancy with stainless steel (SS) weights having density **7.8 g.cm^{-3}.**

The aforesaid *three* steps are frequently used to render the volume of the glassware under calibration, either from the weight of water *contained* or *delivered* by the respected glassware.**

Examples:

1. **Glass Volumes:** The respective and specific **glass volumes** meticulously calculated for the **standard temperature of 20°C** certainly include slight adjustments for the particular **Borosilicate Glass** (*viz.*, **Pyrex or Kimax**) apparatus either undergoing contraction or expansion based on temperature variations.***
2. **Expansion of Water:** Water expands nearly 0.02% per °C around 20°C. Therefore, it is almost necessary to apply **requisite volume (concentration) corrections** by making use of the **'water-density-data'** cited in reference books thereby taking into consideration the corresponding **ratios** of the **relative densities** carefully.

Methods for Calibrating Glassware

Based on the enormous informations with respect to the actual practice and expertise one may generally calibrate glassware upto **five significant figures,** which rightly provides the **maximum degree of precision** one invariably needs either in delivering or filling solutions.

Therefore, it is absolutely necessary and important that the **'net weight of water needs to be of five figures'.** In other words, in case the particular glassware exceeds 10 mL capacity, it all requires to weigh up to 1 mg only. In order to achieve this readily and conveniently one is strongly recommended to make use of a *reasonably good quality* **Top-Loading Balance** rather than a *more sensitive* **'Analytical Balance'.**

The calibration of the *three* most abundantly used glassware are, namely: (*a*) Pipette, (*b*) Volumetric Flask, and (*c*) Burette, which shall now be treated individually in the sections that follows:

(*i*) **Calibrations of Pipette:** The **calibration of a pipette** is usually carried out by first-weighing a **'dry'** Erlenmeyer Flask with a rubber bung or a **'dry'** glass weighing bottle with a glass stopper, which solely depends on the exact volume of water to be weighed. Carefully fill the pipette with distilled water (DW), having a predetermined recorded temperature, and

---

* To correct to weight in vacuum.

** These values are not appreciably different for the **Brass weights** with a density of 8.4 g.cm^{-3}.

*** Volumetric glassware (apparatus) essentially bears a coefficient of expansion of 0.00025 per °C, producing changes 0.0025% per °C; and for 1 mL, it is almost 0.000025 mL per °C.

deliver the entire water right into the **flask or bottle,** employing **adequate pipette handling method,** and stopper the container (bottle or flask) rapidly so as to eliminate any loss due to 'evaporation'. Finally, reweigh the container plus DW to record the weight of water in air duly delivered by the pipette.

(*ii*) **Calibration of Volumetric Flask:** The **calibration of a volumetric flask** is invariably accomplished by first weighing the clean and dry flask, plus its glass-stopper. Fill up the volumetric flask up to the mark with DW carefully [**CAUTION**]*. Now, weigh the filled volumetric flask, and subsequently record the temperature of the water upto 0.1°C,. Thus, the respective increase in weight actually represents the weight in air of the DW contained duly by the volumetric flask.

(*iii*) **Calibration of Burette:** In normal practice, the calibration of a burette is quite akin to the method described for a pipette [as in (*i*) above], except that here **several volumes** shall be delivered sequentially (instead of only one as in pipette). It has also been observed broadly that the '**internal bore of the burette**' is not perfectly cylindrical in nature, and it will be a bit 'wavy' in actual practice. Therefore, consequently the '**actual volume**' delivered would vary between the '**plus**' and the '**minus**' range from the **nominal volumes** distinctly marked on the burette, as increased volumes are duly delivered. At this point in time, one may ascertain the volume at **20% full-volume increments** (*viz.,* an each 10 mL stepwise increment meant for a 50 mL burette) by filling up the said burette each time, and subsequently delivering the '**nominal volume**' into a dry flask.**

It is, however, pertinent to state here that since the '**delivered volume**' may not have to be **quite exact, but in close vicinity to the** nominal volume, hence one may afford **fairly rapid deliveries,** but should definitely wait for nearly 10 to 20 seconds to allow complete '**film drainage**'.

After having accomplished the said sequential operations one may adopt the following *two* steps carefully:

(*a*) Plot a **graphic rapresentation** between **volume correction** *Vs* **nominal volume,** and draw '**straight lines**' between each point, and

(*b*) **Interpolation** is duly carried out at the '**intermediate volumes**' from the lines.

Based on several authentic calibration exercises of '**burettes**' one may conclude that the— '**typical volumes correction for a 50-mL burette may range between $\pm$ 0.05 ML**'.

1.12 METHODS OF EXPRESSING CONCENTRATIONS

The **methods of expressing concentrations** (or **expression of concentrations**) refer specifically to the 'Solution Concentrations' that may be conveniently expressed on a **physical basis** *viz.,* **weight** or **volume.**

---

* **Caution**: No droplets of water should appear on the neck of the flask. If these are present, do blot them with tissue paper carefully

** The burette is duly filled each time to reduce errors due to evaporation considerably. Alternatively, one may also carry out successive deliveries right into the same flask, *i.e.,* fill the flask once only, and thereafter make quick deliveries expressed in this way.

A number of these **expression of concentrations** shall now be treated individually, with a brief description, in the section that follows:

1.12.1 Percent by Weight

It refers to the number of grammes of solute contained in 100 g of solution.

Example: The concentration of strong acids that are available commercially *viz.,* HCl, HNO₃, H₂SO₄, CH₃COOH etc., are usually expressed in this way.

1.12.2 Percent by Volume

It indicated the number of **mililiters (mL)** of solute present in 100 mL of solution.

Example: It is a common way of specifiying solution composition of mixtures of miscible liquids *viz.,* 60% (*v/v*) ethanol *i.e.,* it contains ethanol (60 mL) and water (40 mL) per 100 mL.

1.12.3 Percent Weight/Volume (w/v)

It represents the number of grammes of solute duly present in 100 mL of solution.

Example: It is invariably encountered in enumerating the exact composition of solids in liquids *viz., a* 0.1% (*w/v*) solution of phenolphthalein in ethanol as an indicator.

It is worth while to mention here that there are quite a few **related concentration units** in **milligram percent (mg%),** that distinctly designates the number of mg of solute present in a 100 mL of solution, and the concentration in parts per million (ppm), *i.e.,* the number of grammes of solute contained in 10^6g of solution.

Interestingly, it is absolutely feasible to convert one form of concentration scale into another both conveniently and effectively, if the **'density of solution'** is provided duly.

Likewise, the **chemical methods of expressing concentration** are predominantly based upon either the **chemical formula** or the **combining power.** Following are some of the typical means of **expressing concentration** vividly.

1.12.4 Molarity (M)

Molarity (M) *i.e.,* the number of moles of solute present in 1000 ml (or 1 L) of solution.

1.12.5 Normality (N)

Normality (N) *i.e.,* the number of equivalents of solute contained in 1 L of solution. The normality of a solution is always equal to an integer times its molarity.

Example: To prepare 1 N NaOH solution, we have to dissolve [23+16+1=40] 40 g of NaOH pellets into 1000 mL of distilled water (DW) slowly into a 2 L beaker with mild constant stirring.

1.12.6 Formality (F)

This terminology is usually used by certain analysts to designate the precise number of **formula weights** of solute that are essentially present in 1 L of solution. However, the major objective is to afford a clear cut distinction between the **actual equilibrium concentration of a chemical species** and the **total analytical concentration of the solute** thereby producing that species.

1.12.7 Molality (m)

Molality (m) *i.e.,* the number of moles of solute per 1000 g of solvent.

1.12.8 Mole Fraction

Mole fraction *i.e.,* the number of moles of solute divided by the total number of moles in the solution.

> **Note:** Both molarity and normality are absolutely temperature dependent by virtue of the fact that they are entirely based on volume. However, the molality and mole fraction are quite independent of temperature.

1.13 PRIMARY AND SECONDARY STANDARDS

1.13.1 Primary Standard

Primary standard is referred to as the—'**substance of known purity** (*viz.,* '**AnalaR**'**Grade Reagents**) **whose carefully weighed quantity eventually helps in the standardization of an unknown solution (normality or molarity).**'

In actual practice, the **volumetric (titrimetric) analysis** invariably make use of the **titrant solution** which is invariably either a **strong acid** or a **strong base**. Since, these substances are **not** available commercially as reagents of accurately known concentration; therefore, the **titrant solutions** are usually prepared to be having almost the desired concentration. These prepared solutions are subsequently **standardized** *i.e.,* they are analyzed accurately by titration against a substance (known as the '**Primary Standard**') whose **purity is already known precisely.**

Examples:

(*a*) **Strong Acid Solutions:** The **strong acid solutions** are normally standardized against a variety of pure basic chemical compounds, such as:

   (*i*) Sodium Carbonate [Na_2CO_3],

   (*ii*) Borax [$Na_2B_4O_7.10H_2O$],

   (*iii*) Tris (hydroxymethyl) aminomethane [TRIS; THAM; $(HOCH_2)_3CNH_2$],*

   Koch *et al.* (1975) observed that the commercial samples of TRIS invariably comprise of **occluded mother liquor** as an **impurity;** and, therefore, a careful drying under stringent prescribed conditions may prove to be an absolute necessary to accomplish a '**standard primary grade product**'.

(*b*) **Strong Basic Solutions:** The **strong basic solutions** are invariably standardized against the pure chemical compound [AnalaR-Grade Reagent] **potassium acid phthalate (KHP).**

* Kolthoff IM and Stenger VA: **Volumetric Analysis** Vol. II Interscience, New York, 2nd.edn. 1947.

** Koch WF *et al.; Talanta,* **22: 637, 1975.**

Primary Standard essentially possesses **five** cardinal criteria that it must fulfil, namely:

1. By all means, it must be 100.00% pure; although an impurity ranging between 0.01 to 0.002% is fairly tolerable provided it is known accurately.

2. It must be thermostable at the prevailing '**drying temperatures',** besides it must also remain stable at room (ambient) temperature for an indefiniite period.

> **Note: It is absolutely important and necessary to 'dry' always the primary standard before actual weighing.**

3. It should be available readily, and not too expensive for common usage in an '**Analytical Laboratory'.**

4. It must possess a relatively **high formula weight* (although not always necessary).** This is done invariably in order that a substantially large quantum of it may have to be weighed to get sufficient to titrate. In reality, the corresponding '**relative error'** in actually weighing a **larger amount** of material would essentially be smaller in comparison to that for a **smaller amount.**

5. In case, a **primary standard** is meant to be employed in a specific titration, it must possess largely the **properties required for a titration.**

> **Note: Importantly, the equilibrium of the ensuing reaction must be far to the right hand side in order to accomplish a very sharp end point.**

1.13.2 Secondary Standard

The **secondary standard** refers to '**another standard solution which is exclusively employed for standardization of an unknown solution'.**

Alternatively, if the material (in question) is not readily available in a sufficiently pure form, a solution is usually prepared to produce nearly the desired concentration (say 0.1 N); and ultimately this (*i.e.,* **secondary standard**) is adequately **standardized** by titrating against a weighed quantity of a **primary standard.**

Examples:

(*i*) **Prepared 0.1N NaOH solution** never represents a **standard solution** by virtue of the fact that NaOH **is not pure sufficiently.** Hence, the prepared NaOH solution is duly standardized by titrating a **primary standard acid** *viz.*, **potassium acid phthalate (KHP),** which being a pure solid substance may be weighed accurately.

(*ii*) **Prepared 0.1 N HCl solution** may be standardized volumetrically by the help of '**AnalaR' grade sodium carbonate (Na_2CO_3)** as a **primary standard** (because its exact purity is known).

---

* High Formula Weight: It signifies that a larger weight should be taken for a given number of moles, which eventually minimizes the error in weighing.

RECOMMENDED READINGS

Baiulescu GE *et al.* **Sampling,** Ellis Horwood, New York, 1991.

Gabb MH and Latchem WM: **A Handbook of Laboratory Solutions,** Chemical Publishing, New York, 1968.

Hungerford JM and Christian GD: **Statistical Sampling Errors as Intrinsic Limits on Detection in Dilute Solutions,** *Anal Chem.,*: **58**:2567, 1986.

Klich H and Walker R: '**COMAR—The International Database for Certified Reference Materials**', *Fresenius' J Anal Chem,* **345**: 104,1993.

Mark H: **Principles and Practice of Spectroscopic Calibrations,** Wiley, New York, 1991.

Pitard FF: **Pierre Gy's Sampling Theory and Sampling Practice, Vol. I: Heterogeneity and Sampling,** Vol.II. **Sampling Correctness and Sampling Practice,** CRC Press, Boca Raton, FL., 1989.

Seward RW and Mavrodineanu R: '**Standard Reference Materials: Summary of the Clinical Laboratory Standards— Issued by the National Bureau of Standards**', *NBS*(*NIST*) *Special Publications,* Washington, DC, 260-271, 1981.

Smith BW and Parsons ML: **Preparation and Standard Solutions. Critically Selected Compounds,** *J.Chem. Ed.,* **50**: 679, 1973.

PROBABLE QUESTIONS

1. '**Quantitative Analysis**'—In the *Quality of Drugs.* Justify the above statement with logical explanations.

2. (*a*) Enumerate the '*different techniques*' frequently used in '**Pharmaceutical Analysis**'.

   (*b*) What do you understand by '*Volumetric Analysis*' and '*Gravimetric Analysis*'? How would you differentiate these *two* aforesaid techniques?

3. Give a comprehensive account with respect to the '**Computation of Analytical Results**' with particular reference to:

   (*a*) Addition and Subtraction   (*b*) Multiplication and Division

   (*c*) Rounding Numbers   (*d*) Retention of as many Significant Figures

4. Explain the following aspects explicitely:

   (*i*) Statistical Validation   (*ii*) Validation of a Method

   (*iii*) Quality Control Chart (CCC)   (*iv*) True Value

5. (*a*) Describe briefly the conventional method of analysis *viz.,* Titrimetric Analysis, Gravimetric Analysis, Electrochemical Analysis, and Instrumental Analysis.

   (*b*) Give a '*Comparative Characteristic Features*' of various '**Analytical Techniques**'.

6. Explain the following preliminaries and definitions with regard to '**Pharmaceutical Analysis**':

   (*a*) Minimum Number of Samples   (*b*) Sample Size

   (*c*) Limit of Detection   (*d*) Limit of Quantitation

7. Describe in detatils the **Types of Error** *Vs* **Concept of Error.** Provide appropriate examples in support of youe explicit answer.

8. Explain the following terminologies:

   (*i*) Mean (Average) Deviation   (*ii*) Standard Deviation

   (*iii*) Statistical Treatment of Small Data Sets

9. Discuss the various commonly used methods of '**Expressing Concentrations**'.

10. What do you understand by **Primary and Secondary Standards**? Explain with appropriate examples explicitely.

Contains

2

Acid-Base (Neutralization) Titrations

The **acid-base (neutralization) titration method** essentially comprises of the volumetric (titrimetric) determinations based exclusively on reactions of acids with alkalies, *i.e.,* on neutralization it follows the reaction given below:

$$H^+ + OH^+ \rightleftharpoons H_2O$$

In a broader sense, the neutralization titration solely employed for estimating the exact quantum of **acid (alkalimetry)** or **akali (acidimetry)** duly present in a given solution. Besides, it is also used abundantly to solve a plethora of other diversified problems intimately involving the **'neutralization phenomenon'** in one form or the other.*

Nevertheless, the **acidity** or **basicity** of a solution is frequently regarded to be an important and vital factor in most of the **'chemical reactions'** encountered. Of course, there are quite a few cardinal factors that seem to be having a reasonably strong impact upon the **acid-base (neutralization) titrations**, such as:

- application of **'buffers'** of a given pH so as to maintain and sustain the solution pH at a predetermined level,
- basics of **acid-base equilibria** for the in-depth understanding of **acid-base titrations**, and
- specific effects of acids on certain **chemical reactions** and species.

The various concerned and important aspects of the **Acid-Base (Neutralization) Titrations** shall now be discussed at length in the sections that follows:

2.1 ACID-BASE CONCEPTS (THEORIES)

Acid-base concepts (Theories) have been beautifully expatiated with reasonable logistics within a rather short span of almost 30 years, from Arrhenius (1894) to Lewis (1923), under the following **four** classical theories, namely:

(*i*) Arrhenius theory [H^+ and OH^-],

---

* **Acidimetry** and **Alkalimetry** are two **'terms'** derived from the words **acid** and **alkali**. In usual practice, the estimation of an **'acid'** the solution is titrated with an alkali solution the volume of which is duly measured by a burette. It justifies the name **alkalimetry**. Likewise, the name of the method for estimating the exact quantum of alkali, **acidimetry**, is derived analogously.

   (*ii*) Theory of solvent systems [solvent **cations** and **Anions**],

   (*iii*) Bronsted Theory [Taking and Giving Protons], and

   (*iv*) Lewis Theory [Taking and Giving Electrons].

   The aforesaid *four* classical **acid-base concepts (theories)** shall now be described in the following sections that follows:

2.1.1 Arrhenius Theory [H⁺ and OH⁻]

Arrhenius in 1894, first and foremost introduced a radical theory which rightly expatiates an adequate quantitative description of the **acid-base typical behaviour** in an aqueous medium specifically. According to this theory, an **acid** represents a substance which particularly ionizes (either **partially or completely**) in an aqueous medium (water) to gives rise to the formation of **hydrogen ions** *via* ultimate and intimate association with the **solvent** (*i.e.* water) to result **hydronium ions (H_3O^+)** as shown below:

$$HA \quad + \quad H_2O \quad \rightleftharpoons \quad H_3O^+ \quad + \quad A^-$$

Acid   Water (solvent)   Hydronium ion

   Exactly in the same vein a **base** ionizes in an aqueous medium (water) to produce **hydroxyl ions**. It has been observed that the **weak** (or **partially ionized**) bases invariably undergoes ionization as expressed under:

$$B \quad + \quad H_2O \quad \rightleftharpoons \quad BH^+ \quad + \quad OH^-$$

Base   Water (solvent)   Hydroxyl ion

   In the particular instance of **strong bases** *viz.*, alkali metal hydroxides (*e.g.*, NaOH or KOH) undergo dissociation as given below:

$$M(OH)_n \longrightarrow M^{n+} + nOH^-$$

   Therefore, the **Arrhenius Theory** is evidently and grossly **limited (restricted) to only water as the solvent.**

2.1.2 Theory of Solvent Systems [Solvent Cations and Anions]

The **theory of solvent systems** was first introduced by Franklin in 1905; and hence, it is also sometimes referred to as **Franklin's Theory**. This theory emphatically advocates the vital **solvent system concept of acids and bases**. According to this theory a **'solvent'** undergoes ionization to produce **a cation** and **an anion**, as exemplified under:

$$2H_2O \quad \rightleftharpoons \quad H_3O^+ \quad + \quad OH^-$$

        Water   Hydronium ion   Hydroxyl ion

or
$$2NH_3 \quad \rightleftharpoons \quad NH_4^+ \quad + \quad NH_2^-$$

      Ammonia   Ammonium ion   Iminium ion

   In the present context, therefore, an **acid** may be defined as –**'a solute that yields the cation of the solvent'**; and a **base** as – **'a solute that yields the anion of the solvent'**.

   Examples: Following are some of the typical examples that substantially elaborates the **Franklin's Theory***:

---

   * **Franklin's Theory:** It is very much identical to the **Arrhenius Theory** but is applicable also to quite a few other **ionizable solvents.**

(a) **Ammonium chloride (NH$_4$Cl):** It serves as a **strong acid** in **liquid ammonia** (NH$_3$) *i.e.,* very much akin to HCl in H$_2$O:

or $\quad\quad\quad\quad\quad\quad\quad\quad$ HCl + H$_2$O $\longrightarrow$ H$_3$O$^+$ + Cl$^-$

Whereas, **sodamide (NaNH$_2$)** behaves predominantly as a **strong base** in **ammonia** *i.e.,* quite similar to NaOH in H$_2$O. Interestingly, the two aforesaid compounds *viz.,* **ammonium chloride** and **sodamide,** distinctly ionize to yield the **solvent cation** and **solvent anion** respectively.

(b) **Ethanol (C$_2$H$_5$-OH):** Ethanol undergoes ionization as given below:

$$2C_2H_5\text{-OH} \quad \rightleftharpoons \quad C_2H_5OH_2{}^+ \quad + \quad C_2H_5O^-$$

$\quad\quad\quad$ Ethanol $\quad\quad\quad\quad\quad\quad$ Ethanolium ion $\quad\quad\quad$ Ethoxide ion

From the above eqn. one may conclude that **sodium ethoxide [C$_2$H$_5$ONa]** exceptionally behaves as a **strong base** in the **solvent** (*i.e.,* ethanol).

2.1.3 Bronsted-Lowry Theory [Taking and Giving Protons]

The **Bronsted-Lowry theory** designates prominently the solvent systems that is specifically appropriate for the **ionizable solvents exclusively**; and, therefore, it fails to be of any utility in the **acid-base reactions** particularly in nonionizable organic solvents, for instance: **benzene, dioxane.**

According to the **Bronsted-Lowry theory** an **acid** may be defined as—'**any substance which may be able to donate (give) a proton**' ; and a **base** as—'**any substance that can accept a proton**'.

Hence, a '**half-reaction**' may be expressed as follows:

$$\text{Acid} = \text{H}^+ + \text{Base}$$

Conjugate Pairs: In actual practice, the **acid** and **base** of a '**half-reaction**' are invariably termed as the **conjugate pairs.**

As it is quite well known and evident that '**free protons**' usually fail to occur in a solution; and, hence, there should be definitely a '**proton acceptor**' **(base)** before a '**proton donor**' **(acid)** would be in a position to **release its proton appropriately.** In other words, the **strategical combination of two half-reactions** is an **absolute necessity and prime requirement.**

Table 2.1 illustrates vividly *four* prominent **acid-base reactions** in altogether **different solvent medium:**

Table 2.1 Bronsted-Lowry Acid-Base Reactions					
S.No. Solvent	Acid$_1$	+ Base$_2$	$\longrightarrow$ Acid$_2$	+	Base$_1$
1 Water (H$_2$O)	NH$_4{}^+$	H$_2$O	H$_3$O$^+$		NH$_3$
2 Water (H$_2$O)	HCO$_3{}^-$	OH$^-$	H$_2$O		CO$_3{}^{2-}$
3 Ethanol (C$_2$H$_5$OH)	NH$_4{}^+$	C$_2$H$_5$O$^-$	C$_2$H$_5$OH		NH$_3$
4 Benzene (C$_6$H$_6$)					

Salient Features

The **salient features** of **Bronsted-Lowry theory** are as enumerated under:

1. A substance cannot simply act as an **acid** unless and until a **base** is very much present to accept the protons graciously.

2. Broadly speaking **acids** shall get ionized either partially or completely in the **basic solvents** *viz.*, **ethanol, water,** or **liquid ammonia**, depending solely on the **basicity of the solvent,** and the **strength of the acid.**

3. Importantly, the **ionization phenomenon** is virtually insignificant as observed in either **'neutral'** or **'inert'** solvents.

4. Interestingly, the **'ionization'** taking place in the solvent may not necessarily be a **prerequisite** for a particular **acid-base reaction.**

Example: In Table 2.1, the fourth example wherein **'pieric acid'** does react with **'aniline'** (a base).

2.1.4 Lewis Theory [Taking and Giving Electrons]

Lewis in 1923, first of all postulated the famous and weld recognized **electronic theory** pertaining to **acids** and **bases**. In fact, the Lewis theory emphatically assumes a clear cut and distinct **donation** (sharing) of electrons from a **base** to an **acid**.

In other words, the **Lewis theory** evidently suggests that—**'A substance which can invariably accept an electron pair is termed as an 'acid' ; and a substance that can conveniently donate an electron pair is known as a 'base'.**

It has been duly observed that most abundantly a **base** consists of either a **nitrogen-atom** or an **oxygen-atom** as the predominant, so called **electron donar**. Hence, one may generally consider and recognize the **nonhydrogen-containing substances** as the **acids**.

Example: A few typical examples illustrating vividly the **acid-base reactions as per the Lewis Theory** are as given under:

(i) $\begin{array}{c} H \\ \diagdown \\ O: + H^+ \longrightarrow H_2O : H^+ \ [\text{or } H_3O^+] \\ \diagup \\ H \end{array}$

(ii) $H^+ + OH^- \longrightarrow H: OH$

(iii) $AlCl_3 + :O\diagup^{R}_{\diagdown R} \longrightarrow Cl_3Al : OR_2$
   (Acid)   (Ether as a **Base**)

(iv) H^+ $+ : NH_3 \longrightarrow H: NH_3^+$
   (Solvated)

In this context, the very concept of the **acid** has been altered markedly and pronouncedly to accommodate certain **typical chemical entities** that precisely do not contain H-atom. Hence, as per the **Lewis theory** the following reaction exclusively designates an **acid-base reaction:**

$$: NH_3 \quad + \quad BF_3 \quad \rightleftharpoons \quad H_3N : BF_3$$
$$\text{Base} \qquad\quad \text{Acid}$$

It has rather become a common practice to consider such **nonprotonic acids** (*e.g.*, BF_3) as the 'Lewis Acids'.

In short, one may conclude that the **Lewis theory** has indeed gone a long way to expatiate substantially several critical and wonderful phenomena, for instance: **definite colour changes in indicators**, which may occur specifically in **nonprotonic system**; however, this must display all the characteristic features of the **acid-base reactions**.

It is worthwhile to state here that it is quite possible to make a meaningful comparison of the *three* prominent **acid-base theories**, namely: (*a*) **Arrhenius Theory,** (*b*) **Bronsted Lowry Theory and** (*c*) **Lewis Theory**, briefly as given in Table 2.2 under:

S.No.	Name of theory	Acid	Base
		Table 2.2 A Brief Comparison of Acid-Base Theories	
1	**Arrhenius**	Proton Donor	Hydroxide Donor
2	**Bronsted-Lowry**	Proton Donor	Proton Acceptor
3	**Lewis**	Electron-pair Acceptor	Electron-pair Donor

The **dotted-lines** actually represent the **equivalent definitions**.

2.2 ROLE OF SOLVENT

It has been duly accomplished that in a particular instance when an investigative solute (or substance) is in its vapourized state (gaseous state), it essentially gives rise to an **'absorption spectrum'** which represents the so called isolated molecule(s). Thus, it may be significantly possible to obtain each and every individual **electronic transitions** along with their respective: (*a*) **Associated vibrations**, and (*b*) **Rotational transitions**.

Figure 2.1 (*a*) illustrates distinctly the **vapour-phase spectrum of benzene** critically displaying **all characteristic features of its fine structure**. Therefore, in a situation when a **'solute'** is duly dissolved in a **'liquid solvent'** it undergoes immediate **solute-solvent interactions**, namely:

(*i*) **Dipole-induced dipole interaction,**

(*ii*) **Dipole-dipole interaction,** and

(*iii*) **Dispersion**.

In fact, these interactions remarkably carry out the following *two* major physical phenomena, such as:

(*a*) prevent and check **free rotation**, and

(*b*) alter the probable **vibrational transitions**.

However, the overall **'net result'** being an appreciable extensive loss with respect to the ensuing **'fine structure in the spectrum**, as could be observed for a **benzene solution in ethanol** depicted in Figure 2.1 (*b*). One may critically notice the following *two* salient features, namely:

(*i*) More polar the nature of the solvent, greater is the degree of solute-solvent interaction; and consequently, the lesser the vibrational structure duly revealed in the observed spectrum.

(*ii*) **Hydrocarbon solvent** (*e.g.,* benzene) justifiably produce much greater spectral details in comparison to the **polar solvents** (*e.g.,* ethanol, ethyl acetate, water).

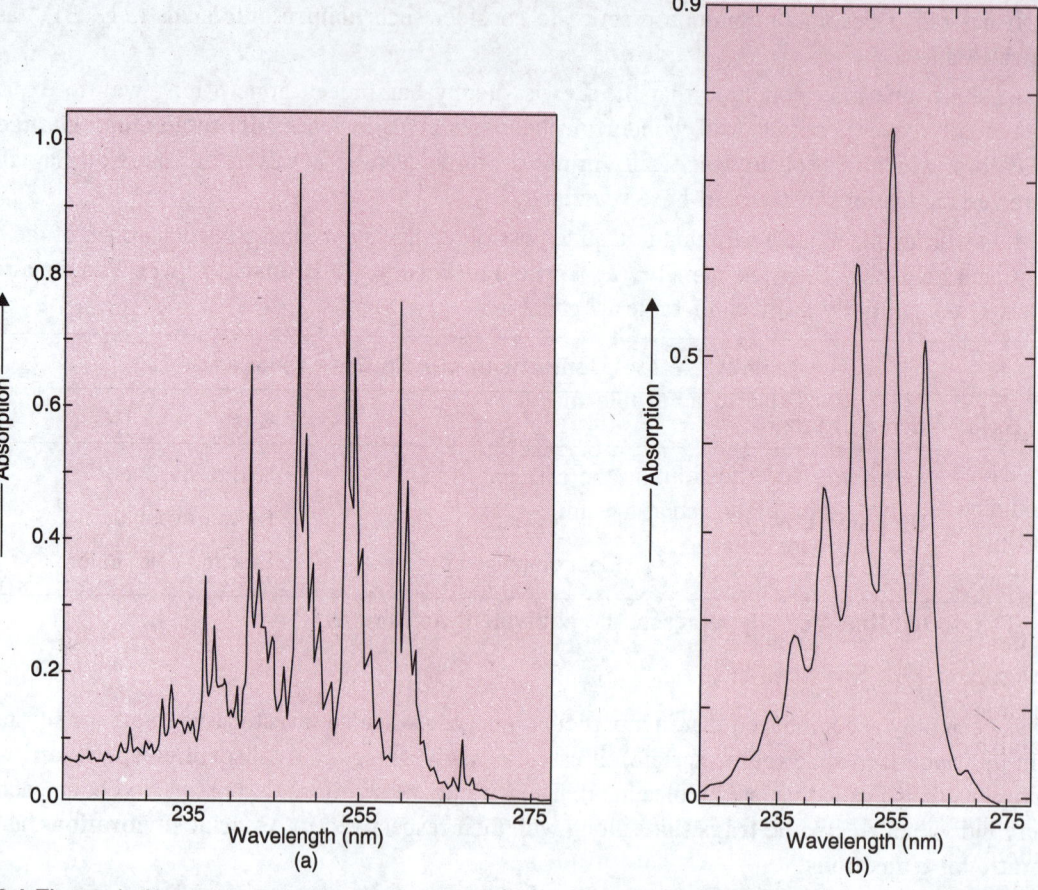

Fig. 2.1 Electronic Absorption Spectrum of Benzene: (a) Benzene vapour; and (b) Benzene in Ethanol solution.

Bathochromic Shift (Red) Hypsochromic Shift (Blue)

In addition to the aforesaid observed **'loss of fine structure,** *via.* passage from the **nonpolar** to the **polar solvents** (*viz.* **benzene to ethanol**), it is distinctly observed that the **wavelength of maximum absorption could alter possibly.** In order to ascertain whether such a **'shift'** could be either a **Bathochromic (Red) shift** or a **Hypsochromic (Blue) shift** rests exclusively upon the precise nature of *two* cardinal factors:

(*a*) nature of the prevailing **solute-solvent interactions**, and

(*b*) nature of the **transition state.**

Example: **Carbonyl [$>$ C = 0] Function:** The **carbonyl function** may undergo *two* different types of **transitions,** such as:

$$n \rightarrow \pi^* \text{ and } \pi \rightarrow \pi^*.$$

---

* The **'atomic nuclei'** happen to be excessively more massive in comparison to the **'electrons'** ; and this principle is usually termed as the **Franck-Condon effect.**

One may, however, consider the above **transitions** in the following *two* altogether different states, for instance:

Ground State

Here, the **electronic distribution** of the ensuing carbonyl moiety [$\diagup C = 0$] may be well represented as given below:

$$\overset{+}{\underset{\delta}{\diagup}} C \overset{\frown}{=} \overset{\delta^-}{O} \quad \left[\begin{array}{c} H \quad O \\ | \quad || \\ H-C-C-H \\ | \\ H \end{array} \right] \text{Acetaldehyde}$$

It ultimately gives rise to a **'dipole moment'** having its **negative pole** directed towards the **O-atom**.

Nevertheless, in a specific solution the carbonyl group containing molecule (*e.g.*, **acetaldehyde**) would be **solvated adequately**, and as a result its **dipole moment** has a tendency to orient the particular solvent molecules present in its close vicinity in order to produce the **most stable solute-solvent system**.

Excited State

In the **excited state** *i.e.*, in the influence of electronic excitation, the electronic distribution shall alter accordingly; and, therefore, it is well known that in the course of the said electronic distribution the ensuing **'atomic nuclei** may not alter their **respective locations**[†]. Hence, the excited state may not get stabilized optimally on account of **solvation**, because the requisite time for the actual reorientation of the solvent molecules would not be available.

Importantly, the realistic actual effect of the solvent upon the energy of the **'excited state'** shall entirely depend on the fact whether the **ensuing excited state** is very much akin electronically to the **'ground state'** or absolutely **'dissimilar'**. In other words, it solely depends on the fundamental question whether the **dipole moment** either gets **enhanced** or **lowered** after excitation.

Table 2.3 categorically summarizes the most justified production of the desired effects upon the specific carbonyl ($-\overset{O}{\overset{||}{C}}-$) bands. Interestingly, the pronounced **'predictions'** are observed to be amazingly successful.

Examples:

(*i*) From the gradual passage from the solvent **hexane (nonpolar)** to the solvent **ethanol (polar)** as the two solvent;

(*ii*) **Acetone** critically undergoes a **'blue shift'** due to its **low-intensity ($n \rightarrow \pi^*$) transitions**, and a **'red shift'** on account of its corresponding **high-density ($\pi \rightarrow \pi^*$) transitions**.

[†] The **'atomic nuclei'** happen to be excessively more massive in comparison to the **'electrons'**; and this principle is usually termed as the **Franck-Condon effect**.

S.No.	Transition	Rrepresentation of excited state	Dipole moment	Excited state: effect of more polar solvent	Energy difference	Shift in wavelength
	Table 2.3 Summary of Predictions of Solvent Effects on Carbonyl Absorption Bonds					
1	Low intensity $[n \rightarrow \pi^*]$	$\overset{}{C} - O^+$	Decreases	Destabilizes	Increases	**Hypsochromic**
2	High intensity $[\pi \rightarrow \pi^*]$	$\overset{+}{C} - O^-$	Increases	Stabilizes	Decreases	**Bathochromic**

2.3 RELATIVE STRENGTHS OF ACIDS AND BASES

Based on the 'Acid-Base-Theories', as discussed in Section 1 above, that whenever either an 'acid' or a 'base' undergoes dissociation in an aqueous medium (*i.e.*, water), it will certainly get **ionized** or **dissociated**. In such a situation, the actual degree of ionization exclusively depend upon the **strength of the acid**. Importantly, it has been observed duly that a 'strong' electrolyte undergoes **complete dissociation**, whereas a 'weak' electrolyte gets **dissociated partially**.

Table 2.4 includes an array of abundantly available electrolytes, a few of them being **strong**, and other **weak** in nature.

S.No.	Strong Electrolytes	Weak Electrolytes
	Table 2.4 Array of Strong and Weak Electrolytes	
1	H_2SO_4 ⊕	CH_3COOH (Acetic Acid)
2	HNO_3	NH_3
3	HCl	C_6H_5OH (Phenol)
4	$HClO_4$	HCOOH (Formic Acid)
5	NaOH	$C_6H_5NH_2$ (Aniline)
6	$NaC_2H_3O_2$ (Sodium Methoxide)	

⊕The first proton is ionized completely in a diluted solution; whereas, the second proton is ionized partially. [$K_i = 10^{-2}$]

2.3.1 Dissociation Constant

The **dissociation constant (Ka)** invariably designates a 'quantitative measure' of the acid strength. As **Ka** refers to an 'equilibrium constant' for an actual ensuing **proton transfer** taking place between **two specific acid base pairs**, there may exist a certain degree of **ambiguity** with respect to its **clear cut interpretation**. Such an 'ambiguity' may be resolved logically and reasonably by selecting critically one of the conjugate pairs as the solvent system *viz.*, **water**. Hence, this particular 'factor' turns out to be **constant**; and the resulting aqueous **Ka (or pKa)** values may be suitably interpreted as the respective measures of the 'acid strength' of the corresponding 'conjugate acid'.

Brown *et al.* (1955)* examined critically the ensuing relationship of the **dissociation constant (pKa)** to the respective **chemical structure**. The **equilibrium** may be expressed by Ka as follows:

$$\text{Conjugate Acid} + H_2O \rightleftharpoons \text{Conjugate Base} + H_3O^+$$

Thus, one may have a distinct **'degree of ionization'** taking place in a **'strong acid'** and a **'weak acid'** as given below:

(a) **Strong Acid** (*viz.,* **HCl**): Hydrochloric acid being a **strong acid** undergoes **complete ionization** as stated under:

$$HCl + H_2O \longrightarrow H_3O^+ + Cl^- \qquad \qquad ...(i)$$

For Eqn: (*i*) an equilibrium constant shall exhibit a value of **infinity** (∞). The proton H^+, liberated by the acid, invariably exists in water (H_2O) as its corresponding **hydrated ion**, termed as the **hydronium ion (H_3O^+)****. It is however, pertinent to state here that the **hydronium ion** (H_3O^+) is usually written as H_3O^+ for simple acceptable convenience, and also to support emphatically the **Bronsted-Lowry concept** *i.e.,* taking and giving protons (see Section 1.3).

(b) **Weak Acid** (*viz.,* **CH₃COOH**): Acetic acid being a **weak acid** that gets **ionized only partially** (*i.e.,* restricted to a few percent exclusively) as expressed under:

$$HOAc + H_2O \rightleftharpoons H_3O^+ + OAc^- \qquad \qquad ...(ii)$$

Equilibrium Constant for Eqn. (*ii*) may be written as under:

$$K_a^0 = \frac{a H_3O^+ . a OAc^-}{a HOAc . a H_2O} \qquad \qquad ...(iii)$$

Where,

K_a^0 = **Thermodynamic acidity constant,**

a = **Activity** of the specified species.

Importantly, the respective **cations** or **anions** of the salt may also undergo **partial hydrolysis** (with water) after they are dissociated duly.

Example: The liberation of the **acetate ion** [OAc^-] from the corresponding **dissociated acetate salt** to give rise to the formation of **acetic acid** [HOAc].

2.3.2 Autoprotolysis

It has been duly observed that in diluted solutions the overall **'activity of water'** almost **remains constant**; and is invariably considered to be as **unity as standard state**. Hence, one may express Eqn. (*iii*) as given under:

$$K_a^0 = \frac{a H_3O^+ . a OAc^-}{a HOAc} \qquad \qquad ...(iv)$$

---

* Brown HC *et al.* Chap. 14, In: *Determination of Organic Structures by Physical Methods*, Braude EA and Nachod FC (eds): Academic Press, New York, 1955.

** **7Higher Hydrates** do exist probably, such as: $H_9O_4^+$.

In other words, **autoprotolysis** refers to the **'self-ionization of a solvent'** to produce eventually a **cation** plus an **anion** viz.,

$$2CH_3OH \rightleftharpoons CH_3OH_2^+ + CH_3O^- \qquad ...(v)$$

Solvent	Cation	Anion
Methanol	Methanolium	Methoxide

Water, in its purest form, undergoes **autoprotolysis** i.e., affords ionization only to a sight extent, and we may express the reaction as stated below:

$$2H_2O \rightleftharpoons H_3O^+ + OH^- \qquad ...(vi)$$

Solvent	Cation	Anion
Water	Hydronium	Hydroxide

Equilibrium constant for the above reaction may be written as:

$$K_w^0 = \frac{a\,H_3O^+ \cdot a\,OH^-}{a\,H_2O^2} \qquad ...(vii)$$

As stated earlier under **'autoprotolysis'** that the **'activity of water'** is found to be **constant** in diluted solutions, hence Eqn. (vii) may be written as under:

$$K_w^0 = a\,H_3O^+ \cdot a\,OH^- \qquad ...(viii)$$

Where, K_w^0 = **Self-ionization Constant (or Thermodynamic Autoprotolysis)**

2.3.3 Molar Equilibrium Constants

In usual practice, the **'molar concentration'** shall be appropriately designated by means of the **'square brackets'** [ ] particularly on either sides of the **species** taken into consideration. Following are some of the typical examples of the **'simplified versions of equations'** for the above cited reactions, namely:

$$HCl \longrightarrow H^+ + Cl^- \qquad ...(ix)$$

$$HOAc \rightleftharpoons H^+ + OAc^- \qquad ...(x)$$

$$K_a = \frac{[H^+][OAc^-]}{[HOAc]} \qquad ...(xi)$$

Where, K_a = **Molar Equilibrium Constant of Acid**

$$H_2O \rightleftharpoons H^+ + OH^- \qquad ...(xii)$$

$$K_w = [H^+][OH^-] \qquad ...(xiii)$$

Where, K_w = **Molar Equilibrium Constant of Water**

Explanations

The nature has meticulously and carefully made, K_w, an even unit number at room temperature (25°C) i.e., the value of $K_w = 1.0 \times 10^{-14}$ at 25°C. In other words, the actual product of the **H$^+$ ion concentration** and the **OH$^-$ ion concentration** in an **aqueous medium** is always equal to 1.0×10^{-14} at **25°C** (i.e., the **room temperature**).

or $$[H^+] [OH^-] = 1.0 \times 10^{-14} \qquad ...(xiv)$$

From Eqn. (*xiv*) one may safely infer (or conclude) that in **pure water**, the concentration of the said two species (*viz.,* H^+ or OH^-) are exactly the same (equal), because except water (H_2O) dissociation there exist no other source(s) that may provide H^+ or HO^- legitimately:

$$\therefore \qquad [H^+] = [OH^-]$$

Thus, we may have:

$$[H^+] [OH^-] = 1.0 \times 10^{-14}$$

or $$[H_+] = 1.0 \times 10^{-7} \, M \equiv [OH^-]$$

Special Point

In an event when an **acid** is added to **water**, one may find out by the help of calculation the actual **OH^- ion concentration,** in case, one is aware of the **H^+ ion concentration** obtained **from the acid.** An **exception** prevails distinctly in a particular instance when the **H^+ ion concentration** emanated from the **acid** is appreciably small *viz.,* either **10^{-6} M** or **even less**; however, any possible contribution duly attributed to [H^+] from the ionization of water may be **ignored completely.**

Example: To determine the OH^- ion concentration from a 1.0×10^{-5} M solution of nitric acid.

Solution: As **nitric acid** happens to be an **inherent strong** electrolyte ; and hence, gets ionized almost completely, the H^+ ion concentration being 1.0×10^{-5} M. Thus, we have:

$$1.0 \times 10^{-5} \, [OH^-] = 1.0 \times 10^{-14}$$
$$[OH^-] = \mathbf{1.0 \times 10^{-9} \ M}$$

2.4 LAW OF MASS ACTION

Guldberg and Waage (1863) first and foremost defined the '**Law of Mass Action**' as — '**The rate of a chemical reaction is proportional to the 'active masses' of the reacting substances that are invariably present at any time**'.

Importantly, one may designate the '**active masses**' as the respective corresponding **pressures** or **concentrations**. Guldberg and Waage eventually put forward an '**equilibrium constant**' by describing judiciously the **equilibrium** as —'**the specific condition when the rates of the forward as well as the opposing (reverse) reactions are almost equal to each other**'.

Let us consider the following chemical reaction:

$$p A + q B \rightleftharpoons r C + s D \qquad ...(i)$$

Where, A, B, C, D = Four different species (substances), and

p, q, r, s = Constant times the respective concentration of each **four** different species.

Guldberg and Waage emphatically suggested that the actual **rate of the forward reaction** is almost equal to a constant times the concentration of each individual species duly raised to the power of the exact number of molecules that are intimately participating in the above reaction [shown in Eqn. (*i*)]:

i.e., $$\text{Rate } f = k_f \, [A]^p \, [B]^q \qquad ...(ii)$$

Where, $\qquad$ Rate f = **Rate of the forward reaction**, and

$\qquad k_f$ = **Rate constant** of the reaction

Importantly, the **rate constant**, kf, is exclusively dependent upon the following *three* cardinal factors, such as:

(*a*) **Temperature** of the ensuing reaction,

(*b*) Presence of the **catalysts**, and

(*c*) **Molar concentrations** of A and B designated by [A] and [B] respectively.

Likewise, Guldberg and Waage represented the **rate of the backward reaction** (*i.e.*, **'opposing'** or **'reverse'** reaction) as stated under:

$$\text{Rate } b = k_b \, [C]^r \, [D]^s \qquad\qquad ...(iii)$$

Therefore, for a **system at equilibrium**, the rate of the forward reaction [Rf] and the rate of the reverse reaction [Rb] are exactly equal. Thus we may have the following expression based on the Eqns. (*ii*) and (*iii*) as:

$$kf \, [A]^p \, [B]^q = kb \, [C]^r \, [D]^s \qquad\qquad ...(iv)$$

Therefore, one may easily obtain the **molar equilibrium constant** [K] (see Section 3.3) by rearranging Eqn. (*iv*) as given below:

$$K = \frac{kf}{kb} = \frac{[C]^r \, [D]^s}{[A]^p \, [B]^q} \qquad\qquad ...(v)$$

Salient Features

The **salient features** of the **molar equilibrium constant** [K] are erumerated as follows:

1. Eqn. (*v*) commands the most precise and correct expression for the ensuing **molar equilibrium constant**; however, the **'mode of derivation bears little specific overall validity apparently'**.

2. The observation in (1) above is by virtue of the fact that the prevailing **rates of reaction** entirely depends upon the **exact mechanism of the ensuing reaction**. This may, however, be estimated accurately by ascertaining the exact quantum of the colliding substances (species); and the expression of the **molar equilibrium constant [K]** depends critically upon the **stoichiometry** of the undergoing chemical reaction.

3. It has been observed that the **'sum of the exponents** as expressed in the **rate constant**, Eqns. (*ii*) and (*iii*), ultimately gives rise to the desired **'order of the reaction'** (*i.e.*, First order; Second order; or Zero order reactions); and, therefore, it may be altogether distinctly different from the observed **stoichiometry** of the prevailing chemical reaction.

   Example: **Rate of Reduction of $S_2O_8^{2-}$ with I$^-$:** The undergoing **'order of the reaction'** may be accomplished from the following chemical reaction:

   $$S_2O_8^{2-} + 3I^- \longrightarrow 2SO_4^{2-} + 3I^-$$

   In the above chemical reaction the precise and accurate **'rate of reduction'** in fact, is actually given by:

   $$kf \, [S_2O_8^{2-}] \, [I^-]$$

   which logically and specifically refers to a **second-order reaction***, and certainly **not** by $kf \, [S_2O_8^{2-}] \, [I^-]^3$, as one may possibly expect from the aforesaid **balanced chemical reaction** thereby predicting a **fourth-order reaction**.

---

* The second-order reaction is governed by the two active species *viz.* [$S_2O_8^{2-}$] and [I$^-$].

4. The exact value of the **molar equilibrium constant [K]** may be calculated empirically by actually determining the concentration of the **four** different species (substances) A, B, C, and D at an **attained equilibrium**.

> **Note: 1.** **More favourable being the observed rate constant of the 'forward reaction' in comparison to the 'backward-reaction'.**
> **2.** **Greater the equilibrium constant plus farther drift to the right (of the chemical reaction), the overall net reaction shall be at equilibrium comfortably.**

Figure 2.2 vividly illustrates the actual commendable progress of an on-going **'chemical reaction'**.

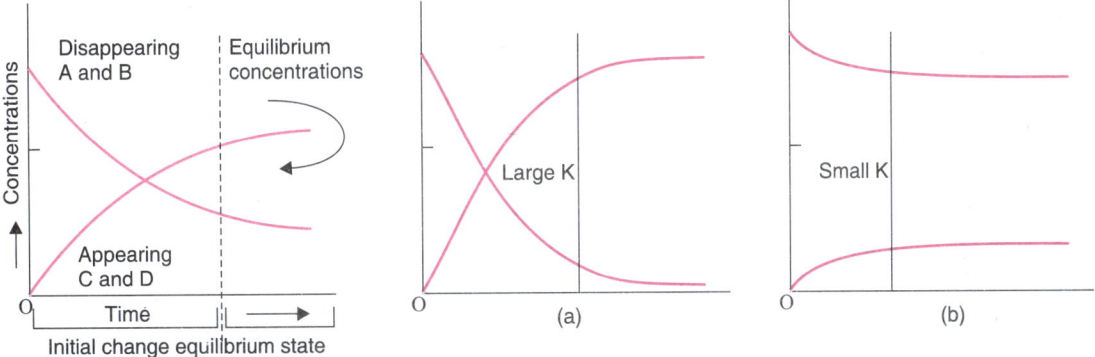

Fig. 2.2 Actual Progress of an On-going Chemical Reaction

Explanation of Various Stages of an On-Going Chemical Reaction as per Fig. 2.2. These are as stated under:

1. At the initial stage *i.e.*, when the reaction between A and B just gets started, one may distinctly observe that the rate of the **forward reaction is usually large** due to the fact that the **concentrations of A and B are also substantially large**; and, in the same vein, the **backward reaction is invariably slow** by virtue of the fact that the ensuing **concentrations of C and D are predominantly small***.

2. With the gradual progress in the on-going chemical reaction one would certainly observe a noticeable decrease in the concentrations of A and B, whereas C and D shall increase correspondingly. As a result the **rate of the forward reaction undergoes a categorical reduction**, whereas that for the **backward reaction affords a proportionate increment**.

3. Ultimately, the **two rates of reaction** (*viz.*, forward and backward) almost **tend to be equal**, and the entire system slumbers into the desired **state of equilibrium**. Importantly, at this critical stage, the concentrations of the individual species A, B, C, and D almost remain constant.**

---

* The rate is really at zero level initially.

** The relative values shall depend solely upon the *two* vital factors *viz.* (*a*) reaction stoichiometry; and (*b*) extent to which the equilibrium remains to right.

4. **Large Equilibrium Constant [K]:** In actual practice one may really observe that the expression of the **molar equilibrium constant** represents evidently the ratio wherein the **numerator** has the **concentrations of the products**, and the **denominator** bears the **concentrations of the reactants***. Therefore, a **large K** normally indicates the equilibrium to lie far to the right as shown in Fig. 2.2 (a).

5. **Small Equilibrium Constant [K]:** For the reaction shown in Fig. 2.2 (b), the rate at which the desired equilibrium is actually attained shall be virtually different for either the **forward reaction** or the **backward reaction**. In other words, if one commences with an admixture of C and D species, the ensuing rate at which the desired equilibrium is eventually approached would be quite faster or slower in comparison to the **converse reaction**.

2.5 COMMON ION EFFECT [SHIFTING THE EQUILIBRIA]

Absolute little change in the 'equilibrium constant [K] may be critically observed in the following *two* events, namely:

    (*i*) concentrations of reacting components may alter, and

    (*ii*) relative concentration of reacting substances may change.

Considering the most typical example whereby a solution of barium chloride [$BaCl_2$] is duly incorporated into a solution of sulphuric acid [H_2SO_4]. At this stage, the prevailing sulphate ion [SO_4^{2-}] is adequately present in a concentration in such a fashion that its ensuing ionic product with the available barium ion [Ba^{2+}] overwhelmingly exceeds the **solubility product (sp)** of barium sulphate [$BaSO_4$]; and therefore, the insoluble precipitate of barium sulphate is duly accomplished:

$$Ba^{2+} + SO_4^{2-} \longrightarrow BaSO_4 \downarrow$$

Importantly, at **equilibrium** the concentrations of Ba^{2+} ions and SO_4^{2-} ions become exactly equal.

Interestingly, if one carefully incorporates to the resulting **supernatant liquid**** an additional small quantum of a soluble barium salt or a soluble sulphate, a slight further precipitation may take place definitely.

Therefore, one may conveniently express the resulting equilibrium constant [K] as given under:

$$K = \frac{[Ba^{2+}] \times [SO_4^{2-}]}{[BaSO_4]} \qquad \qquad ...(1)$$

Two vital and important observations may be derived legitimately from the Eqn. (1), such as:

(*a*) Concentration of **Ba^{2+} ion** is usually increased by the incorporation of a **soluble barium salt** thereby the concentration of SO_4^{2-} ion must get reduced almost simultaneously.

(*b*) Conversely, an increase in the concentration of **SO_4^{2-} ion** by the incorporation of a **soluble sulphate salt**, whereby the ultimate concentration of Ba^{2+} ion must get reduced because their solubility product (sp) practically remains constant.

Obviously, the aforesaid predominantly apparent decrease in the concentration of the respective ions in either instance can be accomplished by the meticulous and careful combination of Ba^{2+} and

---

* Though it happens to be quite arbitrary, but it actually represents the most widely accepted and recognized convention.

** A saturated solution of barium sulphate [$BaSO_4$]

SO_4^{2-} ions to produce the corresponding insoluble barium sulphate ultimately pushing the reaction towards completion forcibly.

Common-ion effect is used profusely to perform the **gravimetric analysis** of pharmaceutical substances in order to drive reactions toward completion specifically.

Calculations Involved: The exact percentage of the investigative substance can be accomplished gravimetrically by the aid of the following expression:

$$\text{Percentage of desired substance} = \frac{\text{Wt. of precipitate} \times \text{Gravimetric factor}}{\text{Wt. of Sample}} \times 100$$

Gravimetric Factor designates broadly the exact number of grammes of the investigative substance **(analyte)** present in 1 g of the substance weighed. However, one may further expatiate the above dictum with the aid of the following examples:

(i) **Gravimetric Factor for Silver Chloride (AgCl):**

1 Mole of AgCl [143.323 g] contains essentially 1 mole of Cl atoms [35.453 g]:

$$\therefore \quad \text{Gravimetric Factor} = \frac{Cl}{AgCl} = \frac{35.453}{143.323} = \textbf{0.2474.}$$

(ii) **Gravimetric Factor for Barium Sulphate (BaSO_4):**

1 Mole of $BaSO_4$ [233.39 g] contains essentially 1 mole of SO_4 atoms [96.06 g]:

$$\therefore \quad \text{Gravimetric Factor} = \frac{SO_4}{BaSO_4} = \frac{96.06}{233.39} = \textbf{0.4116.}$$

2.6 IONIC PRODUCT OF WATER [K_{H_2O}]

Qualitative analysis* significantly advocates that any aqueous solution, irrespective of its nature of reaction, essentially comprises of both **H⁺ and OH⁻ ions** due to the prevalent **'dissociation of water'**. However, its has been duly established that the ultimate product of concentrations of these ions viz., H⁺ and OH⁻, at a given specified temperature remains almost constant.**

The **ionic product of water** [K_{H_2O}] in any aqueous solution at 22°C is given as:

$$K_{H_2O} = [H^+][OH^-] = 10^{-14} \qquad \qquad ...(a)$$

It is, however, pertinent to state here that the **ionic product of water** [K_{H_2O}] increases both rapidly and progressively with the rise of temperature as depicted in Table 2.5.

---

* Alexeyev V: **Course of Qualitative Chemical Semimicroanalysis**, Sec. **19**, Goskhimizdat, 1962.

** Most precisely, it does **not** represent the **product of the concentrations**, but the **product of the activities of the H⁺ and OH⁻ ions**, which virtually remains constant i.e., $a_{H^+} \cdot a_{OH^-} = K_{H_2O}$

Table 2.5 Ionic Product of Water [K_{H_2O}] at Temperature 0–100°C					
Temperature [°C]	Ionic Product of water [K_{H_2O}]	[H^+] = [OH^-]	Temperature [°C]	Ionic Product of water [K_{H_2O}]	[H^+] = [OH^-]
0	0.13×10^{-14}	0.36×10^{-7}	40	3.80×10^{-14}	1.95×10^{-7}
10	0.36×10^{-14}	0.59×10^{-7}	50	5.60×10^{-14}	2.40×10^{-7}
20	0.86×10^{-14}	0.93×10^{-7}	60	12.6×10^{-14}	3.50×10^{-7}
22	1.00×10^{-14}	1.00×10^{-7}	80	34.0×10^{-14}	5.80×10^{-7}
30	1.89×10^{-14}	1.37×10^{-7}	100	74.0×10^{-14}	8.60×10^{-7}

[Adopted From: Alexeyev V: **Quantitative Analysis**, CBS-Publishers, New Delhi, 2005]

The **theory of electrolytic dissociation** advocates that the **acidic characteristic features** of solutions exclusively depend upon the H^+ **ions**, and the corresponding **basic characteristic features** solely on OH^- **ions**. It has been duly established that concentrations of these ions must be absolutely **equal in water** and the same also holds good for the **natural solutions** as follows:

$$[H^+] = [OH^-] = \sqrt{K_{H_2O}} = \sqrt{10^{-14}} = 10^{-7} \text{ g. ion. } L^{-1}$$

In Acidic Solutions. We may have:

$$[H^+] > [OH^-] \; i.e., \; [H^+] > 10^{-7}, \text{ and } [OH^-] < 10^{-7}$$

In Alkaline Solutions. We may have:

$$[OH^-] > [H^+] \; i.e., \; [OH^-] > 10^{-7}, \text{ and } [OH^-] < 10^{-7}$$

From Eqn. (*a*) above it is quite evident that the **Concentrations of H^+ and OH^- ions** are present in an **inverse proportionality**; and, therefore, it may be logically possible and plausible to represent the overall reaction of any solution quantitatively. Thus, by considering simply the concentration of one of these ions, one may precisely determine the concentration of the other ion.

Example: In case, the H^+ ion concentration of a solution is found to be 10^{-11} g-ion. L^{-1}, the OH^- ion concentration would be 10^{-14}: 10^{-11} = 10^{-3}; and, hence, the solution definitely exhibits an **alkaline reaction**.

2.7 pH [or THE pH SCALE]

It has been observed articulately that the prevailing concentration of H^+ or OH^- ion in an aqueous medium (solution) may vary over a reasonably wide range starting from 1 M or greater to 10^{-14} M or even less. In actual practice, it is almost extremely difficult to plot a graph between H^+ concentration against certain variables by virtue of the fact that the '**concentration**' undergoes drastic changes *viz.,* from 10^{-1} M to 10^{-13} M*. Therefore, it is rather more easy, practical, and convenient to '**compress the acidity scale**' by judiciously placing it on a **logarithm basis**.

---

* The range varying between 10^{-1} M to 10^{-13} M seems to be quite common in a volumetric analysis.

Definition

Sorenson put forward the definition of **pH** of a solution as stated below:

$$pH = - \log [H^+] = \log \frac{1}{[H^+]} \qquad \qquad ...(i)$$

In other words, **pH** should be really designated as — $\log a_{H^+}$ *i.e.*, **the measured value of a pH meter using a glass-electrode.**

Salient Features

The **salient features** of **pH** are as given below:

1. Larger the value of pH, smaller is the hydronium ion [H+] concentration.

   Example: Between **two solutions**, the one having the **lower pH is more acidic**, whereas the one with the **higher pH happens to be more alkaline**.

2. The '**minus sign**' is employed invariably due to the fact that most of the concentrations encountered are specifically less than 1 M; and, therefore, this designation bears a positive number.

3. Based on the above glaring facts one may have another **more precise and stricter definition of pH** as: $-\log a_H$.

4. However, the alternative method of notation *viz.*, **p Anything = – log Anything**, may also be employed later for other numerical numbers which can vary by **large quantities**, happen to be **quite large** or **small** (*viz.*, **equilibrium constants**).

   Example: **To determine the pH of a 2.0 × 10⁻⁵ M solution of HCl:** It is known that HCl being a strong acid undergoes complete ionization as:

   $$[H^+] = 2.0 \times 10^{-5} \text{ M}$$
   $$\therefore \quad pH = - \log (2.0 \times 10^{-5})$$
   $$= 5 - \log 2.0$$
   $$= 5 - 0.30$$
   $$= \mathbf{4.70}$$

   i.e., pH of a 2.0 × 10⁻⁵ M solution of HCl is 4.70.

   Likewise, an identical definition can be easily made for the hydroxyl ion (OH⁻) concentration:

   $$pOH = - \log [OH^-] \qquad \qquad ...(ii)$$

   It is, however, pertinent to state at this point in time that instead of the actual concentrations of H+ or OH⁻ ions it is definitely more convenient to designate precisely the respective reaction of a solution by their **negative logarithms**, commonly termed as: **hydrogen and hydroxyl components; pH and pOH**.

   Hence, we may have

   $$pH = - \log [H^+];$$
   and $$pOH = - \log [OH^-]$$

Taking the **logarithms of Eqn. (*i*)**, and also **reverse the signs accordingly,** we may have the following expression:

$$- \log \{H^+\} - \log [OH^-] = 14$$

or $pH + pOH = 14$

Table 2.6 summarizes meticulously the prevailing relationship between the **H^+ and OH^- ion concentrations,** the **pH and pOH values, and reactions of solution(s).**

		Table 2.6 Relationship Existing between [H^+], [OH^-], pH, pOH, and Solution Reaction*			
S.No.	**[H^+]**	**[OH^-]**	**pH**	**pOH**	**Reaction**
1	1	10^{-14}	0	14	
2	10^{-1}	10^{-13}	1	13	A
3	10^{-2}	10^{-12}	2	12	C
4	10^{-3}	10^{-11}	3	11	I
5	10^{-4}	10^{-10}	4	10	D
6	10^{-5}	10^{-9}	5	9	I
7	10^{-6}	10^{-8}	6	8	C
8	10^{-7}	10^{-7}	7	7	Neutral
9	10^{-8}	10^{-6}	8	6	A
10	10^{-9}	10^{-5}	9	5	L
11	10^{-10}	10^{-4}	10	4	K
12	10^{-11}	10^{-3}	11	3	A
13	10^{-12}	10^{-2}	12	2	L
14	10^{-13}	10^{-1}	13	1	I
15	10^{-14}	1	14	0	N
					E

*Upward and downward vertical arrows indicate the directions of acidity and alkalinity increase respectively.

From Table 2.6 one may draw the following inferences, namely:

1. pH and pOH of neutral solutions stands at 7,
2. Acidic solution pH is less than 7, and decreases with increasing acidity,
3. Alkaline solutions pH is more than 7, and increases with increasing alkalinity, and
4. pH increase of one specific unit corresponds to a tenfold decrease of H^+ ion concentration.

2.8 HYDROLYSIS OF SALTS

Hydrolysis may be defined as— **'a reaction which being the reverse of neutralization, whereby the reaction taking place in the course of the titration is reversible and does not attain completion at the end.'**

Sodium acetate [CH_3COONa], which is the **'salt'** of a weak acid [CH_3COOH] and a strong base [$NaOH$] behaves as a **strong electrolyte**, very much akin to all salts, and undergoes **complete**

ionization in due course. Besides, the anion of the salt of a weak acid (in this case acetate ion, CH_3COO^-) distinctly represents a **Bronsted-Lowry base** (see Section 2.1.3), that will specifically **accept the protons** only.

Consequently, the **acetate ion** gets **partially hydrolyzed** in **water** (*i.e.*, a Bronsted-Lowry acid) to result into the formation of *two* major entities *viz.*, (*a*) hydroxide ion [OH^-]; and (*b*) undissociated acetic acid [CH_3COOH] as given below:

$$OAc^- + H_2O \rightleftharpoons HOAc + OH^- \qquad \qquad ...(i)$$

Salient Features of Eqn. (*i*): These are as follows:

1. Acetic acid (HOAc) is obtained in its undissociated form, and, hence, fails to contribute to the pH value.*

2. As it causes hydrolysis, the salt *i.e.*, sodium acetate behaves as a weak base (or the corresponding **conjugate base of acetic acid**—an weak acid).

3. In Eqn. (*i*) the **ionization constant** is equivalent to the basicity constant of the salt (CH_3COONa).

4. The **weaker the conjugate acid**, the **stronger would be the** conjugate base; which means the more strongly the salt (CH_3COONa) shall combine with an available proton (H^+) obtained from the water (H_2O), so as to shift the ensuing ionization to the right hand side in Eqn. (*i*).

5. From (4) above one may gracefully conclude that– **'Equilibria duly attained for these Bronsted-Lowry bases are almost treated similarly to the weak bases that we have already taken into consideration.'**

Hydrolysis Constant

From Eqn. (*i*) we may safely derive an equilibrium constant as given under:

$$K_H = K_b = \frac{[HOAc][OH^-]}{[OAc^-]} \qquad \qquad ...(ii)$$

In Eqn. (*ii*), K_H is invariably termed as the **hydrolysis constant** of the corresponding salt *viz.*, sodium acetate, and it eventually being the same as the **basicity constant**. However, in actual practice one profusely makes use of K_b in order to stress and emphasize that such types of salts are invariably treated in the same manner as is done for any other similar **weak bases**.

From Eqn. (*ii*), the value of basicity constant [K_b], may be easily calculated from the acidity constant [K_a] of acetic acid and K_w. Let us multiply both the numerator and the denominator by [H^+], we may have:

$$K_b = \frac{[HOAc]\overline{[OH^-]}}{[OAc^-]} \cdot \frac{\overline{[OH^+]}}{[H^+]} \qquad \qquad ...(iii)$$

The two components inside the dotted-line in Eqn. (*iii*) represents K_w, and the remaining components designates $1/K_a$. Therefore, Eqn. (*iii*) may be rewritten as:

---

* The ionization is usually termed as **hydrolysis** of the respective **salt ion**.

$$K_b = \frac{K_w}{K_a} = \frac{1.0 \times 10^{-14}}{1.75 \times 10^{-5}} = 5.7 \times 10^{-10} \qquad \qquad ...(iv)$$

From Eqn. (iv), one may observe that the relatively small value of K_b suggests abundantly that the acetate ion [OAc$^-$] is definitely a weak base (Bronsted-Lowry concept) having merely a small extent of ionization.

Thus, from Eqn. (iv) we may have the expression:

$$K_w = K_a K_b \qquad \qquad ...(v)$$

Eqn. (v) evidently affirms that — **'the product of K_a of any weak acid and K_b of its corresponding conjugate base is found to be always equivalent to K_w.'**

2.9 HENDERSON-HASSELBALCH EQUATION

Henderson-Hasselbalch Equation essentially connects the pH of a solution comprising of comparable and significant concentrations of a conjugate acid-base pair to the ratio of these concentrations. It indeed represents the **ionization constant equation**. It may be employed advantageously and usefully for duly calculating the pH of a **weak-acid solution** containing its salt specifically.

Therefore, the generalized form may be written pertaining to a weak acid HA which ultimately gets ionized to its salt, A$^-$ and H$^+$ as expressed under:

$$HA \rightleftharpoons H^+ + A^- \qquad \qquad ...(i)$$

$$pH = pK_a + \log \frac{[A^-]}{[HA]} \qquad \qquad ...(ii)$$

$$pH = pK_a + \log \frac{[\text{Conjugate Base}]}{[\text{Acid}]} \qquad \qquad ...(iii)$$

$$pH = pK_a + \log \frac{[\text{A Proton Acceptor}]}{[\text{A Proton Donor}]} \qquad \qquad ...(iv)$$

2.10 BUFFER SOLUTION

The critical examination of the **'titration curves'** would reveal explicitly that there are *two* absolutely distinct **types of regions**, namely:

(a) **pH Change being Abrupt:** In this particular instance, when the **pH change is abrupt**, as observed in the region of the **titration curve**, the **curves are practically vertical in nature** wherein even the additions of extremely small quantities of **acid** or **alkali** shall cause an enormous change in the pH of solution.

(b) **pH Change being very Small:** In this specific case, when the **pH change is very small**, the **curves appear to be flat and almost horizontal in shape**. It obviously shows that at the corresponding titration stages the ensuing pH of the solution gets altered to a very small extent only by the addition of either acid or alkali. Importantly, such solutions are said to exert **'buffer action'** or are broadly termed as **'buffer solution'**.

In other words, such a solution which strategically holds the pH from being undergoing any further changes is called a **'buffer solution'**, because it predominately resists a change in pH with the subsequent addition of a small quantum of acid or base.

In reality, the terminology **'buffer'** is aptly and rightly applied to such solutions due to the fact, just as:

- buffer stocks of food grains/staple foods to encounter any unforeseen calamities, and
- buffer of railway carriages to resist shocks, exactly in a similar manner the **buffer solutions** usually resist the action of various factors that may alter the pH.

Advantage

The very introduction of an **appropriate buffer** into a reacting system renders the pH of the solution to remain constant firmly despite the formation of an acid or a base in the reaction medium.

Following are some of the most **typical examples** that would fairly substantiate the fundamental concept and need for the **'buffer solution'** in pharmaceutical analysis.

1. **Effect of 0.1 N NaOH upon a mixture of 0.1 M CH_3COOH and 0.1 M CH_3COONa (Solution-I):**

   Explanations

   (*i*) The ratio $b/a = 1.0$

   (*ii*) According to the following equation:

   $$pK_a = pH - \log \frac{b}{a} \qquad ...(a)$$

   Hence, the pH = pK_a or pH = **4.76**

   (*iii*) Add 1.0 mL of 0.1 N NaOH to 100 mL of solution-I, and to determine the **pH of the resulting solution.**

   (*iv*) It may be **'assumed'** that NaOH exactly converts an equivalent quantum of acetic acid CH_3COOH) and sodium acetate (CH_3COONa).

   (*v*) After addition of NaOH, the resulting solution should essentially comprise of:

   $(100) (0.1) - (1) (0.1) = 10 - 0.1 = 9.9$ m mole of CH_3COOH, and $(100) (0.1) + (1) (0.1)$ $= 10 + 0.1 = 10.1$ m mole of CH_3COONa, present in $(100 + 1) = 101$ mL of solution.

   (*vi*) The new acquired ratio $b/a = 1.02$, its logarithm being 0.01, and Eqn. (*a*) gives the new pH as **4.77** (instead of 4.76).

   (*vii*) In fact, the addition of 1 mL of 0.1 N NaOH could only cause an apparent change in pH to the extent of 0.01 unit.

> **Note:** In case, the addition of the same volume NaOH (*i.e.*, 1 mL of 0.1 N NaOH) to a 100 mL of a strong acid (having pH 4.76), the ultimate pH would have been altered to almost ≃ **11.**

2. **Separation of Zn^{2+} from the rest of group III cations by precipitation:** The various steps involved are as given under:

   (*i*) Zn^{2+} is invariably separated from the rest of group III cations by precipitation with H_2S (hydrogen sulphide) (*ii*) In actual practice, the black ZnS (zinc sulphide) is more or less completely precipitated even at **pH 2**; whereas, CoS (cobalt sulphide), NiS (nickel sulphide), and other group III sulphides fail to get precipitated under identical experimental parameters.

(*iii*) Interestingly, if the initial solution is first and foremost neutralized, added a reasonably sufficient quantum of a **'buffer solution'** of **pH 2***, and subsequently H$_2$S is made to pass through the solution, whereby Zn^{2+} gets precipitated completely (as ZnS) despite the underlying fact that an acid (*i.e.*, HCl) is duly formed in the reaction mixture, as given under:

$$ZnCl_2 + H_2S \longrightarrow ZnS\downarrow + 2HCl \qquad \qquad ...(b)$$

Interestingly, all the rest of the group-III cations shall remain very much in solution.

An appropriate **'buffer solution'** exclusively meant for this critical and effective separation is a mixture of free formic acid [HCOOH] together with a particular **'salt' of the same acid** *viz.*, **sodium formate** [HCOONa] or **ammonium formate** [HCOONH$_4$]. Actually the resulting mixture is commonly termed as the **'formate buffer mixture'**.

Mechanism of Action: The **formate buffer mixture** exerts its action due to the formation of a strong acid *viz.*, HCl [as shown in Eqn. (*b*)] in the reaction that reacts with the **respective formate** (*i.e.*, the salt of formic acid), and produces ultimately an equivalent quantum of the relatively **weaker formic acid [HCOO]** as stated under:

or
$$\left. \begin{array}{l} HCOONH_4 \longrightarrow NH_4CL + HCOOH \\ HCOO^- + H^+ \longrightarrow HCOOH \end{array} \right\} \qquad ...(c)$$

From Eqn. (*c*) one may safely conclude that almost the entire H$^+$ ions duly introduced into the solution do combine specifically with the HCOO$^-$ [formate ions] to yield HCOOH, and hence do not remain free at all; and, therefore, the pH of the ultimate solution fails to alter appreciably *i.e.*, remains pegged at pH 2.

Interestingly, one may observe almost the same thing when an **'alkali'** is duly incorporated into a solution essentially containing a **'formate buffer'**. Thus, the OH$^-$ ions of the alkali practically do not remain free at all, but do combine almost instantly with liberated H$^+$ ions from the formic acid [HCOOH], and we have:

$$OH^- + HCOOH \longrightarrow H_2O + HCOO^- \qquad \qquad ...(d)$$

From Eqn. (*d*) one may rightly infer that the pH of the resulting solution almost remains unchanged.

2.11 NEUTRALIZATION CURVES [TITRATION CURVES]

In actual practice we may have come across a titration of a **weak acid** with a **strong base**. However, the terminology **'neutralization'** invariably employed as a synonym of **'titration'**. Based on certain calculations intimately associated with the titrations one may distinctly take notice of the fact that the ensuing pH at the **equivalence point (end-point)** is **not** usually as observed normally at **neutrality**; and, therefore, this usage is evidently not so accurate and precise, but is certainly widespread.

---

* Formate Buffer Mixture (pH 2).

Figure 2.3 illustrates explicitly a calculated **titration curve** representing the titration between a 10 mL of 0.2 M of a **weak acid** ($pK_a = 5.00$) and a 0.2 M **strong base**.

Salient Features

The **salient features** of Figure 2.3 are as enumerated under:

1. The actual volume observed at the end point is 10 mL, and it may be observed that this situation particularly takes place at the **inflection point** (or **end point**). **importantly**, at this most critical point the resulting curve significantly exhibits the steepest slope.

2. Besides, at the **end point** every bit of the **weak acid** has been converted completely to its respective conjugate base.

3. **Midpoint of the titration** *i.e.*, at a point when practically one-half of the exact end point volume has been added duly, obviously almost one-half of the weak acid gets adequately converted to its corresponding **conjugate base** and hence, their prevailing concentrations are nearly equal.

4. In accordance with the following expression:

$$pH = pK_a + \log \frac{[\text{Conjugate Base}]}{[\text{Conjugate Acid}]}$$

We may have $pH = pK_a$ at the **midpoint** of this titration. Therefore, this particular relationship has been duly indicated in Fig. 2.3.

5. It is known that the ensuing slope of the titration curve at any point represents an exact measure of the rate of change of pH in accordance with the corresponding addition of a **'known volume'** of the **titrant**.

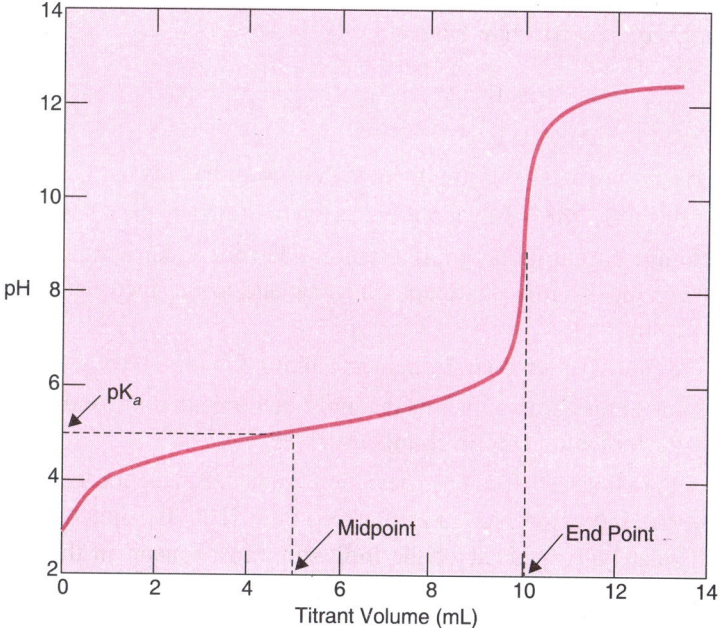

Fig. 2.3 Calculated Titration Curve Between a Weak Acid [0.2 N, 10 mL, pK$_a$ 5.00] and a Strong Base [0.2 N].

6. It is definitely quite obvious from Fig. 2.3 that this **"specific slope"** has *two* distinct meaningful status, namely:

    (*a*) **At End Point**— The slope is **maximum**, and

    (*b*) **At Midpoint**— The slope is **minimum.**

2.12 ACID-BASE INDICATORS

An **acid-base indicator** may be defined as – 'a compound whose conjugate acid and conjugate base duly formed show altogether different colours.

It has been observed that there exists absolutely no definite kind of limitation(s) imposed upon the charge type of the indicator. In fact, the **indicators** are invariably employed to detect the **equivalence point (end point)** in a titration. However, it is absolutely important to choose a particular indicator which is entirely based upon certain array of well defined simple principles as described here under.

Let us take into consideration hydroiodic acid [HI] as the **indicator acid**, which would undergo dissociation in an aqueous medium as expressed below:

$$HI \rightleftharpoons H^+ + I^-$$

Hence, the acid dissociation constant $[K_I]$ is usually given as:

$$K_I = \frac{[H^+][HI^-]}{[HI]} \qquad \qquad ...(i)$$

Importantly, the **acid form of HI** is invariably responsible for attributing the specific **acidic colour** to the indicator solution, whereas the **iodide ion $[I^-]$** imparts the particular **basic colour** to the indicator solution. In actual practice, the specific colour invariably picked up by human eyes is strategically associated with the relative concentrations of these *two* distinct forms of the **indicator**. Thus, by rearranging Eqn. (*i*) we may have:

$$\frac{[I^-]}{[HI]} = \frac{K_I}{[H^+]} \qquad \qquad ...(ii)$$

Eqn. (*ii*) gives rise to *two* vital and important conclusions, namely:

    (*a*) **Colour of the indicator** is duly monitored and controlled by the respective **pH of the solution,**

    (*b*) **Colour change** during an on-going titration does not occur abruptly (of an **indicator**), but takes place gradually in a continuous manner due to the fact that pH of the medium also alters continuously.

Sensitivity of Human-Eye *vis-a-vis* Indicator Colour Change

Following are some of the cardinal factors that must be borne in mind with regard to the **sensitivity of human eye *vis-a-vis* indicator colour change,** such as:

    1. *To detect the first and foremost deviation from the authentic and pure **acid colour** in a solution of the **indicator**, the corresponding ratio $[I^-]/[HI]$ should be at least 1/10 or 0.1, *i.e.,* approximately 10 percent of the **indicator** must remain in the **basic form.**

---

* The statement of facts in (1) and (2) solely apply to the **two-colour indicators**.

2. Likewise, nearly 10% of the **indicator** should be present in the **acidic form** to detect any acid colour.

3. It must be understood clearly that these prevailing limits for $[I^-]/[HI]$ lying between 0.1 to 10 bear absolutely no relevant theoretical significance whatsoever. However, these ensuing meaningful limits are more or less related to the sensitivity of the human eyes, and to a great extent to the specific indicator being used.

4. Nevertheless, certain **indicator colour** are predominantly more quickly detected than the others.

5. One may arrive at the definitive pH values at which the prevailing limits of the observable colour change take place are calculated easily and conveniently.

6. From Eqn. (*i*) we have the following expression:

$$pH = pK_I + \log \frac{[I^-]}{[HI]} \qquad \qquad ...(iii)$$

Thus, we have:

(*a*) **Limit on the acid side** is given by:

$$\frac{[I^-]}{[HI]} = 0.1$$

or $\qquad\qquad pH = pK_I - 1 \qquad$ [From Eqn. (*iii*)] $\qquad\qquad ...(iv)$

(*b*) **Limit on the base side** is given by the following expression:

$$\frac{[I^-]}{[HI]} = 10$$

or $\qquad\qquad pH = pK_I + 1 \qquad$ [From Eqn. (*iii*)] $\qquad\qquad ...(v)$

Therefore, the **range of pH** within which the **indicator** is capable of changing its observed colour is given by the following expression:

$$pH = pK_I \pm 1 \qquad\qquad ...(vi)$$

i.e., Eqn. (*vi*) is obtained by combining Eqns. (*iv*) and (*v*).

7. **Transition Interval:** In fact, the Eqn. (vi) is known as the **transition interval** of the **respective indicator**; and, therefore, evidently depends upon the pK_I value of the **indicator**.

The overwhelmingly greatest importance of the **transition interval** in **indicators** amply suggest, support, and ascertain why the **indicators** having altogether **different chemical structures undergo specific change in colour at different pHs**.

2.13 THEORY OF INDICATORS

Since more than hundred years the investigations of '**indicators**' centered mostly and exclusively around their **empirical characteristic features**. Nevertheless, such investigations altogether failed to touch upon specifically **physico-chemical phenomena** that intimately get involved when an **indicator changes its colour distinctly**. This all happened perhaps due to the absolute lack of the **general chemical theory** that may prove to be the fundamental basis of the so called '**theory of**

indicators'. Importantly, such useful basic informations shall not only provide a reasonably acceptable viewpoint for most of the available divergent experimental data, but also unfold the intricacies involved with respect to the various physico-chemical processes associated with the change in colours of indicators.

2.13.1 Ionic Theory of Indicators

Arrhenius (1987) first of all introduced the **electrolytic dissociation phenomena** to explain the change in colour of indicators. Later on, Oswald (1894) successfully postulated the **'ionic theory of indicators'**, which suggested broadly that the — **'neutralization indicators are weak organic acids or bases wherein the specific undissociated molecules altogether differ in colour from their respective ions'**.

    Example: **Colour change of litmus [Azolitmic Acid]:** As per the **ionic theory indicators, the azolitmic acid** present in **litmus** contains **undissociated molecules** which exhibit purely a **red colour** whereas its **respective anions** give **blue colour**. Let us denote any **indicator acid** as **HInd**, and its corresponding **anions** by **Ind⁻**.

    Hence, we may represent the **'dissociation of Litmus'** as expressed under:

$$HInd \quad \rightleftharpoons \quad H^+ \quad + \quad Ind^- \qquad \qquad ...(a)$$

Litmus		Litmus Anion
[Undissociated]		[Dissociated]
RED		**BLUE**

Salient Features

The **salient features** of **Litmus** are as enumerated below:

1. **Litmus** when dissolved in water provide *two* types of products *viz.*, **undissociated molecules** and its **ions,** which combinedly attributes an **intermediate violet colour** to the resulting solution.

2. **Addition of an Acid:** When a drop of an acid [HCl] is added to an aqueous solution of litmus, the equilibrium in Eqn. (*a*) is drifted to the left-hand side. Alternatively, the added H⁺ ions get duly combined with **Ind⁻ anions** present in the solution to yield **undissociated molecules [HInd]** which ultimately renders the solution **red in colour**.

3. **Addition of an Alkali:** When a drop of an alkali [NaOH] is added to an aqueous solution of litmus, the dissociation equilibrium of the indicator gets shifted to the left, and ultimately the solution acquires the colour of the undissociated **IndOH molecules**. Now, when an acid is being added (which removes OH⁻ ions) the equilibrium gets shifted to the right, and consequently the solution acquires the colour of **Ind⁺ cations**.

    Conclusively, **Oswald's ionic theory of indicators** explains explicitly the distinct changes in the colours of indicators when the H⁺ or OH⁻ ions are duly incorporated to the respective solutions. Another most advantageous outcome of Oswald's theory is that it legitimately permits **definite quantitative interpretations**.

Disadvantages

The major glaring disadvantage of Oswald's theory being that the colouring of organic compounds solely depends upon the prevailing structure of their molecules. Consequently, an apparent distinct colour change may evidently take place exclusively as a result of **certain concrete intermolecular rearrangement** that critically **alters the basic fundamental structure of the indicator**.

2.13.2 Chromophore Theory of Indicators

The **chromophore theory of indicators** finally came to the rescue of putting forward a plausible explanation to the most acceptable and widely recognized mechanism how the indicators function actually. The fundamental concept of the said theory emphasizes the underlying fact that the colour of the **organic compounds** is specifically attributed to the articulated presence in these molecules **(indicators)** of some strategically positioned **radicals** (*viz.*, **atomic moieties**), or **functional group having double bonds**, termed as 'chromophores'.

In fact, the host of **chromophores** that happen to be present in the array of indicators essentially include the **nitro group [O = N →]***, that may be conveniently converted into the corresponding **hydroxy amino function [HO—N→]***; and the **azo moiety [–N=N–]**, that under appropriate parameters gets duly transformed into the corresponding hydroazo group [=N–NH]. Interestingly, the conversion of *three* conjugate double bonds present in benzene (benzenoid) into the corresponding quinoid form as shown below:

Benzene	Benzene
[Benzenoid form]	[Quinoid form]

The above self-explanatory typical examples do throw an ample light to understand the basics of the **'chromophore theory of indicators'** ; that is predominantly responsible for the definitive critical changes taking place in various **indicators at the inflection point (end point)**. Besides, the aforesaid moieties, there are quite a few other **chromophores** that essentially cause colour changes

in **indicators**, such as: (*a*) presence of **double bonds** $\left[-C=C-; =C-C=C-;-C=N-; \right]$

that are close to each other; and (*b*) presence of **carbonyl groups in different fractional moieties**

$$\left[\overset{O}{\underset{\|}{-C-}}; \overset{O}{\underset{\|}{-C-Cl}}; \overset{O}{\underset{\|}{-C-OH}}; \overset{O}{\underset{\|}{-C-OR}}; \overset{O}{\underset{\|}{-C-H}} \right].$$

---

* The **arrows [→]** present in these formulae of organic compounds imply the presence of the **semipolar coordinate bonds**, whereby a pair of electrons is completely donated to the electron deficient atom.

Auxochromes

The particular colour of organic compounds (*e.g.,* indicators) is also categorically influenced by the intimate presence of another altogether different kind of functional moieties invariably known as '**auxochromes**'. Remarkably, as a clear cut distinction from the **chromophores**, the auxochromes cannot of their own characteristic feature attribute (confer) a specific colour to a compound, but when present very much along with the **chromophores** they combinedly potentiate as well as augment the colour of the later *i.e.,* **chromophores**), and ultimately intensifying (deepen) the generated colour caused by them.

Examples: A few most typical and important examples of the **auxochromes** are as stated under:

(*a*) **Functional Groups** *e.g.,* hydroxyl [—OH]; amino [—NH$_2$];

(*b*) **Substituted Functional Groups** *e.g.,* replacement of H-atoms duly in:

Hydroxyl Moiety [—OH] *viz.,* —OCH$_3$ (methoxy); —OC$_2$H$_5$ (ethoxy);

Amino Moiety [—NH$_2$] *viz.,* —N(CH$_3$)$_2$ (dimethyl amino); —N(C$_2$H$_5$)$_2$ (diethyl amino);

Explanation of Chromophoric Theory

The **chromophoric theory** may be further expatiated on the basis of the specific colour change taking place in an **indicator** as a consequence of an '**isomeric change**. That is, an **intramolecular rearrangement** that virtually alters the chemical structure of an **indicator** thereby essentially differing in properties.

It is, however, pertinent to state here that there are indeed several factors which essentially modulate the **chromophoric theory** such as:

- Intramolecular regrouping (rearrangement) affords the formation (or disappearance) of functional moieties that solely influence the colour (*i.e.,* **chromophores** and **auxochromes**), and hence alter the colour of the **indicators**.

- Inter-conversion of isomeric forms is a reversible phenomenon commonly observed amongst the **indicators**.*

- Chromophoric theory largely promulgates that any **neutralization indicator** invariably comprises of various distinct **tautomeric forms** that usually differ from each other both in **colour** and in **equilibrium**.

In a broader perspective, one may illustrate the **Chromophore theory of indicators** explicitly with the help of the following **classical examples:**

1. *para*-**Nitrophenol Indicator:** The **tautomeric change** which takes in *para*-**nitrophenol** may be expressed as follows:

---

* The reversible isomerism encountered is usually termed as '**tauto-merism**', and the corresponding isomers, as **tautomers**.

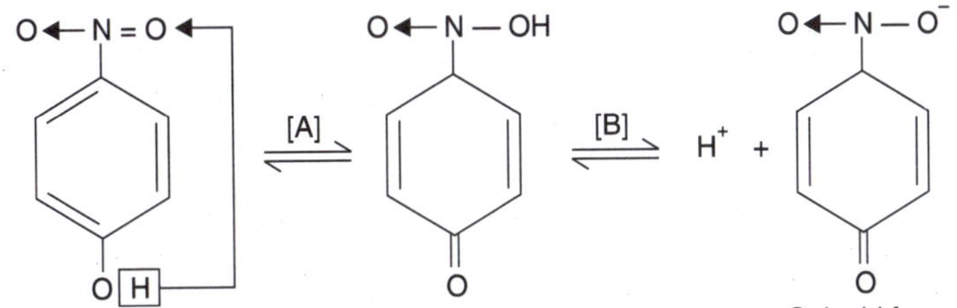

$O \leftarrow N = O \leftarrow$	$O \leftarrow N - OH$	$O \leftarrow N - O^-$
Benzenoid form Colourless (I)	Quinoid form Yellow (II)	Quinoid form Yellow (III)

The above scheme of reactions give rise to such vital facts as:

(*a*) Conversion of the benzene nucleus (**benzenoid form**) into the corresponding **quinoid form** *i.e.,* from structure (I) to structure (II).

(*b*) The solution when made **alkaline** the formation of the quinoid nucleus (II) into being which renders the colours change from colourless to **yellow in *p*-nitrophenol.**

(*c*) When the resulting solution is duly acidified the ensuing equilibrium between the *two* prevailing **tautomeric forms** gets shifted to the **opposite direction** (see III); and, therefore, the **indicator changes from yellow to colourless.**

(*d*) In the specific instance of *p*-nitrophenol the **yellow tautomer** (II) behaves as an **acid.** It may be observed from structure (II) that the **—OH moiety** present in this tautomeric form is an integral component of the $O \leftarrow N—OH$ moiety *i.e.,* it is duly attached to an

oxidized N-atom, as we usually come across either in nitric acid $\left[NHO_3; O \leftarrow N—OH \right]$ or nitrous acid [HNO_2; $O = N—OH$].

(*e*) The various **structural analogy** must correspond to an analogy in characteristic features in such a manner that all the **three** enumerated compounds *viz.,* I, II, and II essentially exhibit **particular acidic properties** *i.e.,* capable of aptly splitting off H-atom from the hydroxy (OH) moieties as H$^+$ ions when present in an aqueous medium.

Presence of Two Equilibria [A] and [B]: From the foregoing statement of facts one may logically infer that the *para*-nitrophenol must possess *two predominant* **equilibria**, namely:

(*i*) **Equilibria [A]** — existing between the *two* **tautomers*** (I) and (II), and

(*ii*) **Equilibria [B]** — existing between the *two* **dissociation components**** (II) and (III).

---

* It may be called as the 'tautomeric equilibria'.

** It may be referred to as the 'dissociation equilibria'.

Interestingly, the very existence of these *two* **equilibria** *viz.,* [A] and [B] discussed above actually go a long way to vividly understand the intricacies of the ensuing bondage taking place between the **reaction of solution** and the **colour of a given indicator**.

(*f*) Let us consider that we are provided with a yellow solution of *p-nitrophenol.* *Two* situations may arise, namely:

Situation-I: Approximately a large segment of the **indicator** is present in solution as the **anions** **(III)** that are in equilibrium along with a relatively small quantum of the **undissociated molecules of tautomer (II)**; and the latter are in perfect equilibrium with the **tautomer (I)**.

Situation-II: When an acid [H⁺] is carefully incorporated to solution, the prevailing **equilibrium** **[B]** gets duly shifted to the left. That is, a large segment of the **indicator anion** gets adequately combined with the H⁺ ions of the acid to give rise to the formation of **undissociated molecules** of the **tautomer (II)** having a yellow colouration.

2. **Orange I [or ∝-Naphthol Orange or Tropaeollin 000 No. 1] Indicator:**

The **acid form (yellow)** of **Orange I** has the following chemical structure:

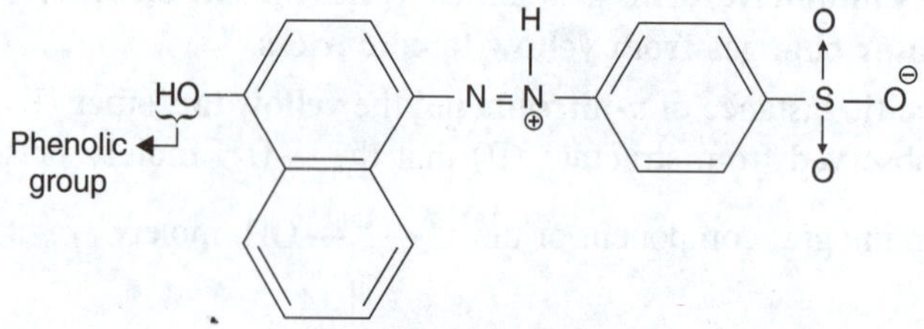

Orange I (A)
[Acid Form (Yellow)]

The conversion of (A) to its corresponding **base form** by carrying out the dissociation of the respective phenolic moiety finally leads to the **delocalized structure** (B), which being **red in colour**.

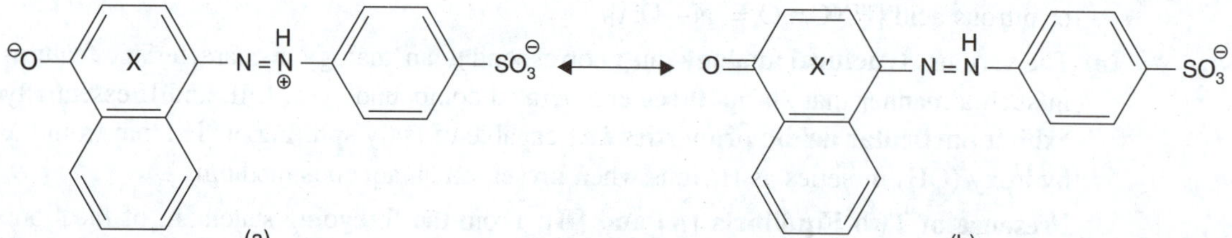

Orange I (B)
[Basic Form (Red)]

In the **delocalized structure (B)** it may be observed critically that the structure (*a*) bears these features, namely:

• Ring (X) in its **benzenoid form**,
• Phenolic O-atom has –ve charge,
• The azo-N-atom closer to the benzene ring has a +ve charge, and

- *para*-Sulphonic acid moiety possesses a –ve charge;

whereas, the corresponding structure (*b*) has the following features, such as:

- Ring (X′) is in its **quinoid form**,
- –vely charged phenolic O-atom is now present as the ketonic form,
- The azo–N–atom closer to the benzene ring has an imino (–NH–) moiety, and
- *p*-Sulphonic acid group bears a –ve charge.

Note: The quinoid form of Orange I (structure B (*b*)] is solely responsible for the actual colour change in such indicators which essentially possess a phenolic moiety.

3. **Methyl Orange: Methyl Orange** is an **aminoazo indicator** that almost provides **identical electronic distribution**, as depicted under structure (C):

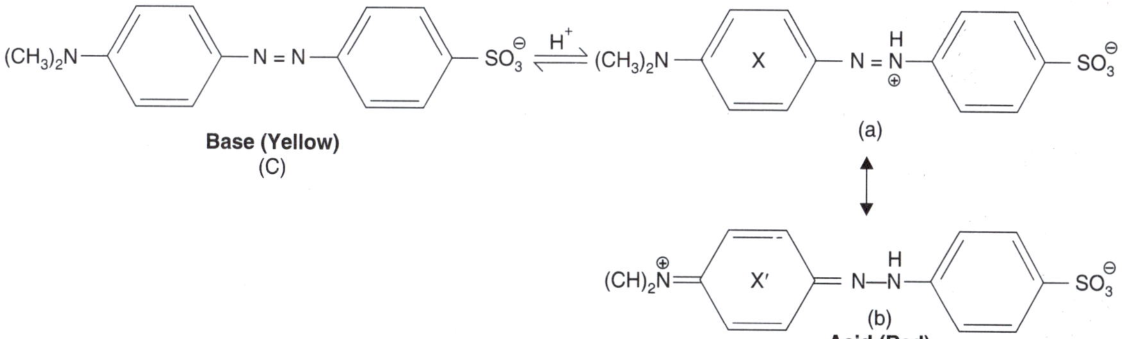

Base (Yellow)
(C)

(a)

(b)
Acid (Red)
(D)

As described under Orange I [Section (2)] above, here (D) duly represents the delocalized structure of **methyl orange** which is **red** in colour in an **acidic environment**. The **quinoid nucleus** in [(D) (*b*)] above, as obtained from the **benzenoid nucleus** in [(D) (*a*)], is exclusively responsible for the colour change. However, **methyl orange** displays yellow colour in its **base form** (c).

4. **Phenolphthalein: Phenolphthalein** is an **acidic indicator**. It has been duly observed that one of the **benzene nuclei** [marked X] in the **phenolphthalein** molecule undergoes **quinoid rearrangement**; and ultimately the following equilibrium is duly obtained in solution:

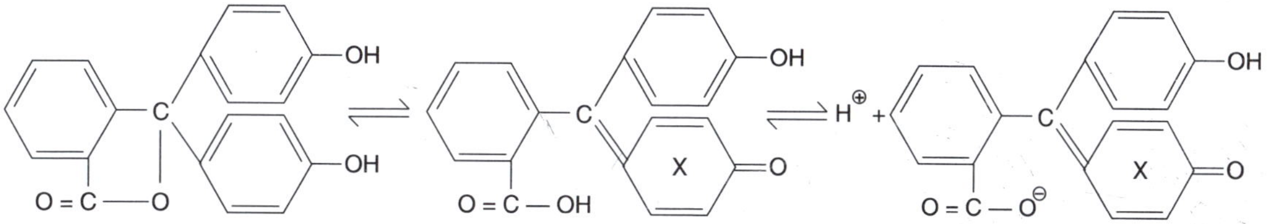

Colourless
[Benzenoid form]

Red
[Quinoid form]

Red
[Quinoid form]

Note: The introduction of OH⁻ ions into the solution predominantly shifts the equilibrium to the right direction, and finally results in a change of colour to red.

Phenolphthalein is usually used as a 0.1% (w/v) and 1% (w/v) solution in 50% (v/v) ethanol.

2.14 CHOICE OF INDICATORS

In usual practice, it has been proved and established that the **neutralization process** is not invariably accompanied by apparent and visible alterations, for instance: **change in the colour of the solution**. It has, therefore, necessitated the absolute inclusion and usage of an appropriate **indicator** right into the titrated solution so as to strategically visualize the critical colour change in determining the precise and accurate inflection point (equivalence point or end point).

It has been adequately dealt with earlier that at the equivalence point the solution has duly attained a definite and specific pH value. In other words, that pH value at the equivalence point has a major role to play *i.e.*, where an **indicator** usually changes its colour sharply and abruptly to conclude the on-going titration to a virtual end. Thus, from the burette reading one obtains the '**titre value**' which on being used in the calculations gives the exact assay of the '**analyte**'*.

In short, the chemical substances that particularly change colour in accordance with pH are invariably employed as the **neutralization indicators**, such as: litmus, phenolphthalein, methyl red, methyl orange, and a host of other substances.

Specific Criteria of an Indicator

Following are some of the specific criteria of an **indicator**, such as:

(*i*) Colour change must prevail over a definite narrow range of pH,

(*ii*) Range solely depends upon the characteristic features of indicator, and

(*iii*) Range seems to be absolutely independent of the nature of the reacting acid and base.

Based on the aforesaid *three* cardinal criteria usually encountered with respect to the **critical colour of an indicator** one may observe that at the equivalence point the change in colour occurs with certain **deviation** from it. And this observed deviation gives rise to a certain degree of error commonly referred to as the '**indicator error**' in titration. The actual depth and magnitude of this errors invariably varies over a reasonably wide range, depending upon the **particular indicator employed**, besides the type of **alkali and acid employed in the specific titration (reaction)**. Here, two obvious situations may arise, such as:

- **Use of a Correct Indicator** — minimises error significantly and the ensuing results fall very much within the usual limits of analytical error, and

- **Use of an Unsuitable Indicator** — enhances errors beyond the limits of acceptance; and hence the results are totally rejected (ignored).

In **pharmaceutical analysis**, we normally come across on array of **pH indicators**, which predominately exhibit their extremely divergent dissociation constant. By virtue of these glaring and supportive evidences the ranges of various commonly used indicators mostly embrace the **entire pH scale** ranging between **pH 0 to pH 12**. Table 2.7 records the ranges to the most vital and important

---

* **Analyte**: The chemical substance present in a sample that needs to be estimated by a standard method of assay.

pH indicators that are recommended and used profusely in **Official Compendia** (*viz.,* BP, USP, IP, Eur. P., and Int. P) and other **Standard Procedures** employed in the **pharmaceutical analysis**.

Indicator	Solvent	Concentration used (%)	Nature of Indicator [A: Acid; B: Basic]	Observed Colour		Operational pH Range
				Acid Form	**Alkaline Form**	
1 **Alizarin Yellow**	Water	0.1	A	Yellow	Violet	10.1 – 12.0
2 **Thymolphthalein**	Ethanol (90%)	0.1	A	Colourless	Blue	9.3 – 10.5
3 **Phenolphthalein**	Ethanol (60%)	0.1 and 1.0	A	Colourless	Red	8.0 – 10.0
4 **Cresol Purple**	Ethanol (20%)	0.05	A	Yellow	Purple	7.4 – 9.0
5 **Natural Red**	Ethanol (60%)	0.1	B	Red	Yellow-Brown	6.8 – 8.0
6 **Phenol Red**	Ethanol (20%)	0.1	A	Yellow	Red	6.4 – 8.0
7 **Bromothymol Blue**	Ethanol (20%)	0.05	A	Yellow	Blue	6.0 – 7.6
8 **Litmus (Azolitmin)**	Water	1.0	A	Red	Blue	5.0 – 8.0
9 **Methyl Red**	Ethanol (60%)	0.1 and 0.2	B	Red	Yellow	4.2 – 6.2
10 **Methyl Orange**	Water	0.1	B	Red	Yellow	3.1 – 4.4
11 **Bromophenol Blue**	Water	0.1	A	Yellow	Blue	3.0 – 4.6
12 **Tropeoline 00**	Water	0.01; 0.1; 1.0	B	Red	Yellow	1.4 – 3.2
13 **Crystal Violet**	Water	—	—	Green	Violet	0.0 – 2.0

Table 2.7 Ranges of Most Vital and Important pH Indicators

2.15 MIXED INDICATORS

In a broader sense, certain **pharmaceutical analysts** in particular and analytical chemists in general invariably prefer to make use of the **mixed indicator**, which when intimately constituted may give rise to an extremely **sharp colour change** duly **spread over a narrow pH interval**. The *two individual indicators* to be mixed must fulfil the following *two* essential criteria, namely:

(*a*) To possess usually almost **identical transition intervals**, and

(*b*) To select these indicators in such a manner that their **acid colour** combine to **produce a hue** (*i.e.,* colour or tint) which represents the complement (See Table 2.8) of the hue obtained by the combination of their **respective base colours**.

Consequently, one may critically observe an extremely sharp colour change occasionally having a passage *via* a **colourless phase** or a **gray phase**.

Table 2.8 summarizes emphatically the prevailing accurate and precise correlation of colour with wavelength of the visible light.*

	Table 2.8 Precise Correlation of Colour with Wavelength of Visible Light		
S.No.	**Wave Length (nm)**	**Colour**	**Complement Colour**
1	400 – 450	Violet	Yellow-Green
2	450 – 480	Blue	Yellow
3	480 – 490	Green-Blue	Orange
4	490 – 500	Blue-Green	Red
5	500 – 560	Green	Purple
6	560 – 575	Yellow-Green	Violet
7	575 – 590	Yellow	Blue
8	590 – 625	Orange	Green-Blue
9	625 – 730	Red	Blue-Green

Kolthoff (1937)** observed that a **mixed indicator** consisting of **bromocresol green** plus **methyl red** exhibit a distinct **red colour** in the **acid form**, and **green** in the **base form**; however, the **actual transition** remains very sharp at pH 5.1. Likewise, a few such other pairs of **mixed indicators** that find their abundant usage in the domain of 'analytical chemistry' are namely: **thymol blue – phenolphthalein; cresol red – thymol blue; bromothymol blue – phenol red,** and the like.

Table 2.9 includes the various, composition of **mixed indicator**, their **respective colours** seen in 'acid' and 'base' form, **indicator exponent (pT)**, and **special remarks**.

			Table 2.9 Composition of Mixed Indicators			
S.No.	**Composition of Two Indicator Solutions**	**A : B***	**Observed Colour**		**pT**	**Special Remarks**
			Acid Form	**Base Form**		
1	A = Methyl Orange [0.1% in H_2O] B = Indigo Carmine [0.25% in H_2O]	1:1	Violet	Green	4.1	Quite convenient and easy to do titration in artificial light.
2	A = Bromocresol Blue [0.2% in ETOH] B = Methyl Red [0.2% in ETOH]	3:1	Red	Green	5.1	Exceptionally sharp change in colour. (contd.)

---

* It is known that below 400 nm the ensuing colour slowly becomes invisible as it sails into the UV region; above 750 nm it passes directly into the IR region.

** Kolthoff IM: **Acid-Base Indicators**, Macmillan, New York, 1937.

3	A = Neutral Red [0.1% in H_2O] B = Methylene Blue [0.1% in H_2O]	1:1	Blue-Violet	Green	7.0	Must be always stored in a dark bottle to avoid deterioration by UV light.
4	A = Phenolphthalein [0.1% in 50% ETOH] B = ∝-Naphtholphthalein [0.1% in 50% ETOH]	3:1	Pale Pink	Violet	8.9	Exhibits pale green colour at pH = 8.5.
5	A = Thymol Blue [0.1% in 30% ETOH] B = ∝-Naphtholphthalein [0.1% in 50% ETOH]	1:3	Yellow	Violet	9.0	Displays green colour at pH = 9.0.

*Exact volume proportions in which the two solutions A and B are mixed thoroughly before use.

Salient Features of Mixed Indicators

These are as follows:

1. **Mixed indicators** may be employed for detecting the **pH changes between** the range 0.1 to 0.15.

2. **Mixed indicators** are, therefore, found to be quite easy and convenient in a situation when the **pH change** on the **titration curve is not so large.**

3. When there is **no distinct sharp pH change** accomplished, the use of the **mixed indicators** do help overwhelmingly to enable carry out the titrations efficaciously.

   Example: A beautiful typical example to justify the application of the **mixed indicators** in analytical chemistry is the titration of **NH_4OH solution** with **acetic acid** in the presence of **Neutral Red + Methylene Blue (Mixed Indicator)** [See No: 3 in Table 2.9]. Since, it is a well known fact that in '**titration by the neutralization method at least one of the reacting substances should be a strong electrolyte**'; and hence, the above titration between NH_4OH/CH_3COOH is just not practicable in the presence of a '**Single indicator**'.

2.16 UNIVERSAL INDICATORS

The pH values at which the '**limits of observed colour change**' invariably take place are calculated easily and conveniently. From the following expression:

$$K_I = \frac{[H^+][I^-]}{[HI]} \qquad \text{where, } K_I = \text{Acid dissociation constant;}$$

or

$$pH = pK_I + \log \frac{[I^-]}{[HI]} \qquad \qquad ...(a)$$

Thus, we may have from Eqn. (a):

For the achievable limit on the acid side, $\frac{[I^-]}{[HI]} = 0.1$;

or

$$pH = pK_I - 1 \qquad \qquad ...(b)$$

For the achievable limit on the base side, $\dfrac{[I^-]}{[HI]} = 10$;

or

$$pH = pK_I + 1 \qquad \qquad ...(c)$$

Therefore, one may accomplish the **pH range** within which the **indicator** may be seen to be changing colour usually given by the expression duly obtained by combining together the Eqn. (b) and Eqn. (c) as follows:

$$pH = pK_I \pm 1 \qquad \qquad ...(d)$$

Eqn. (d) is termed as the '**transition interval**' of the indicator, which predominantly depends upon the pK_I (*i.e.,* **acid dissociation constant**) of the **indicator**. This perhaps is the fundamental reason why various **indicators** having altogether **definite structural variants** invariably **change** colour at **different pH's**.

In case, an **array of indicators** are mixed thoroughly in such a fashion that their ensuing '**transition intervals' get overlapped significantly**, in such a situation it may be quite feasible, plausible, and possible to observe **colour change** explicitly over a rather **broad spectrum of pH**. Importantly, under such a situation one may safely and concretely obtain a **rough estimate** of the **pH** of the solution by critically noting the **indicator colour**.

Nevertheless, when such a **universal indicator** is applied to a filter paper meticulously, the resulting '**pH paper**' articulately gives rise to a rather exceptionally simple means of measuring pH accurately to within a close limit of ± 1 **unit** by dipping it into the **investigative solution**, and subsequently comparing the **observed colour** *vis-a-vis* a series of **known standards**.

Following are a few typical examples of **universal indicators**, such as:

(a) **Mixture of Methyl Red and Thymol Blue Indicator:** It is regarded to be the **simplest universal indicators** not only due to its composition, but also on account of its most convenient preparation* and usage in the domain of **pharmaceutical** analysis. In fact, the **universal indicator** comprised of a **mixture of methyl red and thymol blue indicator** aptly undergoes the following **colour changes with pH**:

pH	4	5	6	7	8	9	10
Colour	Red	Orange	Rose Yellow	Yellow	Pale Green	Green	Blue Green

(b) **Kolthoff's Universal Indicator [EIV-1]:** It is a mixture of many indicators, which essentially gives the following **colour changes** with respective pH:

pH	2/LESS	3	4	5	6	7	8	9	10/MORE
Colour	Red Rose	Red Orange	Orange	Yellow Orange	Lemon Yellow	Yellow Green	Green	Blue Green	Violet

2.17 POLYPROTIC SYSTEM

It has been observed that the **diprotic acids [H$_2$A]** [*e.g.*, H$_2$SO$_4$ (sulphuric acid); H$_2$CrO$_4$ (chromic acid] may be titrated in a **stepwise manner**, with great case and fervour, just like the titration of the diprotic base, Na$_2$CO$_3$ (sodium carbonate). In order to accomplish reasonably sharp and distinct **equivalence point (end point)** breaks for the desired titration of the **first proton K$_{a_1}$** must be at least $10^4 \times$ K$_{a_2}$ *i.e.*, the breaks for the **first proton** should be ten thousand fold to those of the **second proton**, K$_{a_2}$. In a situation, when K$_{a_2}$ is found to be strategically located between the range of 10^{-7} and 10^{-8} for a successful titration, consequently one may obtain an end point break for carrying out the titration of the second proton easily.

Likewise, the **triprotic acids [H$_3$A]** *e.g.*, H$_3$PO$_4$ (phosphoric acid); H$_3$BO$_4$ (boric acid)] may also be titrated efficaciously, but the actual titration of the **third proton, K$_{a_3}$**, is invariably found to be too meagre and small to accomplish a good and point break for the titration of the **third proton, K$_{a_3}$**.

Figure 2.4 shows the titration curve for a **diprotic acid [H$_2$A]** *Vs* **sodium hydroxide [NaOH]** as given under:

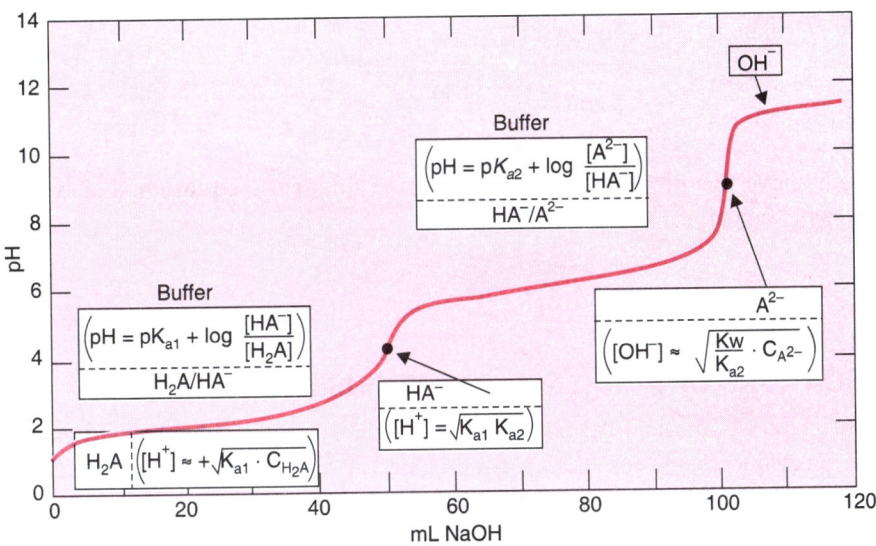

Fig. 2.4 Plot of Titration of Diprotic Acid *Vs* Sodium Hydroxide
[Adapted from: Christian GD: Analytical Chemistry John Wiley & Sons Inc. New York, 6th edn. 2004]

Explanation

The explanation of the various segments of the above titration curve are as given below explicitly:

1. pH observed at the very initial stage of the titration may be estimated precisely from the ensuing ionization of the **first proton, K$_{a_1}$**, provided the solution is available at a not so diluted state.

2. In a situation, when the available quantum of **first proton, K_{a_1}** is observed to be not so abundant, whereas the quantity undergoing dissociation may be ignored compeletly *vis-a-vis* the analytical concentration of the diprotic acid $[H_2A]$, the approximate equation thus obtained may be employed strategically to calculate $[H^+]$ ultimately.

3. In the course of titration up to the **first inflection point (end point)**, the development of an **HA^-/H_2A buffer region** is duly accomplished.

4. However, at the **first equivalence point (end point)** there exists a solution of **HA^+ ions**, and hence:

$$[H^+] \approx \sqrt{K_{a_1} K_{a_2}}$$

where, K_{a_1} = first proton; and K_{a_2} = second proton, in the prevailing **diprotic acid**.

5. Beyond this point (Fig. 2.4) a **buffer** having an **A^{2-}/HA^-** prevails predominantly.

6. Ultimately, at the **second inflection point (equivalence point)**, the pH is accurately estimated by the ensuing hydrolysis of A^{2-} (*i.e.,* the respective salt).

7. At this material time, if one observes distinctly that the resulting salt, A^{2-}, happens to be not too strong a base, the following given approximate equation may be suitably employed to duly calculate $[OH^-]$ (See Fig. 2.4):

$$[OH^-] = \sqrt{\frac{K\omega}{K_{a_2}} \cdot C_{A^{2-}}}$$

In case, the above line of action is not feasible, the **quadratic equation** should be employed to solve the following equation:

$$K_b = \frac{K\omega}{K_{a_2}} = \frac{[HA][OH^-]}{[A^-]}$$

2.18 APPLICATIONS OF ACID-BASE TITRATIONS

The actual applications of the acid-base titrations in the domain of the '**pharmaceutical analysis**' shall be discussed according to the methods recommended in the '**Official Compendia**' *viz.,* **Indian Pharmacopoea [IP]; British Pharmacopoea [BP]; United States Pharmacopoea [USP]; European Pharmacopoea [Euro.P.]** and **International Pharmacopoea [Int.P.]**.

The following chemical substances shall be treated separately in details:

2.18.1 Assay of Sodium Hydroxide [NaOH]

Sodium hydroxide can be assayed by **titrimetric analysis** using sulphuric acid.

Chemicals Required: Sodium hydroxide (Pellets) 1.5 g ; sulphuric acid 1 N;

Method: Accurately weigh approx. 1.5 g of sodium hydroxide and dissolve it in 40 mL of **CO_2-free distilled water*** (DW). Cool the resulting solution and titrate with 1 N sulphuric acid by making

---

* It may be obtained by boiling distilled water from 20-30 minutes

use of phenolphthalein solution [0.1% *w/v* in 50% *v/v* EtOH] as an indicator. Record the exact volume of acid solution from the burette reading (titre value) when the pink colour of the solution gets discharged almost completely.

Reactions: The inflection point end point) duly obtained with phenolphthalein as an indicator actually represents complete neutralization of the total NaOH as depicted in the following equation:

$$2\ NaOH + H_2SO_4 \longrightarrow Na_2SO_4 + 2H_2O \qquad\qquad ..(i)$$
$$2(40.0)$$

Nevertheless, in a cold solution, with phenolphthalein as an indicator, the equivalence point of titration of sodium carbonate with 1 N H_2SO_4 is exhibited duly when the sodium carbonate gets transformed into sodium bicarbonate as given under:

$$2\ Na_2CO_3 + H_2SO_4 \longrightarrow Na_2SO_4 + 2\ NaHCO_3 \qquad\qquad ...(ii)$$
$$2(106)$$

At this critical point in time, add **methyl orange** solution and continue with the above titration until one arrives at a **persistent pink colour**. Thus, we may have:

With Phenolphthalein 1 mL of 1 N $H_2SO_4 \equiv 0.040$ g (or 40 mg) of total alkali calculated as NaOH;

With Methyl Orange 1 mL of N $H_2SO_4 \equiv 0.0106$ g of Na_2CO_3;

Explanations: The following *four* different aspects expatiates the above assay adequately:

1. The usual titration of phenolphthalein equivalence point (end point) mainly caters for *two* purposes:

   (*a*) Neutralization of sodium hydroxide, and

   (*b*) Conversion of Na_2CO_3 to $NaHCO_3$.

2. When the Na_2CO_3 gets converted to $NaHCO_3$ *i.e.,* $[CO_3^{2-} + 2H^+ \rightleftharpoons 2\ HCO_3^-]$, the H^+ ion remains usually at a low ebb because the CO_3^{2-} is strongly basic in character, whereby the pH of the resulting mixture varies between 8 to 9.8. At this juncture when phenolphthalein changes colour till the conversion of Na_2CO_3 to $NaHCO_3$ is complete.

3. The resulting HCO_3^-, as in (2) above, is weakly basic in nature due to: $HCO_3^- + H^+ \rightleftharpoons$ H_2CO_3, and the $NaHCO_3$ thus formed practically remains unneutralized even though H^+ has been enhanced to the extent where phenolphthalein affords a change in colour.

4. **Neutralization** of the **generated NaHCO_3** gets duly completed only when H^+ ion has been increased by further incorporation of acid, as could be seen by the change in colour of methyl orange at pH ranging between 3.2 to 4.4.

   The underlying reaction is designated by equation:

$$2\ HaHCO_3 + H_2SO_4 \longrightarrow Na_2SO_4 + 2\ CO_2 \uparrow + H_2O \qquad\qquad ...(iii)$$
$$2(84.01)$$

Calculations: In reality, the total volume of 1 N H_2SO_4 consumed in the titration was actually required to neutralize NaOH and Na_2CO_3, thereby converting the latter *first* to $NaHCO_3$ at the **phenolphthalein equivalence point (end point)**, and secondly to H_2CO_3 (unstable/transient) at the **methyl orange end point (inflection point)**.

From Eqn. (*i*), it may be seen that the equivalent weight of NaOH is 40.00 g. Therefore, 1 mL of the total amount of 1 N H_2SO_4 consumed is equivalent to 40.00 mg or 1 meq of NaOH. Thus, the total alkalinity calculated as NaOH may be expressed as under:

$$\%NaOH = \frac{mL. \times 1 \times meq\ wt \times 100}{wt\ of\ sample}$$

Volume of 1 N H_2SO_4* required to neutralize $NaHCO_3$ [as in Eqn. (*iii*)] is almost equivalent to the volume needed to yield $NaHCO_3$ from Na_2CO_3 [as in Eqn. (*ii*)].

Therefore, from Eqn. (*ii*) we may calculate:

Each mL of 1 N $H_2SO_4 \equiv 106.0$ mg of Na_2CO_3

Hence, the amount (%) of Na_2CO_3 present in the sample (analyte) is given by the following expression:

$$\%\ Na_2CO_3 = \frac{mL. \times 1 \times meq\ wt \times 100}{wt\ of\ sample}$$

2.18.2 Assay of Calcium Carbonate [CaCO₃]

The underlying principle for the assay of **calcium carbonate** is the liberation of CO_2 by the interaction with an acid. The excess of 'acid' is now back-titrated with an alkali using a suitable and sensitive acid-base indicator (*viz.,* **methyl orange**). The following reaction takes place:

$$2\ HCl + CaCO_3 \longrightarrow CaCl_2 + CO_2 + H_2O$$

i.e., 1 L of 1 N acid $\equiv \dfrac{1}{2}$ of calcium carbonate.

However, one may also express the 'analytical results' in terms of **percentages**. Therefore, in the assay of **calcium carbonate** it can be determined what percentages of **calcium, carbon** and **oxygen** it actually contains. Keeping in view the above factual observation it is quite logical that $CaCO_3$ may be regarded as a compound of **calcium oxide [CaO]** with **carbonic anhydride [CO₂]**; and, therefore, the composition of this salt is invariably expressed in **percentages of the oxides CaO and CO₂**.

> **Note:** The use of HCl is usually preferred to H_2SO_4 [BP-1948] so as to avoid the formation of the sparingly soluble calcium sulphate [$CaSO_4$], that is generated when $CaCO_3$ is duly decomposed by H_2SO_4 [0.1 N].

Methodology

The various steps involved in the assay of **calcium carbonate** are as enumerated under:

1. A weighed quantity of $CaCO_3$ is dissolved in a measured volume of 0.1 N HCl (duly diluted with water).

---

* The actual difference between the acid consumed to a **methyl orange** end point and the acid consumed to a **phenol-phthalein** end point.

2. CO_2 is removed by boiling the solution and then cooling the solution to ambient temperature,

3. The excess of acid is precisely determined by carrying out the titration with 0.1 N NaOH, employing methyl orange as an indicator.

2.18.3 Assay of Phosphoric Acid [H_3PO_4]

The fundamental theoretical basis for the assay of **phosphoric acid** is its titration with 0.1 N NaOH to the **sodium phosphate [Na_2HPO_4]** equivalence point using **phenolphthalein** as an **indicator**. Thus, we have:

$$2\ NaOH + H_3PO_4 \longrightarrow Na_2HPO_4 + 2\ H_2O$$

However, it is always desirable to perform the above titration in the presence of **sodium chloride [NaCl]** so as to provide a rather more accurate and distinct end-piont*. The changes in pH in the course of the above titration may be understood clearly from the following *three* obseived variable dissociation constants, namely:

$$K_1 = \frac{[H^+][H_2PO_4^-]}{[H_3PO_4]} = 1 \times 10^{-2}:\ pK_1 = 2$$

$$K_2 = \frac{[H^+][HPO_4^{3-}]}{[H_2PO_4^-]} = 1.5 \times 10^{-7}:\ pK_2 = 6.8$$

$$K_3 = \frac{[H^+][PO_4^{3-}]}{[HPO_4^{3-}]} = 2.5 \times 10^{-12}:\ pK_3 = 11.6$$

These constants usually refer to dilute solutions, but vary to certain extent with the concentration. Rapid **pimps** or **changes** of pH take place usually at the **first** and **second** equivalence points, that are calculated from the equations:

$$\frac{pK_1 + pK_2}{2} = 4.4 \text{ corresponding to } \mathbf{NaH_2PO_4}, \text{ and}$$

$$\frac{pK_2 + pK_3}{2} = 9.2 \text{ corresponding to } \mathbf{Na_2HPO_4}.$$

RECOMMENDED READINGS

Bishop E: **Indicators**, Pergamon, Oxford, 1972.

Convington AK *et al.*: **Computer Simulation of Titration Curves with Applications in Aqueous Carbonate Solution**, *Anal. Chem. Aeta.*, **130**: 103, 1981.

---

* As per Smith [*Qutr. Jr. of Pharmacy*, **2**: 238, 1928] the same identical end point is given, without using NaCl, using **cresolphthalein** as **indicator** (pH range: 8.2 to 9.8). Kolthoff strongly recommends the use of **thymolphthalein** as **indicator**, and titrating to the first perceptible blue colour.

Day RA Jr. and Underwood AL: **Quantitative Analysis**, Prentice Hall of India Pvt Ltd., New Delhi, 6th edn. 1993.

deLevie R: **A Spreadsheet Workbook for Quantitative Chemical Analysis**, McGraw Hill, New York, 1992.

Ewing GW: **Analytical Instrumentation Handbook**, Marcel Deckker Inc., New York, 1997.

Frieser H and Fernado Q: **Ionic Equilibria in Analytical Chemistry**, John Wiley, New York, 1963.

Green JM: **A Practical Guide to Analytical Method Validation**, *Anal. Chem.*, **68**, 305 A, 1996.

Guenther WB: **Unified Equilibrium Calculations**, Wiley, New York, 1991.

Kateman G and Pippers FW: **Quality Control in Analytical Chemistry**, Wiley, Chichester, 1981.

Kenkel J: **A Primer on Quality in the Analytical Laboratory**, CRC Press, Boca Raton, FL, 2000.

Laitinen HA and Harris WE: **Chemical Analysis**, McGraw Hill, New York, 2nd edn, 1975.

McAlpine R.K: **Change in pH at the Equivalence Point**, *J.Chem. Ed.*, **25**: 694, 1948.

Miller JM and Crowther (Eds.): **Analytical Chemistry in a GMP Environment: A Practical Guide**, Wiley, New York, 2000.

Pearson RG: **Recent Advances in the Concept of Hard and Soft Acids and Bases**, *J. Chem. Educ.*, **63**: 687, 1986.

Perrin DD and Dempsey B: **Buffers for pH and Metal Ion Control**, Chapman and Hall, London, 1974.

Pietrzyk DJ and Frank CW: **Analytical Chemistry**, Academic Press, London, 2nd edn., 1979.

Rosenthal D and Zuman P: Acid-Base Equilibria, Buffers and Titration in Water, In: **Treatise on Analytical Chemistry**, (eds) Kolthoff IM and Elring PJ, John Wiley and Sons, New York, 2nd edn. vol. 2., 1979.

Schrimer RE: **Modern Methods of Pharmaceutical Analysis.**, CRC Press, Boston, 2nd edn., Vol. 1, 1991.

Stoeppler M *et al.*, (Eds): **Reference Materials for Chemical Analysis: Certification, Availability, and Proper Usage**, Wiley, New York, 2001.

PROBABLE QUESTIONS

1. Explain the Acid-Base (Neutralization) Titrations. Discuss the underlying theoretical aspects of **Neutralization Titrations** with specific reference to:

    (*i*) Arrhenius Theory

    (*ii*) Theory of Solvent systems

    (*iii*) Bronsted-Lowry Theory

    (*iv*) Lewis Theory

2. Discuss the specific **'Role of Solvent'** in Acid-Base Titrations. Give suitable examples in support of your answer.

3. Give a comprehensive account on the **'Relative Strengths of Acids and Bases'**. Explain the terms:

    (*a*) Dissociation Constant

    (*b*) Autoprotolysis

    (*c*) Molar Equilibrium Constants

4. Describe the **Ionization Law of Mass Action.** Explain diagramatically the progress of an on-going chemical reaction.

5. Write a **detailed account** on the following:

    (*a*) Common-Ion Effect

    (*b*) Ionic Product of Water [K_{H_2O}]

    (*c*) Polyprotic System

6. Explain explicitly the following terminologies:
   (*a*) The pH Scale
   (*b*) Hydrolysis of Salts
   (*c*) Buffer solutions
7. (*a*) Give a brief account on the '**Henderson Hasselbalch Equation**'.
   (*b*) Discuss the '**Neutralization Curves**'.
8. What do you understand by '**Indicators**'. Explain the following:
   (*a*) Theory of Indicators
   (*b*) Acid-Base Indicators
9. Describe the **Chromophore Theory of Indicators** with specific reference to:
   (*i*) *para*-Nitrophenol Indicators
   (*ii*) Phenophthalein
   (*iii*) Methyl Orange
10. Write an Exhaustive account on the following vital aspects of **indicators**, namely:
    (*a*) Choice of Indicators
    (*b*) Mixed Indicators
11. Write an essay on the '**Universal Indicators**'. Give appropriate examples wherever necessary.
12. Discuss thse '**Applications of Acid-Base Titrations**' with particular reference to:
    (*i*) Assay of Sodium Hydroxide
    (*ii*) Assay of Calcium Carbonate
    (*iii*) Assay of Phosphoric Acid.

Contains

3.1 Concepts of Oxidation and Reduction

3.2 Reduction-Oxidation (Redox) Reactions

3.3 Standard Oxidation Potential

3.4 Strengths and Equivalent Weights of Oxidizing and Reducing Agents

3.5 Nernst Equation [Effects of Concentrations on Potentials]

3.6 Theory of Redox Titrations

3.7 Equilibrium Constants of Oxidation-Reduction Reactions

3.8 Side Reactions in Redox Titrations

3.9 Oxidation-Reduction Titration Curves [Redox Titration Curves]

3.10 Redox Indicators

3.11 Redox Cell Representations [Electrochemical Cells]

3.12 Measurement of Electrode Potentials [or Half-Reaction Potentials]

3.13 Titrations Based on Redox Reactions

3

Oxidation-Reduction Titrations

In **'Pharmaceutical Analysis'** the most important field of activity as an excellent class of titrations is the **'oxidation-reduction titrations'** or **'redox titrations'**, wherein an **oxidizing agent** and a **reducing agent** duly interact with each other effectively.

Importantly, one may distinctly and discretely observe an appreciable contract in **oxidation-reduction titrations** to **neutralization** and **precipitation** methodologies, in which the titration reaction(s) essentially comprises of specific ions thereby critically giving rise to the **'undissociated molecules'** of either a **weak electrolyte** *viz*, weak acid, water or a **precipitate** *viz*., silver chloride [AgCl], barium sulphate [$BaSO_4$]. In a rather broader perspective, **oxidation-reduction titrations (or oxidimetry)** predominantly involves oxidation-reduction reactions that are intimately associated with the actual transfer of electrons.*

3.1 CONCEPTS OF OXIDATION AND REDUCTION

The definitions of oxidation and reduction are as given under:

Oxidation: Oxidation may be defined as — **'a loss of electrons to an oxidizing agent (that undergoes reduction aptly) to yield a more positive or higher (elevated) oxidation state.**

Reduction: Reduction may be defined as — **'a gain of electrons from a reducing agent (that undergoes oxidation swiftly) to give a lower or more negative oxidation state'.**

However, one may accomplish a much better in depth and better understanding of these reactions *via.* all representations (electro chemical cells), measurement of electrode potentials etc., which will be treated elsewhere in this chapter.

In other words, the aforesaid **'exchange of electrons'** ultimately leads to definitive alternations in the valence of the corresponding atoms or irons; **the valence of an oxidized atom or ion is enhanced (increased), and the valence of a reduced atom or ion is decreased.**

Example: A few typical examples consist of the conversions of:

(*i*) Fe^{2+} (ferrous ion) into Fe^{3+} (ferric ion);

---

* The modern concepts of the oxidation-reduction phenomenon as the specific processes that involves electrons transfer, and it was duly postulated by Pisarzhersky (1910-14).

(*ii*) Cu into Cu^{2+} (cupric); and

(*iii*) Cl^- (chloride) into Cl_2 are nothing but **oxidations**, by virtue of the fact that in all these **three instances** the respective valence of the atom or ions get duly enhanced (from $+ 2$ to $+ 3$; from $- 1$ to 0; and from 0 to $+ 2$).

3.2 REDUCTION-OXIDATION (REDOX) REACTIONS

A **reduction-oxidation reaction**, invariably termed as a **redox reaction**, may be defined as one which takes place rapidly between *two* typically specific entities, one being a **reducing agent** and the other an **oxidizing agent**. Thus, we have:

$$O_{x_1} + Red_2 \rightleftharpoons Red_1 + O_{x_2} \qquad \ldots(a)$$

From Eqn. (*a*) it may be observed that:

- O_{x_1} gets reduced to Red_1, and likewise Red_2 gets oxidized to O_{x_2}.

- O_{x_1} being the **oxidizing agent**, whereas Red_2 is the respective **reducing agent.**

- Tendency of a reducing or oxidizing substance will be exclusively dependent upon the reduction potential.

The above statement of facts and logistics may be further expatiated as enumerated under:

An **oxidizing substance** shall usually adore a tendency to get **associated with an electron or electrons**, and subsequently be reduced to a **lower level of oxidations status**:

$$M^{a+} + ne^- \longrightarrow M^{(a-n)+} \qquad \ldots(b)$$

For **example:** $\quad Ce^{4+} + e^- \longrightarrow Ce^{3+}$

$\qquad\qquad$ Ceric Form $\qquad\qquad$ Cerous Form

$\qquad\qquad$ **[Oxidized]** $\qquad\qquad$ **[Reduced]**

Likewise, a **reducing substance** will invariably exhibit a tendency to **release an electron or electrons**, and in turn get oxidized:

$$M^{a+} \longrightarrow M^{(a+n)^+} + ne^- \qquad \ldots(c)$$

For **example:** $\quad 2Cl^- \longrightarrow Cl_2 + 2e^-$

Following are a few typical examples of very **strong oxidizing** and **reducing substances (agents)** namely:

(*a*) **Very Strong Oxidizing Agents** *e.g.*, Permanganate ion $[MnO_4^-]$, Dichromate ion $[Cr_2O_7^{2-}]$, Free chlorine $[Cl_2]$, Free bromine $[Br_2]$, Ferric ion $[Fe^{3+}]$, Arsonite $[AsO_4^{3-}]$, Free iodine $[I_2]$, Stannic ion $[Sn^{4+}]$.

(*b*) **Very Strong Reducing Agents** *e.g.*, Alkali metals [Li, K, Na], Alkaline earth metals [Ca, Sr, Ba], Hydrogen arsenide $[AsH_3]$, Vanadium ion $[V^{2+}]$, Titanium ion, $[Ti^{3+}]$, Sulphide ion $[S^2]$.

In conclusion, it may be added that if the **oxidized state** of a metal ion is duly **complexed**, it is rendered to have these **characteristic features**, namely:

- becomes certainly more stable,

- rather becomes more difficult for undergoing reduction, and

- decreased tendency to take on electrons.

Similarly, if the **reduced form** fails to undergo **complexation**, it becomes rather **more stable**; and, therefore, **easier to accomplish** duly.

3.3 STANDARD OXIDATION POTENTIAL

Having gained a rather substantial exposure to the basic fundamental concepts with regard to the **oxidizing** and **reducing agents** one may observe critically that they do **differ amongst themselves in strength** *viz.*, in their respective **chemical activity**.

Nevertheless, the following **cardinal observations** are worth noting, such as:

- **Strong oxidizing agents** do exert a marked and pronounced tendency to gain electrons.
- Evidently such **strong oxidizing agents** are capable of withdrawing electrons from several reducing agents, even though they are **comparatively weak***.
- Contrarily, the **weak oxidizing agents** possess relatively a much less marked tendency to gain electrons.
- Obviously such **weak oxidizing agents** are capable of oxidizing exclusively the **strongest reducing agents****.

Therefore, it may be inferred without any reasonable doubt that the actual prevailing **'direction of an oxidation-reduction (redox) reaction** may be predicted with utmost certainty only if certain distinctly **quantitative characteristic feature** of the **relative force** pertaining to the respective **oxidizing and reducing agents** involved is **known precisely.** In fact, this particular **quantitative characteric property** is termed, as the **'redox potential'.**

Needless to mention here that the very underlying **concept of oxidation potential** predominantly implies even much greater marked and pronounced significance in the present context of **'quantitative analysis'.**

However, in actual practice it is observed that one seldomnly comes across in a **redox system** either an absolutely pure oxidizing agent or an absolutely pure reducing agent; whereas, their respective solutions invariably comprise of the products of their reduction or oxidation respectively.

Examples:

(*i*) **Ferric-Ferrous System [Fe^{3+}/Fe^{2+} System]:** In this typical instance, the respective **reductant Fe^{2+} (ferrous ion)** always does contain certain quantum of Fe^{+3} **ion** duly produced from it; and hence, distinctly possesses **oxidizing characteristic features.**

(*ii*) **Other Oxidants [MnO_4^- ; Cl_2]:** Both MnO_4^- (permanganate ion) and Cl_2 (chlorine) usually contain insignificantly minute quantum of the admixtures of the corresponding reducing agents they mostly produce critically, for instance: Cl^- (chloride ion), Mn^{2+} (manganese ion) and the like.

Based on the aforesaid fundamental factual findings it would be definitely perhaps more correct and appropriate to consider and regard the respective **'redox potentials'** of the ensuing **oxidation-**

---

* They may yield electrons with a little difficulty.

** They may yield electrons with great ease and rapidity.

reduction couples *viz.*, Fe^{3+}/Fe^{2+} system ; MnO_4^{2-}/Mn^{2+} system; Ce^{4+}/Ce^{3+} system etc., more preferably and logically than those of the potentials (observed) of the individual oxidants or reductants.

Oxidation Potentials

The actual determination of the desired **oxidation potentials** of the **different couples** (*viz.* Fe^{3+}/Fe^{2+} ; Ce^{4+}/Ce^{3+}) experimentally and quantitatively one should always take into account that their corresponding values do not exclusively depend upon the individual strengths of the oxidizing and reducing agents (forming the **'couple'**), but also related directly upon the ensuing ratio of their respective concentrations.

Therefore, it is absolutely necessary to strictly accomplish fairly **'comparable results'**, and for this the concentrations of the two species should always be rendered to be the **same** *i.e.*, generally equivalent to a unity. Thus, the **oxidation potentials** duly obtained stringently under such experimental parameters are broadly termed as **standard oxidation potentials**, normally designated as E_o.

Determination of Standard Oxidation Potential [E_o]

In order to obtain a reasonably accurate and fairly comparable results with respect to **standard oxidation potentials [E_o] estimation** it is always advisable that various divergent **oxidation-reduction couples** must at all times be essentially **paired together** invariably with the same **standard couple**.

Standard Hydrogen Electrode: **Standard hydrogen electrode** is commonly employed for the determination of **standard oxidation potential**. This is emphatically a $2H^+/H_2$ **couple** having the **activity of the prevailing H^+ ions** almost equivalent to **1 g ion. L^{-1}**, and at a H_2–**gas pressure of 1 atm.** However, the actual potential of the **standard hydrogen electrode** is assumed to be equal to zero conventionally. Therefore, in order to carry out the precise determination of the **standard oxidation potential** of any specific system *viz.*, Fe^{3+}/Fe^{2+}, Ce^{4+}/Ce^{3+}, MnO_4^{2-}/Mn^{2+}, it is adequately combined with a **standard hydrogen electrode** in the form of a **Galvanic Cell** (which shall be treated separately at length in this Chapter elsewhere).

3.4 STRENGTHS AND EQUIVALENT WEIGHTS OF OXIDIZING AND REDUCING AGENTS

This particular section has two distinct and different aspects, as stated below, which need to be discussed separately.

    (*a*) Strengths of oxidizing and reducing agents, and

    (*b*) Redox equivalent weights [Equivalents weights of oxidizing and reducing agents].

3.4.1 Strengths of Oxidizing and Reducing Agents

It is well known that the actual **strengths of oxidizing agents** usually **increase**, whereas the corresponding **strengths of reducing agents** normally decrease according to the **increasing oxidation potential**.

    Example:

    (*a*) **Strongest oxidizing agents** – are namely:

        Permanganate ions [MnO_4^-] in acidic environment: $E_0 = + 1.51$ V;

Dichromate ions $[Cr_2O_7^{2-}]$ in acidic environment	: $E_0 = +1.36$ V;
Free Chlorine $[Cl_2]$	: $E_0 = +1.36$ V;
Free Bromine $[Br_2]$	: $E_0 = +1.07$ V;
Ferric ions $[Fe^{3+}]$	: $E_0 = +0.77$ V;
Arsonate ions $[AsO_4^{3-}]$	: $E_0 = +0.57$ V;
Free Iodine $[I_2]$	: $E_0 = +0.54$ V;
Stannic ions $[Sn^{4+}]$	: $E_0 = +0.15$ V;

(b) **Strongest reducing agents** — are namely:

Hydrogen Arsenide $[AsH_3]$: A powerful reducing agent;

Strongest reducing ions— are namely:

Titanium ion $[Ti^{3+}]$	: $E_0 = +0.10$;
Stannous ion $[Sn^{2+}]$	: $E_0 = +0.15$;
Iodide ion $[I^-]$	: $E_0 = +1.09$;
Arsenate ion $[AsO_3^{2-}]$	: $E_0 = +0.57$;

3.4.2 Redox Equivalent Weights [Equivalent Weights of Oxidizing and Reducing Agents]

Very much akin to the application of **acid-base titration results**, it has been duly proved and established that in the **redox titrations** one may make use of the conceptualized knowledge of 'equivalents' in the **expression of concentrations** most easily and conveniently. The **equivalent** in a **redox reaction** specifically refers to that segment of a mole which intimately corresponds to the loss or gain of one 'mole' of electrons. In other words, the most ideal and the simplest definition solely based on this particular concept is—'**the equivalent weight of a chemical entity (substance) is equal to the molecular weight divided duly by the exact number of electrons which one molecule gains or loses in the reaction.**'

Calculations: Based on the known '**half-reaction**', one may calculate the **equivalent weight** conveniently and rapidly. In order to elaborate the aforesaid fact, we may consider the reduction of permanganate ion* $[MnO_4^-]$ in an acidic medium; and thus the half-reaction may be expressed as follows:

$$MnO_4^- + 8H^+ + 5e \rightleftharpoons Mn^{2+} + 4H_2O|$$

Hence, $KMnO_4 \equiv 5e$

Therefore, the equivalent weight of potassium permanganate $[KMnO_4]$ can be calculated as MW/5 under these parameters:

or	158.0 g $KMnO_4 \equiv 5000$ mLN
or	31.60 g $KMnO_4 \equiv 1000$ mLN
or	3.16 g $KMnO_4 \equiv 1000$ mL of 0.1 N $KMnO_4$

---

* *i.e.* the usage of permanganate as an oxidizing agent.

At this point in time one may logically conclude that the equivalent weight of a substance exclusively depends upon the reaction wherein it gets involved intimately. Thus, in an **acidic solution**, equivalent weight (EW) is equal to 1/5th of the molecular weight (MW) [*i.e.*, MW/5] for $KMnO_4$; whereas, in a **basic solution** the half-reaction may be written as given below:

$$MnO_4^- + 4H^+ + 3e \rightleftharpoons MnO_2 + 2H_2O$$

Therefore, the equivalent weight of $KMnO_4$ is MW/3 under these experimental conditions. Conclusively, the **normality of a redox titrant** may, therefore, represent an absolutely **ambiguous quantum** unless the reaction is specified explicitly.

Analytical Method Using Two or More Redox Reactions

In a particular **analytical method** that makes use of either **two** or **more redox reactions**, one may arrive at a **deviated** or **distorted equivalent** after the necessary calculations.

In order to expatiate this phenomenon, let us consider a '**sample**' that has been duly reacted with a **second substance**; and eventually the resulting **reaction product** is assayed duly by a **redox titration.** Ultimately, the equivalent weight of the '**sample**' is precisely estimated by the **specific equation** that describes exclusively the '**final determinant titration**'.

Example: Iodate $[IO_3^-]$ ion Reacting with Iodide $[I^-]$ ion in an Acidic Medium:

It refers particularly to an unusual reaction wherein both the **oxidant $[IO_3^-]$** as well as the **reductant $[I^-]$** finally give rise to the **some substance $[I_2]$.**

Thus, we have:

$$IO_3^- + 5I^- + 6H^+ \rightleftharpoons 3I_2 + 3H_2O \qquad ...(a)$$

Therefore, according to the half-reaction we may have:

$$2IO_3^- + 12H^+ + 10e \rightleftharpoons I_2 + 6H_2O \qquad ...(b)$$

Hence, the equivalent weight of iodate is MW/5 ; that it would be only when the reaction [as per Eqn. (*a*)] follows rigidly throughout this entire analysis. However, in actual practice the liberated iodine in Eqn. (*a*) is duly titrated with standardized thiosulphate (*i.e.* sodium thiosulphate solution) so as to complete the analysis duly. Thus, we may have:

$$2S_2O_3^{2-} + I_2 \longrightarrow S_4O_6^{2-} + 2I^- \qquad ...(c)$$

Thiosulphate ion   Tetrathionate ion

[Bivalent]   [Bivalent]

Therefore, from the half-reaction, $2e + I_2 \rightleftharpoons 2H^-$, one may obviously observe that the ensuing equivalent weight in the overall final reaction would be MW/2. Hence, from Eqn. (*a*) one may evidently conclude and infer that each mole of iodate $[IO_3^-]$ ion yields six equivalents of iodine $[I_2]$, so ultimately the equivalent weight of iodate $[IO_3^-]$ in this particular analysis is MW/6.

Hence, $KIO_3 \equiv 6e$

Therefore, the equivalent weight of potassium iodate [KIO_3] can be calculated as MW/6 under these conditions:

or $\qquad\qquad$ 214.0 g $KIO_3 \equiv$ 6000 mLN

or $\qquad\qquad$ 35.66 g $KIO_3 \equiv$ 1000 mLN

or $\qquad\qquad$ 3.57 g $KIO_3 \equiv$ 1000 mL of 0.01 N KIO_3

3.5 NERNST EQUATION [EFFECTS OF CONCENTRATIONS ON POTENTIALS]

It has been well established that whenever a metal M is carefully incorporated in a solution having its own ions M^{n+}, eventually an electrode potential gets established critically across the two electrodes, the actual value of which is given precisely by the **Nernst Equation** as expressed under:

$$E = E^- + (RT/nF) \, {}^1n \, a \, M^{n+} \qquad ...(a)$$

Based on Eqn. (a) the relationship to a **cationic electrode** may be expressed as given below:

$$E = E^- \, Y^{n+}, Y + (RT/nF) \, {}^1n \, a \, Y^{n+} \qquad ...(b)$$

Likewise, to an **anionic electrode**:

$$E = E^- \, X^{n-}, X - (RT/nF) \, {}^1n \, a \, X^{n-} \qquad ...(c)$$

or $\quad$ to a **redox electrode:**

$$E = E^-_{\text{ox.red}} + (RT/nF) \, {}^1n \, \frac{a_{OX}}{a_{\text{red}}} \qquad ...(d)$$

where, $\;$ E $\;=$ Standard Electrode Potential (SEP)*

$\qquad$ a $\;=$ **Thermodynamic activity of the ion** to which the electrode is sensitive,

$\qquad$ R $\;=$ Gas constant (8.314 $JK^{-1} \, mol^{-1}$),

$\qquad$ T $\;=$ Absolute temperature (K),

$\qquad$ F $\;=$ Faraday (96,487 coul deg^{-1} of electrons), and

$\qquad$ n $\;=$ Number of electrons actually involved in the specific electrode reaction.

It is, however, pertinent to mention here that the specific **thermodynamic activity of the ion**, designated by **'a'**, must be employed emphatically in the **Nernst Equation**. In actual practice one makes use of the prevailing **'concentrations'** in these particular instances due to the underlying fact that titrations predominantly encounter reasonably **large potential changes**; and, therefore, the ultimate errors are considerably small by doing so.

Standard Potentials

In a **redox system**, when the ensuing concentrations of both the oxidized and reduced states (together with all other species) were attainable at **unit activity**, they are invariably termed as **standard potentials**, duly represented by $\mathbf{E°}$.

---

* That is, reduction potential of the half-cell involved.

Nernst was pioneer in providing a practical applicability to the said observation by establishing remarkable **'quantitative relationships'** between **potential** and **concentrations**. Importantly, this specific observed potential is solely dependent upon the prevailing concentrations of the species; and, therefore, distinctly varies from the above mentioned **'standard potential'**.

Alternatively, Nernst described this particular potential dependence by the following expression, commonly known as the **Nernst Equation**:

$$a\,O_x + ne^- \rightleftharpoons b\,Red$$

or

$$E = E° - \frac{2.3026\,RT}{nF}\log\frac{[Red]^b}{[OX]^a}$$

Where, E = Reduction potential at the specific concentrations,

n = Number of electrons involved in the half-reaction (*i.e.* equivalents mole^{-1}),

R = Gas constant (8.3143 V coul deg^{-1} mol^{-1})

T = Absolute temperature, and

F = Faraday constant (96,487 coul eq^{-1})

Note: 1. **Concentration of pure substances viz., liquids [H_2O] and precipitates viz., silver chloride [AgCl], barium sulphate [$BaSO_4$], is always taken as unity.**
2. **The log term of the reduction half-reaction is the ratio of the right-side concentrations over the left-side concentrations.**

3.6 THEORY OF REDOX TITRATIONS

The **oxidation-reduction titrations** (or **redox titrations**) usually make use of a highly sensitive electrolytic cell that essentially consists of *two* different and typical types of electrodes, such as:

(*a*) Indicator Electrode, and

(*b*) Reference Electrode.

Indicator Electrode: The **indicator electrode** invariably used in a **redox titration** consists of a **'noble metal'*** which simply acts as a vitally important centre of electron transfer from the **bulk of the solution** to the **prevailing external circuit.** In usual practice, one may usually employ a **Platinum Electrode** for this purpose.

Reference Electrode

The most commonly used **reference electrode**, which eventually completes the **cell**, is the **Saturated Calomel Electrode (SCE).** Importantly, the observed potential of the ensuing **'cell'** varies articulately in proportion to the prevailing concentrations of the **various titration reactions entities.** At this point in time the following *two* different modes of **half-reactions** occur usually, such as:

(*i*) Presence of **two redox × half-reactions** in the ensuing titration solution, and

(*ii*) Presence of another half-reaction at the reference electrode (SCE).

---

* A metal that is almost insert in extreme concentrations of acid, alkali, and reagents *e.g.,* Pt., Au, Ag etc.

In usual practice, the presence of **two redox × half-reactions** are totally ignored and hence not accounted for as a cell. The very incorporation of the **requisite titrant** into the **'sample'** gives rise to an almost instantaneous **'equilibrium'** taking place critically between the said *two* **redox couples.**

Interestingly, because these **two redox couples** exist very much in **equilibrium**, and hence their **potentials are almost identical.** Ultimately this ensuing potentials is measured precisely in relation to the reference electrode (SCE).

The above conceptualized theories and critical observations may be further elaborated with the help of the following typical example:

Example: **Titration of Fe^{2+} ion by Ce^{4+} ion in 1 M HNO_3:**

The various half-reactions are as given below:

$$Fe^{2+} \rightleftharpoons Fe^{3+} + e \qquad\qquad E^{\circ}_{Fe^{2+}, Fe^{3+}} = -0.77 \text{ V}$$

$$Ce^{4+}e \rightleftharpoons Ce^{3+} \qquad\qquad E^{\circ}_{Ce^{4+}, Ce^{3+}} = +1.61 \text{ V}$$

Following sequence of events take place, namely:

(*i*) Platinum (Pt) wire and saturated calomel electrode (SCE) are used as indicator and reference electrodes repetitively.

(*ii*) Potential remains undefined before the incorporation of the **'titrant'**.

(*iii*) The moment certain quantum of ceric (Ce^{4+}) ion is added to the respective solution, it gives rise to an equivalent quantum of ferrous (Fe^{2+}) ion, and in turn gets reduced to its cerous (Ce^{3+}) form.

(*iv*) Actually, after each addition of the **'titrant'**, the respective **equilibrium** is duly accomplished; and, therefore, one would expect the **potential of the iron couple** should almost **equalize the potential of the cerium couple**. Thus, we may have:

$$E_{Fe^{3+}, Fe^{2+}} = E'_{Ce^{4+}, Ce^{3+}}$$

Each of the above **two couples** is appropriately expressed by the **Nernst Equation** as stated below:

For Iron Couple:

$$E_{Fe^{3+}, Fe^{2+}} = E^{\circ}_{Fe^{3+}, Fe^{2+}} - 0.059 \log \frac{[Fe^{2+}]}{[Fe^{3+}]}$$

For Cerium Couple:

$$E_{Ce^{4+}, Ce^{3+}} = E^{\circ}_{Ce^{4+}, Ce^{3+}} - 0.059 \log \frac{[Ce^{3+}]}{[Ce^{4+}]}$$

Note: The potential is usually expressed related to the Standard Hydrogen Electrode (SHE).

The relevance of the **Nernst Equation** may be examined critically at *two* cardinal stages during a **Redox titration**, namely: (*a*) Before the Equivalence Point; and (*b*) At the Equivalence Point, which shall now be discussed briefly in the sections that follows:

3.6.1 Before the Equivalence Point

In this specific situation, one may make use of the **Nernst Equation** based upon the above cited **Iron Couple** in an easy and convenient manner by virtue of the fact that the **necessary concentrations** may be duly **calculated** from the **available titration data.**

Example: Let us add 3.5 mL of 0.1 N Ce^{4+} (ceric) ion into a 10 mL of 0.1 N Fe^{2+} (ferrous) ion:

Thus, the **concentration of Fe^{2+} ion** shall be equal to:

$$[(10)\ (0.1) - (3.5)\ (0.1)]/13.5 = (10 + 3.5)$$

and the corresponding Fe^{3+} **ion** will be equal to:

$$[(3.5)\ (0.1)]/13.5$$

The **standard potential** is given as + 0.77 V.

Therefore, the resulting **Iron Couple Potential**, corresponding to the **saturated calomel electrode (SCE)** will be:

$$E_{Fe^{3+}, Fe^{2+}} = 0.77 - 0.059 \log (6.5/3.5) = \mathbf{0.75\ V}$$

Because, the potential of **SCE** is itself given to be + 0.24 V *Vs* the SHE, the potential of the corresponding **Platinum Electrode** is given by $(0.75 - 0.24 =) \pm \mathbf{0.51\ V}$ *Vs* the SCE. One may, therefore, easily calculate the **'observed potential'** in this way till one reaches value in the close vicinity of the equivalence point.

3.6.2 At the Equivalence Point

Interestingly, **at the equivalence point**, the desired relationship of **equality** *viz.*, $[Fe^{3+}] = [Ce^{3+}]$ holds good based upon the very definition of the equivalence point. Thus, the ensuing concentrations of the Fe^{2+} **(ferrous) ions** and the Ce^{4+} **(ceric) ions** happen to be **finite**, inspite of being present in too small a quantity. Hence, the following equilibrium:

$$Fe^{2+} + Ce^{4+} \rightleftharpoons Fe^{3+} + Ce^{3+}$$

very much ensure that $[Fe^{2+}] = [Ce^{4+}]$

Adding all the equations with respect to the potential of the corresponding **indicator electrode**, we have:

$$2E = E^{\circ}_{Fe^{3+}, Fe^{2+}} + E^{\circ}_{Ce^{4+}, Ce^{3+}} + 0.059 \log \frac{[Fe^{3+}][Ce^{4+}]}{[Fe^{2+}][Ce^{3+}]}$$

Now, based upon the **observed equalities**, the ultimate and final term becomes zero; and, therefore, **at the equivalence point** the prevailing potential at the **Indicator Electrode** *Vs* **SHE** may be expressed as given below:

$$E = \frac{E^{\circ}_{Fe^{3+}, Fe^{2+}} + E^{\circ}_{Ce^{4+}, Ce^{3+}}}{2}$$

$$E = \frac{+0.77 + 1.61}{2} = +1.19 \text{ V } \textit{Vs} \text{ SHE.}$$

Therefore, the equivalence point potential is given by **+ 0.95 V** *Vs* SCE.

Importantly, the aforesaid figure may be judiciously employed and exploited in order to select a proper **redox indicator** for the titration.

Suitable Visual Indicator: In reality, the **redox titration** between **Ferrous ion (Fe^{2+}) by ceric ion (Ce^{4+})** the most **suitable visual indicator** would be **Ferroin** that essentially has a **transition potential of + 1.06 V** *Vs* **SHE.**

Potential at the End Point. It is indeed quite feasible and plausible to calculate the **potential at the end-point** based upon the equation which evidently expresses the **Ce^{4+} – Ce^{3+} [ceric–cerous] concentration dependence.**

3.7 EQUILIBRIUM CONSTANTS OF OXIDATION-REDUCTION REACTIONS

It has been amply proved and established that there exists a scope as well as a possibility of precisely changing the track of the redox reactions in the opposite direction, is obviously due to the consequence of the reversibility of these reactions. Thus, evidently the resulting **chemical equilibrium** gets duly established in the net **reversible reactions**. In such circumstances, one may calculate the desired **equilibrium constant** with great ease and fervour only if the **oxidation potentials of both redox systems are known**.

Carrying out the calculation for the reaction:

$$\underset{\text{Stannous ion}}{Sn^{2+}} + \underset{\text{Ferric ion}}{2Fe^{3+}} \rightleftharpoons \underset{\text{Stannic ion}}{Sn^{4+}} + \underset{\text{Ferrous ion}}{2Fe^{2+}}$$

First and foremost let us express the equations for the oxidation potentials of the systems **Sn^{4+}/Sn^{2+} and Fe^{3+}/Fe^{2+}:**

$$E_{Sn^{4+}/Sn^{2+}} = 0.15 + \frac{0.059}{2} \log \frac{[Sn^{4+}]}{[Sn^{2+}]} \qquad \qquad ...(a)$$

$$E_{Fe^{3+}/Fe^{2+}} = 0.77 + 0.059 \log \frac{[Fe^{3+}]}{[Fe^{2+}]} \qquad \qquad ...(b)$$

Interestingly, Eqn. (*a*) and Eqn. (*b*) clearly display the following vital observations, namely:

(*i*) Concentrations of Sn^{4+} (stannic) ion and Fe^{2+}(ferrous) ion increase as the reaction comes into effect.

(*ii*) Concentrations of Fe^{3+} (ferric) ion and Sn^{2+} (stannous) ion decrease as the reaction proceeds.

(*iii*) Potential of the **First-Pair** initially gets **lowered** and then increase gradually.

(*iv*) Potential of the **Second Pair** gets **decreased** slowly.

(*v*) Ultimately an equilibrium is duly attained between the *two* aforesaid potentials [step (*iii*) and (*iv*)].

It is, however, pertinent to state here that the ensuing actual **'transference of electrons'** is possible exclusively when there exists a **potential difference**, that should eventually cease provided the latter vanishes completely *i.e.*, when the following equilibrium gets established adequately.

$$E_{Sn^{4+}/Sn^{2+}} = E_{Fe^{3+}/Fe^{2+}} \qquad \qquad ...(c)$$

Now, substituting the respective values of $E_{Sn^{4+}/Sn^{2+}}$ and $E_{Fe^{3+}/Fe^{2+}}$ from Eqns. (*a*) and (*b*) into the Eqn. (*c*) we have:

$$0.15 + \frac{0.059}{2} \log \frac{[Sn^{4+}]}{[Sn^{2+}]} = 0.77 + 0.059 \log \frac{[Fe^{3+}]}{[Fe^{2+}]}$$

or $\qquad \frac{0.059}{2} \log \frac{[Sn^{4+}]}{[Sn^{2+}]} - \underbrace{0.059 \frac{[Fe^{3+}]}{[Fe^{2+}]}}_{X} = 0.77 - 0.15 \qquad \qquad ...(d)$

In Eqn. (*d*) the **'second component'**, marked as 'X', in the L.H.S.* may be rewritten as given below:

$$0.059 \log \frac{[Fe^{3+}]}{[Fe^{2+}]} = \frac{0.059}{2} 2 \log \frac{[Fe^{3+}]}{[Fe^{2+}]} = \frac{0.059}{2} \log \frac{[Fe_3{}^+]^2}{[Fe_2{}^+]^2}$$

Inserting the above value of the derived **'second component'** into the Eqn. (*d*) we have:

$$\frac{0.059}{2} \log \frac{[Sn^{4+}]}{[Sn^{2+}]} - \frac{0.059}{2} \log \frac{[Fe^{3+}]^2}{[Fe^{2+}]^2} = 0.77 - 0.15$$

or** $\qquad \frac{0.059}{2} \left[\log \frac{[Sn^{4+}]}{[Sn^{2+}]} - \log \frac{[Fe^{3+}]^2}{[Fe^{2+}]^2} \right] = 0.62$

or $\qquad \log \frac{[Sn^{4+}][Fe^{2+}]^2}{[Sn^{2+}][Fe^{3+}]^2} = \frac{0.62 \times 2}{0.059} \qquad \qquad ...(e)$

The above expression in Eqn. (*e*), immediately following the **'logarithm sign'** precisely designates the **'equilibrium constant' K**; and, therefore, Eqn. (*e*) may be expressed as follows:

$$\log K = \frac{0.62 \times 2}{0.059} \approx 21$$

or $\qquad \qquad \boxed{K \simeq 21}$

Conclusively, the aforementioned result evidently confirms that at equilibrium the product of the Sn^{4+} and Fe^{2+} concentrations stands at **10^{21} folds** the product of the concentrations of the corresponding **unconverted Sn^{2+} and Fe^{3+}**.

---

   * **LHS** = Left Hand Side.

  ** Taking the coefficient (0.059/2) outside the bracket.

Important Inference. The exceptionally high observed numerical value (*viz.*, 10^{21} times) of the attained equilibrium constant, K, predominantly and emphatically infers that the ensuing redox reaction almost accomplishes near completion.

Confirmation of Derived Conclusion. In other words, one may logically confirm the aforesaid derived conclusion by calculating the concentration ratios between $[Fe^{2+}]$: $[Fe^{3+}]$ and $[Sn^{4+}]$: $[Sn^{2+}]$ at equilibrium as observed at the **inflection point** (or **equivalence point**). The equation of the redox reaction is expressed as under:

$$2Fe^{3+} \quad + \quad Sn^{2+} \quad \rightleftharpoons \quad 2Fe^{2+} \quad + \quad Sn^{4+} \qquad ...(f)$$

Ferric ion   Stannous ion   Ferrous ion   Stannic ion

From Eqn. (*f*), it is quite evident that the ensuing **'molar concentrations'** of **Ferric $[Fe^{3+}]$** and **Ferrous $[Fe^{2+}]$ ions** must be **two folds** at **equilibrium state** in comparison to the prevailing concentrations of the corresponding **Stannous $[Sn^{2+}]$** and **Stannic $[Sn^{4+}]$ ions** *i.e.,*

$$[Fe^{3+}] = 2[Sn^{2+}] \quad \text{and} \quad [Fe^{2+}] = 2[Sn^{4+}]$$

Therefore, dividing the latter equation with the former we may have:

$$[Fe^{2+}]/[Fe^{3+}] = [Sn^{4+}]/[Sn^{2+}] \qquad ...(g)$$

It has been duly established earlier that:

$$K = \frac{[Fe^{2+}]^2 \, [Sn^{4+}]}{[Fe^{3+}]^2 \, [Sn^{2+}]} = 10^{21} \qquad \text{[From eqn. (e)]}$$

Considering Eqn. (*g*) we have at the **Equivalence Point (End Point)** the following expression:

$$[Fe^{2+}]^3/[Fe^{3+}]^3 = [Sn^{4+}]^3/[Sn^{2+}]^3 = \mathbf{10^{21}}$$

or

$$[Fe^{2+}]/[Fe^{3+}] = [Sn^{4+}]/[Sn^{2+}] = 3\sqrt{10^{21}} = \mathbf{10^7} \qquad ...(h)$$

The results obtained in Eqn. (*h*) vividly depicts that at the **inflection point (equivalence point)** at equilibrium there exists almost **10 million** ($\equiv 10^7$) **Sn^{4+} (stannic)** or **Fe^{2+} (ferrous) ions** to each and every prevailing **Sn^{2+} (stannous)** or **Fe^{3+} (ferric) ions** respectively very much remaining in solution.

3.8 SIDE REACTIONS IN REDOX TITRATIONS

Preamble: There is a major hinderance and intricate complication that predominantly obstructs the application of redox phenomena specifically in the **titrimetric analysis (volumetric analysis)** by virtue of the **several side reactions** which use up **an unknown quantum of the standard solution**. Consequently, the exact and precise determination almost turn out to be quite impossible in these **redox titrations** provided adequate steps are not taken as a **preventive measure** to stop these **side reactions efficaciously**.

Example: **Permanganate determination of Fe^{2+} (ferrous) ion in an acidic medium:**

Thus, ionically we have:

$$5Fe^{2+} + MnO_4^- + 8H^+ \longrightarrow 5Fe^{3+} + Mn^{2+} + 4H_2O \qquad ...(i)$$

From Eqn. (*i*), it is absolutely obvious that eight (8) **H⁺ ions** have been actually consumed in the above **redox reaction;** and, therefore, it must be carried out in an **acidic medium.** Interestingly, the exact nature of the acid that helps categorically in the introduction of the H⁺ ions has a vital role as well as significance.

First Choice of Acid

Ideally, in actual practice the usage of **sulphuric acid [H_2SO_4]** is the **first choice** based on the fact that the exact amount of permanganate [MnO_4^-] ion actually consumed corresponds quite accurately to the respective ferrous [Fe^{2+}] ion content, and consequently an accurate and correct result is duly accomplished in the assay procedure.

Second Choice of Acid

Hydrochloric acid [HCl] or the corresponding **Chlorides** [Cl^-] invariably demands the presence of $KMnO_4$ actually taken to be excessively high thereby ascertaining the fact that permanganate [MnO_4^-] ion is definitely and positively used up in some sort of **side reactions.** One may distinctly experience the pungent characteristic odour of **chlorine (gas)** in the course of the redox titration, which evidently confirms that following is the predominant 'side reaction':

$$10Cl^- + 2MnO_4^- + 16H^+ \longrightarrow 2Mn^2 + 8H_2O + 5Cl_2 \uparrow \qquad ...(ii)$$

Chloride Ion   Permanganate Ion   Acid   Chlorine (Gas)

From Eqn. (*ii*) the **free chlorine** liberated helps to oxidize the available **ferrous (Fe^{2+}) ions** to the corresponding **ferric (Fe^{3+}) ions** as given below:

$$2Fe^{2+} + Cl_2 \longrightarrow 2Fe^{3+} + 2Cl^- \qquad ...(iii)$$

From Eqn. (*iii*) one may safely conclude that if the entire chlorine [Cl_2] remained in solution, the quantum of iron being oxidized by it will be more or less exactly the same (*i.e.* equivalent) to the quantum of permanganate [MnO_4] ion duly consumed in the adequate generation of chlorine [Cl_2] by the Eqn. (*ii*) above.

> **Note:** In actual common practice, a certain portion of the liberated chlorine [Cl_2] by Eqn. (ii) gets evaporated from the ensuing reaction medium inadvertently, which eventually accounts for the excessive amount of $KMnO_4$ being apparently consumed for the redox titration.

3.9 OXIDATION-REDUCTION TITRATION CURVES [REDOX TITRATION CURVES]

In **oxidation-reduction titrations** (**redox titration** or **oxidimetric titration**) one may critically observe that the ensuing concentrations of the chemical entities (substances) or ions which eventually get intimately involved in the chemical reaction do undergo concentrations changes. Therefore, the observed **oxidation potential of the solution (E)** should also change simultaneously very much akin to the change in the **pH of solutions** almost continuously in the course of a titration as could be seen in a **neutralization titration.**

Thus, a plot between the observed oxidation potentials at different points in the titration *Vs* the volume of titrant added, we obtain a desired **redox titration curve.**

Example: Calculation and plotting the redox titration curve between a Ferrous Iron Salt and Potassium Permanganate in an acidic medium:

Ionic equation for the reaction between Fe^{2+} ion and MnO_4^- ion in acidic medium is as given under:

$$MnO_4^- + 5Fe^{2+} + 8H^+ \rightleftharpoons Mn^{2+} + 5Fe^{3+} + 4H_2O \qquad ...(a)$$

Eqn. (a) is obviously a **reversible reaction**; and, therefore, at any material time the solution must contain the initial **'original ions'** plus the **'generated ions'** obtained in the course of the on-going chemical (redox) reaction. Alternatively, at any specific stage during the completion of the redox titration the solution should invariably comprise of **two redox systems** *viz.* Fe^{3+}/Fe^{2+}, and MnO_2^-/Mn^{2+}. Obviously, we must have *two* altogether separate equations for the approximate and precise calculation for the **observed oxidation potential** of the solution, designated as E:

$$E = 0.77 + \frac{0.059}{1} \log \frac{[Fe^{3+}]}{[Fe^{2+}]} \qquad ...(b)$$

$$E = 1.151 + \frac{0.059}{5} \log \frac{[MnO_4^-][H^+]^8}{[Mn^{2+}]} \qquad ...(c)$$

Interesting, both these Eqns. (b) and (c) practically give the **same result**, which suggests clearly that either of the two Eqns. may be employed effectively based on its convenience.

Applicability of Eqns. (b) and (c):

Eqn. (b) — It has been observed that as long as not all the available Fe^{2+} (ferrous) iron has been duly converted, it may be quite easy and convenient to calculate the **Fe^{3+} (ferric) iron** along with the **Fe^{2+}(ferrous) iron** concentrations at any specific stage during the titration.* Hence, Eqn. (b) is definitely more convenient as well as useful in this particular instance.

Eqn. (c) — Conversely, in a situation when a reasonably excess quantum of permanganate $[MnO_4^-]$ ion is available, it is rather convenient and easy to calculate precisely the ensuing concentrations of the prevailing MnO_4^- and Mn^{2+} ions in solution; and, therefore, relatively much more difficult to calculate the actual concentrations to the residual Fe^{2+} (ferrous) ions. Hence, Eqn. (c) must be employed in this particular case for the eventual calculation of the **observed oxidation potential E.**

Calculations Involved

Considering the **calculations involved** with respect to the **oxidation potential** of a solution at which a definite volume (say 50 mL) of potassium permanganate $[KMnO_4]$ solution has been duly incorporated into a definite volume (say 100 mL) of ferrous sulphate $[FeSO_4]$ solution having the **identical normality** (say 0.1 N).

Obviously, at this particular juncture only **half of the Fe^{2+} ions** duly contained in **100 mL of the original solution** get duly converted into the **respective Fe^{3+} ions**. Thus, we may express the **observed oxidation potential** (E) as given below**:

---

* Because the concentrations of the permanganate $[MnO_4^-]$ ions that mostly remain unconverted, due to the reversibility of the reaction, prove to be really much more complicated, difficult, and unreliable.

** As the Nernst Equation refers to the specific ratio of the concentrations existing between $[Fe^{3+}]$: $[Fe^{2+}]$, hence it may be replaced by the **equal ratio of the volumes** of the titrated and untitrated portions of the solution *i.e.*, the ratio in the present instance is 50 : 50.

$$E = 0.77 + \frac{0.059}{1} \log \frac{50}{50}$$

or
$$E = 0.77 \text{ V} \qquad \qquad \qquad ...[A]$$

Salient Features Pertaining to Redox Titration Curve

The various **salient features** that are related intimately to the **redox titration curve** are as enumerated under:

1. The particular **'critical points'** strategically located in the vicinity of the end point (equivalence point) which essentially correspond to ± 0.1 mL of $KMnO_4$, because these points specifically determine the actual magnitude of the ensuing **break of potential**.

2. **Points having the abrupt change:** At this specific point almost 99.9 mL of the standardized $KMnO_4$ solution has been duly added *i.e.*, precisely 0.1 mL lower than the amount actually needed by the **desired redox reaction equation**. In other words, the exact volume of unoxidized residual Fe^{2+} ions in solution is 0.1 mL, and all the **remaining Fe^{2+} ions**, duly contained in 99.9 mL of the original solution have undergone complete conversion into **Fe^{3+} ions** after the titration. Therefore, we may have the **observed oxidization potential (E)** as stated under:

$$E = 0.77^* + \frac{0.059}{1} \log \frac{99.9}{0.1}$$

or
$$E = 0.944 \text{ V} \qquad \qquad \qquad ...[B]$$

3. **'E' at the end of the break:** In order to find out exactly the observed oxidation potential, E, at the end of the break, *i.e.*, the stage when 100.1 mL (or 100 + 0.1 mL) of the permanganate solution has been duly incorporated (obviously, of this volume 100 mL had already been used up in the redox reaction with the available Fe^{2+} ions, so as to reduce the MnO_4^- ion present in it to the corresponding Mn^{2+} ions. Therefore, the resulting solution evidently comprises of the additional excess amount (+ 0.1 mL) of permanganate which is available in the form of **MnO_4^- ions**. Therefore, we may have the ratio $[MnO_4^-] : [Mn^{2+}]$ at this particular point as 0.1 : 100, and hence the **observed oxidation potential (E)** can be expressed as given below:

$$E = 1.51^* + \frac{0.059}{5} \log \frac{0.1 \times [H^+]^8}{100} \qquad \text{[From Eqn. } (a)\text{]}$$

Let us assume that the $[H^+]$ in the solution as 1 g ion. L^{-1}, we may have:

$$E = 1.51 + \frac{0.059}{5} \log 10^{-3}$$

or
$$E = 1.475 \text{ V} \qquad \qquad \qquad ...[C]$$

4. **'E' at the equivalence point (end point):** This is the last and the final calculation which may be accomplished by the multiplication of Eqn. (*b*) by 5 so as to equalize the coefficients of the

---

* The potential (E_0) in terms of V for the highest/lowest degree of oxidation for Fe^{3+} and Fe^{2+} is **+ 0.77** ; and for MnO_4^- + $8H^+$ and Mn^{2+} + $4H_2O$ is **+ 1.51** [as per Standard Tables].

logarithmic terms of Eqns. (b) and (c) equal. Thus, the *two* said equations are respectively **add up term by term**[*] as given below:

$$E = 0.77 + 0.059 \log \frac{[Fe^{3+}]}{[Fe^{2+}]}$$

$$5E = 5 \times 1.51 + 0.059 \log \frac{[MnO_4^-]}{[Mn^{2+}]}$$

or $$6E = 0.77 + 5 \times 1.51 + 0.059 \log \frac{[Fe^{3+}][MnO_4^-]}{[Fe^{2+}][Mn^{2+}]} \qquad ...(d)$$

Evidently, at the **equivalence point** the quantum of permanganate (MnO_4^-) ions incorporated precisely corresponding to the redox reaction **Eqn. (a)**; and, therefore, at the **'equilibrium'** there should always be available **5 Fe^{2+} ions** for each of the **MnO_4^- ion** remaining in the ensuing solution. Consequently, at the equivalence point the observed **molar concentration** of the Fe^{2+} ions is found to be five folds the concentration of corresponding MnO_4^- ions. Thus, we may have:

$$[Fe^{2+}] = 5[MnO_4^-] \qquad ...(e)$$

Likewise, one may also observe at the equivalence point by following expression:

$$[Fe^{3+}] = 5[Mn^{2+}] \qquad ...(f)$$

Therefore, dividing Eqn. (f) by Eqn. (e), we may have:

$$\frac{[Fe^{3+}]}{[Fe^{2+}]} = \frac{[Mn^{2+}]}{[MnO_4^-]}$$

or $$\frac{[Fe^{3+}][MnO_4^-]}{[Fe^{2+}][Mn^{2+}]} = 1$$

Because, log 1 = 0, hence from Eqn. (d) we may have:

$$6E = 0.77 + 5 \times 1.51$$

or $$E = \frac{0.77 + 7.55}{6}$$

$$= 1.387 \text{ V}$$

i.e.,   E = 1.387 V   ...[D]

Nevertheless, it is quite possible to record the actual variations of the observed oxidation potential in the course of a redox titration engaged between 100 mL of ferrous sulphate [$FeSO_4$] solution against potassium permanganate [$KMnO_4$] solution essentially having the same normality (say $\simeq$ 0.1 N), and at [H^+] is equal to unity (*i.e.*, 1).

---

[*] In usual practice, the H^+ ion concentration is taken as 1 M. However, in both these equations 'E' represents the observed oxidation potential of the given solution; and, therefore, essentially possess the **same value**.

Table 3.1 summarizes the observed oxidation potential (E) in terms of V during titration carried out between 100 mL of $FeSO_4$ solu. *Vs* $KMnO_4$ solution (having the same normality).

S. No	Vol. of $KMnO_4$ Soln. Added (mL)	Excess volume of $FeSO_4$ (mL)	Excess volume of $KMnO_4$ (mL)	$\dfrac{[Fe^{3+}]}{[Fe^{2+}]}$	$\dfrac{[MnO_4^-]}{[Mn^{2+}]}$	Calculations involved For Oxidation Potential (E)	Oxidation Potential (E) (V)
1	50	50	—	50 : 50 = 1	—	E = 0.77 + 0.059 log 1	0.77 [Eqn. (A)]
2	91	9	—	91 : 9 ≃ 10	—	E = 0.77 + 0.059 log 10	0.829
3	99	1	—	99 : 1 ≃ 100	—	E = 0.77 + 0.059 log 100	0.887
4	99.9	0.1	—	99.9 : 0.1 ≃ 1000	—	E = 0.77 + 0.059 log 1000	0.944 [Eqn. (B)]
5*	100 [End Point]	—	—	—	—	$E = \dfrac{0.77 + 5 \times 1.51}{5 + 1}$	1.387 [Eqn. (D)]
6	100.1	—	0.1	—	0.1 : 100 = 0.001	$E = 1.51 + \dfrac{0.059}{5} \log 0.001$	1.475 [Eqn. (C)]
7	101.0	—	1.0	—	1 : 100 = 0.01	$E = 1.51 + \dfrac{0.059}{5} \log 0.01$	1.487
8	110.0	—	10.0	—	10 : 100 = 0.1	$E = 1.51 + \dfrac{0.059}{5} \log 0.1$	1.498
9	200	—	100	—	100 : 100 = 1	$E = 1.51 + \dfrac{0.059}{5} \log 1$	1.510

Table 3.1 Observed Variations of the Oxidation Potential (E) During Titration of $FeSO_4$ Solution (100 mL) *Vs* $KMnO_4$ Solution Having Same Normality (at $[H^+]$ = 1)

*From Table 3.1, it is quite clear that the **end point (equivalence point)** is indicated at **V = 1.387**, which is **not the exact mid-point** of the break, as may be seen in the Redox Titration Curve-Figure 3.1. It is a clear cut deviation from the respective titration curves obtained duly by the neutralization technique.

Redox Titration Curve: In a rather broader perspective if one considers the observed standard potentials in relation to the respective oxidizing and reducing agents taken as E_0^1 and E_0^2, and their corresponding **'stoichiometric coefficients'** as '*a*' and '*b*' respectively, the ultimate desired **oxidation potential** (E) of the solution at the **equivalence point (inflection point)** is usually given by the following expression:

$$E = \frac{bE_0^1 + aE_0^2}{a + b}$$

Figure 3.1 illustrates explicitly the **redox titration curve** of the **Ferrous sulphate [FeSO₄] solution** *Vs* the **Potassium Permanganate [KMnO₄] solution** [at $[H^+] = 1$]; however, the necessary desired calculation of the said titration curve is duly provided in Table 3.1.

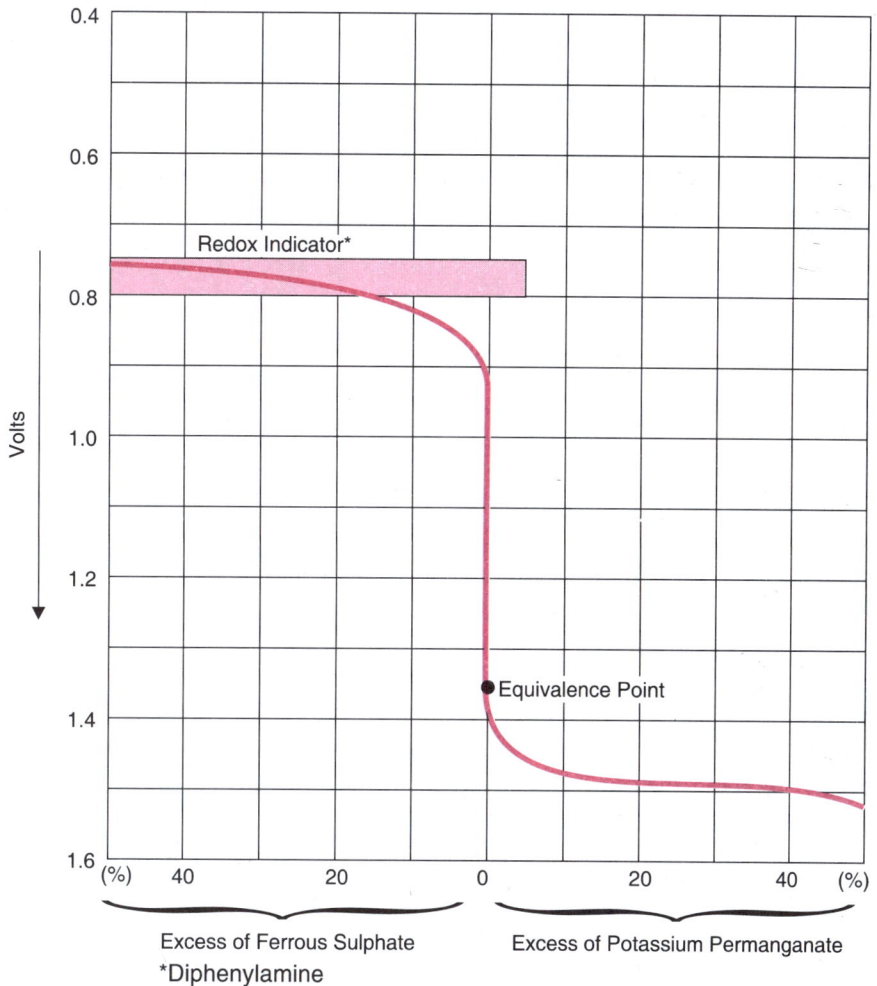

Fig. 3.1. Redox Titration Curve of Ferrous Sulphate Soln. *Vs* Potassium Permanganate solution
[AT [H⁺] = 1]. [SCALE: X-AXIS = 1 CM (≡ 10 %) ; Y-AXIS = 1 CM (≡ 0.1 VOLT)]

Salient Features

The **salient features** of Figure 3.1 are as enumerated under:

1. Redox titration (oxidimetric titration) curves and acid-base titration curves do have more or less the same general pattern.

2. An almost **'abrupt change'** of potential in the vicinity of the **end-point** (**equivalence point**) is observed invariably and specifically, whereas the curve tends to be flat in the **'regions'** either before or after the end-point, which suggests emphatically that the **observed oxidation potential, 'E',** undergo actual changes in a rather exceptionally gradual mode during the **redox titration**.

3. The wisdom and skill must be used in the proper selection and usage of the **redox indicator** (in this instance **'diphenylamine'**) to locate the exact and precise determination of the **end-point**.

4. In actual practice, the **vast magnitude of the potential change** obviously depends upon the apparent difference existing between the **standard oxidation potentials** of the *two* engaged systems *i.e.*, the greater the difference, the greater would be the actual change of the potential.

5. Most significantly, the **redox titration curves** are normally found to be absolutely independent of the so called **'dilution factor'** by virtue of the cardinal fact the **Nernst Equation** [see Section-3.5] essentially comprises of the ratio of the concentrations of the ensuing oxidized and reduced states, and of course, this fails to alter with dilution at all*.

Advantages of Redox Titration Method vis-a-vis Neutralization Titration Method

The glaring differences that evidently exist between the **redox titration** and **acid-base titration** techniques, whereby the former proves to be more advantageous than the latter, are as given under:

1. Redox titration curve is independent of dilution *vis-a-vis* neutralization method.

2. 'Break' observed on the redox titration curve may be extended significantly when one of the ions generated in the reaction gets successfully combined in the form of a definite complex formation.

   Example: **Ions** *viz.*, PO_4^{3-}, F^- etc., that specifically combine with Fe^{3+} ions to give rise to the formation of **stable complexes** *viz*, $[Fe(PO_4)_2]^{3-}$, are duly introduced into the solution.

3.10 REDOX INDICATORS

Redox indicators usually may be defined as —**'substance that can be reversibly oxidized or reduced, having different distinct colour in the individual oxidized and reduced forms.'**

Alternatively, the **redox indicators** are invariably regarded as highly coloured specific dyes which are categorically either weak reducing or weak oxidizing agents that may be oxidized or reduced; and certainly the emanated colours of the oxidized and reduced states happen to be altogether different.

Theory: Theoretically, the respective oxidation form of the indicator and so its colour will solely depend upon the oxidation potential at a given point in the titration procedure. Therefore, both the **half-reaction** and the **Nernst Equation** may be expressed for the redox indicator as stated under:

$$Ox_{Ind} + ne^- \rightleftharpoons Red_{Ind} \qquad ...(a)$$

$$E_{Ind} = E^°{}_{Ind} - \frac{0.059}{n} \log \frac{[Red_{Ind}]}{[Ox_{Ind}]} \qquad ...(b)$$

---

* Perhaps this could be the most logical and acceptable explanation that one may make use of more dilute solutions in **redox titration** in comparison to the **neutralization titration** procedures.

where, E_{Ind} = Oxidation potential of indicator, and

$E°_{Ind}$ = Standard oxidation potential of the system.

Salient Features of Eqns. (a) and (b): The various vital and important **salient features** of Eqn. (a) and (b) are as enumerated under:

1. In reality, the **half-reaction potential** in the course of the redox titration determine specifically $E°_{Ind}$; and, therefore, the ratio of $[Red_{Ind}]/[OX_{Ind}]$*. Consequently, the ratio, and hence, the **change in colour** will be affected corresponding to the **change in potential** during the on-going titration.

2. Let us take into consideration that the **ratio** *viz.* $[Red_{Ind}]/[Ox_{Ind}]$, as in the specific instance of acid-base indicators, should undergo a change from 10/1 to 1/10 so as to observe a sharp colour change, we may essentially require:

$$E°_{Ind} = 2 \times (0.059/n)V$$

Assuming $n = 1$, $E°_{Ind} = 2 \times (0.059/1)$ V = 0.118 V

or $E°_{Ind} = 0.12$ V

i.e., a 0.12 V change is needed.

3. In a situation, when $E°_{Ind}$ almost approaches quite close to the **equivalence point potential of the redox titration**, at which stage there prevails a rather quick change in potential in slight excess of **0.12 V**, a **definite colour change** takes place at the **equivalence point (end-point)** predominantly.

4. Evidently, the very existence of a **H+ ion dependence** in the ensuing **indicator reaction** [see Eqn. (a)], shall cause a critical appearance in the corresponding **Nernst Equation**, [see Eqn. (b)]. Thus, consequently the potential at which the **indicator changes its particular colour** shall take the place of $E°_{Ind}$ by the corresponding **H+ ion.**

5. Conclusively, the **redox indicators** exclusively and predominantly shall possess a **definite transition range** duly spread out over a certain potential. As a result, this ensuing transition range should invariably fall very much within the **observed steep end point break** [see Figure 3.1] of the **redox titration curve.**

6. The overall net **redox indicator reaction** should not only be **rapid** in its performance, but also be **reversible** in nature.

Obviously, a slow reaction or an irreversible one** shall eventually lead to *two* cardinal drawbacks seriously, such as:

(a) Gradual noticeable colour change, and

(b) Absence of sharp detectable equivalence point.

---

* It seems to be analogous to the ratio of the different stages of a **pH indicator** being estimated by the pH of the solution.

** It is quite comparable to the specific requirement that the specific requirement that the pK*a* value of an acid-base indicator should be close to the pH of the **end point** (equivalence point).

Redox Indicator Variants

As to date quite a few **redox indicators** are largely available, and abundantly applicable in a broad spectrum of **redox titrations**.

Table 3.2 summarizes **redox indicator variants** along with their specific colour change in 'Reduced State', 'Oxidized State', and various values of E° in terms of V. However, the common indicators are duly arranged in the particular order of the **decreasing standard potentials.**

| S.No. | Redox Indicator | Colour | | Solution | E° at [H⁺] = 1 |
		Reduced State [OX$_{Ind}$]	Oxidized State [Red$_{Ind}$]		(V)
	Table 3.2 REDOX Indicator Variants **[Arranged in Decreasing Order of Standard Potential 'V']**				
1	Diphenylamine – 2, 2′ – dicarboxylic acid	Blue-Violet	Colourless	—	1.26
2	Nitroferroin	Red	Pale Blue	1 M H$_2$SO$_4$	1.25
3	Phenylanthranilic Acid	Red-Violet	Colurless	—	1.08
4	Ferroin	Red	Pale Blue	1 M H$_2$SO$_4$	1.06
5	Erioglucin A	Red	Green	—	1.00
6	Diphenylamineazo-sulphonic Acid	Red-Violet	Colourless	—	0.85
7	Diphenylaminesulphonic Acid	Colourless	Purple	Diluted Acid	0.84
8	Diphenylamine	Colourless	Violet	1 M H$_2$SO$_4$	0.76
9	Methylene Blue	Blue	Colourless	1 M Acid	0.53
10	Indigotetrasulphonate	Colourless	Blue	1 M Acid	0.36
11	Neutral Red	Red	Colourless	—	0.24

Characteristic Features of Some Typical Redox Indicators: These are as follows:

1. **Diphenylamine: Diphenylamine indicator** essentially has standard potential, E° = 0.76 V, and $n = 2$; and, therefore, its range varies from **0.73 V to 0.79 V** as indicated below:

From:
$$E_1 = 0.76 - \frac{0.059}{2} \simeq 0.73 \text{ V}$$

To:
$$E_2 = 0.76 + \frac{0.059}{2} \simeq 0.79 \text{ V}$$

Explanations: The **diphenylamine indicator** distinctly behaves at *two* different levels of V as stated under:

At 0.73 V: *i.e.*, either **at 0.73 V or below** the reduced form of the indicator is exceptionally predominant; and, therefore the solution remains **absolutely colourless.**

At 0.79 V : *i.e.*, either **at 0.79 V or above** the oxidized form of the indicator is invariably found to be predominant; and, hence the solution remains **distinctly violet.**

However, between the range 0.73 V and 0.79 V, the **redox indicator diphenylamine** alters the colour of the **'solution'** slowly from **colourless to violet colour**.

2. **Ferroin [*or* tris (1, 10-phenanthroline) iron (II) sulphate]:** It is regarded to be one of the best **redox indicators**, which is extensively and beneficially used in several titrations with **cerium (IV)**. It is duly oxidized from the red colour to a pale blue colouration at the equivalence point (*i.e.*, in its reduced form).

3. **Diphenylamine Sulphonic Acid:** It is abundantly employed as an extremely useful and highly specific **redox indicator** for titrations with dichromate $[Cr_2O_7^{2-}]$ ion in an **acidic medium exclusively.** Importantly, the observed potential of the $[Cr_2O_7^{2-}]/[Cr^{3+}]$ couple is found to be distinctly lower than the corresponding cerium couple. Therefore, the indicator is essentially required with a lower $E°$, but utmost care must be taken adequately in disposing of Cr (VI) because it proves to be a serious environmental pollutant which is **carcinogenic** in nature. The final colour at the end point is **purple.**

Importantly, the **redox indicator** employed may solely depend upon the sample under titration because the magnitude of the **'equivalence point break'** is also proved to be dependent on the observed potential of the said **sample half-reaction.**

3.11 REDOX CELL REPRESENTATIONS [ELECTROCHEMICAL CELLS]

In actual practice, the **redox cell representations** or the **electrochemical cells** are broadly made use of in the precise and accurate measurement of the **spontaneous redox reactions.** In fact, we invariably come across with *two* different types of **electrochemical cells**, namely:

(*a*) **Voltaic (Galvanic) Cells:** In **voltaic (galvanic) cells** one usually encounters a **spontaneous chemical reaction** to cause the **production relevent electrical energy** (*i.e.*, **electricity**)*.

(*b*) **Electrolytic Cells:** In **electrolytic cells** one may observe critically that the **electrical energy is usually employed** to forcibly direct a nonspontaneous chemical reaction to take place *i.e.*, to proceed in the reverse direction in a voltaic cell.

In other words, in an electrolytic cell, the reaction is forced the other way duly by the application of an **'external voltage'** sufficiently **greater** than and specifically **opposite** to the **spontaneous voltage.**

Difference of Applicability of Voltaic Cells and Electrolytic Cells:

Voltaic Cells	Electrolytic Cells
It is of immense utility in the **potentiometric titrations** wherein the change in the electrode potential is noted during the titration, at the equivalence point, and even beyond it.	It is of great importance in the **voltammetry** where in the electroactive substances *viz.*, **metal ions** get reduced duly at an electrode to yield a measurable current by applying a suitable potential to get the spontaneous reaction to take place.**

---

* It takes place when the cell-circuit is closed, as we switch on a flashlight. The cell-voltage is determined by measuring the potential difference of the ensuing two half-reactions. Once the reaction gets completed the voltage becomes zero.

** Ultimately, the current which duly results from the forced electrolysis is directly proportional to the concentration of the ensuing electroactive force.

Voltaic (Galvanic) Cells *vis-a-vis* Spontaneous Reaction

Let us take into consideration the **redox reaction** involving the **Fe^{2+}/Ce^{4+} system** in a **voltaic cell:**

$$Fe^{2+} + Ce^{4+} \rightleftharpoons Fe^{3+} + Ce^{3+} \quad \text{...}(a)$$

Figure 3.2 shows the diagrammatic representation of a **Voltaic Cell** containing: two separate glass cells 1 and 2; salt bridge (or electrolytic bridge) 3; platinum electrodes 4 and 5; micro ammeter [μ A] 6; and Fe^{2+} solution – 7; Ce^{4+} solution – 8.

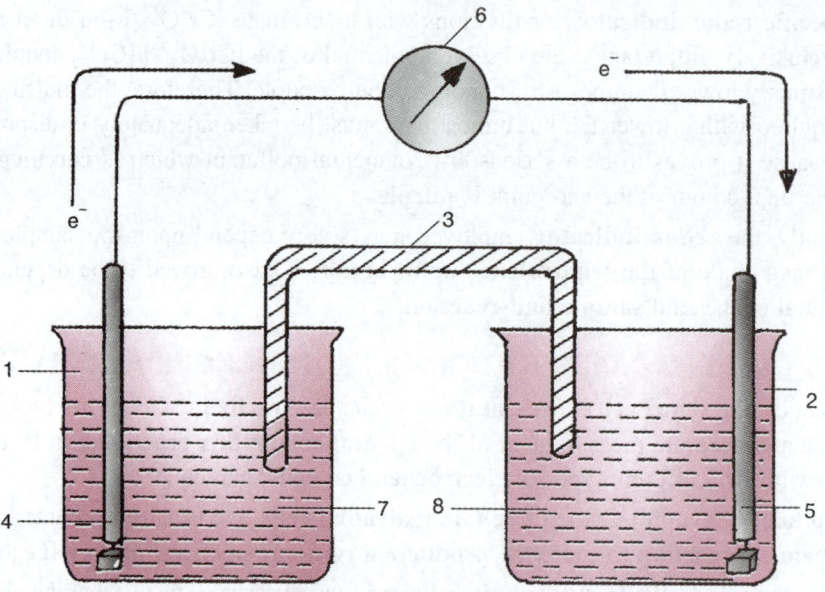

Fig. 3.2 Diagram of a Voltaic Cell

Explanation: The various steps that are involved sequentially in a redox voltaic cell are duly explained as under:

1. When a solution comprising of **Fe^{2+} (ferrous) ions** is made to interact with another having **Ce^{++} (ceric) ions**, there exists a certain definite tendency amongst the ions to undergo transference of electrons.

2. At this stage, let us assume that the said two ions *viz.* Fe^{2+} and Ce^{3+}, are kept individually in two **glass cells 1 and 2** respectively which is duly connected by a **salt bridge (or electrolytic bridge)*3** . However, no reaction can actually take place because the solutions fail to make any direct contact.

3. Now, carefully introduce an inert **platinum electrode** in each of the two solutions (**4 and 5**), namely: **Fe^{2+} (ferrous) solution (7)**, and **Ce^{4+} (ceric) solution (8)**; and ultimately, connect the two electrodes. Thus, the prevailing set up essentially gives rise to a desired **voltaic cell**.

---

* **Salt Bridge:** It specifically permits charge transfer *via.* the solution but checks mixing of the solutions randomly. Importantly, a **salt bridge** is **not always needed**, but invariably required when either the reactants or the products of the reaction at the **anode** or **cathode** do interact with each other so as to avoid their mixing freely.

4. A **micro ammeter** [μ A] **(6)** is strategically connected in between the two **platinum electrodes (4 and 5)** in a series which meticulously indicates the slightest flow of current (caused due to the actual transference of electrons in between the two **glass cells 1 and 2**). Thus, *two* separate reactions normally come into play at **anode** and the **cathode** as indicated under:

   At the Anode: $\qquad Fe^{2+} \longrightarrow Fe^{3+} + e^-$ $\qquad\qquad\qquad\qquad\qquad$ ...(*b*)

   At the Cathode: $\qquad Ce^{4+} + e^- \longrightarrow Ce^{3+}$ $\qquad\qquad\qquad\qquad\qquad$ ...(*c*)

   In fact, Eqn. (*b*) represents **ferrous (Fe^{2+}) ions being oxidized** at the platinum electrode (**anode**); whereas, Eqn. (*e*) designates explicitly the flow of the '**released electrons**' *via* the wire to the other **glass vessel (2)** at which the corresponding **ceric (Ce^{4+}) ions being reduced** at the platinum electrode (**cathode**). The actual feasibility of the above phenomena could only be possible due to the fact that there exists a predominant overwhelming tendency for these ensuing ions to allow transferences of electrons.

5. The overall net result being the redox reaction expressed in Eqn. (*a*), which might have taken place otherwise, in case, the Fe^{2+} and Ce^{4+} ions were added simultaneously in a **single glass vessel** (instead of two separately).

6. Each of the *two* **platinum electrodes (4 and 5)** shall essentially adopt an **electrical potential** which is adequately and precisely estimated by the prevailing inherent tendency of the respective ion to either specifically **taken on (accept)** or **give off (release) electrons**; and hence, this underlying phenomena is commonly termed as the '**Electrode Potential**'.

7. A proper measuring device to record the slightest extent of the ensuing change in electrode potential by the help of highly sensitive **micro ammeter (μA)** placed in between the two electrodes shall show up the '**difference in the potentials**'. Thus, one may observe **larger potential difference**, corresponding to the definitely greater reactivity for the interaction taking place between Fe^{2+} and Ce^{4+} ions.

3.12 MEASUREMENT OF ELECTRODE POTENTIALS [or HALF-REACTION POTENTIALS]

In actual practice, any *redox reaction* usually consists of the **half-reactions**, such as:

$$Fe^{2+} \longrightarrow Fe^{3+} + e^- \qquad\qquad\qquad ...(i)$$
$$Ce^{4+} + e^- \longrightarrow Ce^{3+} \qquad\qquad\qquad ...(ii)$$

Importantly, a **half-reaction** can never come into being by itself. Hence, to make it really happen there must prevail an **electron donor** [Eqn. (*i*)] *i.e.*, a *reducing agent* , and an **electron acceptor** [Eqn. (*ii*)] *i.e.*, an *oxidizing agent*. Nevertheless, each **half-reaction** shall meticulously give rise to a definite quantum of potential, which in turn will be duly accepted by an absolutely inert electrode *viz.* Pt-electrode, strategically dipped in the solution respectively.

Measurement Accomplished

Had it been actually possible and feasible to measure that potentials of practically **all half-reactions,** one could have easily and conveniently determined which would be the most befitting **oxidizing** and **reducing agents** that will interact. As luck would have it, as to date there exists no reasonably acceptable manner and means to precisely measure the ensuing electrode potentials. It is, however, pertinent to state here that the actual **difference** between the two electrode potentials is possible to measure using the electrochemical instrumental devices. Interestingly the electrode potential of the half-reaction*:

$$2H^+ + 2e^- \rightleftharpoons H_2 \qquad\qquad ...(iii)$$

has arbitrarily been assigned a value equivalent to 0.000 V. Thus, at standard experimental parameters one may rightly define arbitrarily the potential of the said **half-reaction** as '**zero**'. In fact, all other potentials are invariably measured relative to this (as a reference).

The arbitrarily assigned value of 'zero' for the **electrode potential of the half-reaction** is usually termed as the '**normal hydrogen electrode (NHE)**', or sometimes also referred to as the '**standard hydrogen electrode (SHE)**'

Methodology: The various steps involved in the determination of **NHE** or **SHE** are as described under:

(1) It essentially comprises of a '**platinized platinum electrode**'** packed in a glass tube, upon which H_2-gas is bubbled slowly. In reality, the **Pt-black** helps in the catalysis of reaction Eqn, (*iii*).

(2) In actual practice, the ensuing potential differences between the **half-reaction in Eqn. (*iii*)** plus the **other half-reactions** have been accurately measured by the help of the voltaic cells, and these values, **E(V)**, are arranged in a decreasing order in Table 3.2.

(3) Importantly, the potentials are solely dependent on the concentrations; besides all **standard potentials** invariably turn to for information related to specific parameters of unit activity for **all available species**.***

*Gibbs-Stockholm Electrode Potentials Convention **** [GSEPC]*

In GSEPC one usually expresses the **half-reaction** as a '**reduction**'; and, consequently, the potential increases substantially due to the prevailing tendency for the above reduction caused (*i.e.*, of the corresponding oxidized state of the **half-reaction**) enhances ultimately.

The aforesaid statement of facts can be further expatiated by the aid of the following concrete example.

Example: Let us consider the redox electrode potential for the system:

$$Sn^{4+} \quad + \quad 2e^- \quad \rightleftharpoons \quad Sn^{2+} \qquad \text{which stands at } + \textbf{0.15 V.}*****$$

    [Stannic State]   [Stannous State]

---

* The reaction in Eqn. (*iii*) may also be expressed as: $H^+ + e^- = 1/2\ H_2$. In whatever way one may write the reaction, it hardly affects its potential.

** An electrode coated with fine '**platinum black**' by electroplating Pt on the electrode.

*** That is, one atmosphere partial pressure in the particular instance of gases, as for hydrogen in the normal hydrogen electrode (NHE).

**** **GSEPC** was dully adopted at the 17th conference of the **IUPAC** (International Union of Pure and Applied Chemistry) in Stockholm in the year 1953. Further, in the Gibbs-Stockholm convention, one invariably expresses the half-reaction as a reduction.

***** Alternatively, the ensuing potential of the half-reactions with reference to the **normal hydrogen electrode [NHE]** in a cell, as depicted in Figure 3.2, shall be 0.15 V {See Section: 4.1).

Evidently, the above cited redox couple exhibits distinctly a much greater (*viz*, more + ve) reduction potential in comparison to the normal hydrogen electrode (NHE); therefore, the Sn^{2+} (stannous) ion remarkably displays a significantly much stronger tendency to undergo '**reduction**' than the corresponding H^+ ion has.

General Conclusive Observations: There are certain exclusively general conclusive observations with reference to the ensuing **electrode potentials**, namely:

(*a*) **The more positive the electrode potentials, the stronger an oxidizing agent the oxidized form is, and the weaker a reducing agent the reduced form is; and**

(*b*) **The more negative the reduction potential, the weaker an oxidizing agent is the oxidized form is, and the stronger a reducing agent the reduced form is.**

Examples: There are *two* glaring examples:

(*i*) **Reduction potential for $Ce^{4+} + e^- \rightleftharpoons Ce^{3+}$:** The reduction potential for this system is **extremely positive**; and therefore, Ce^{4+} (ceric) ion represents a strong oxidizing agent whereas, Ce^{3+} (cerous) ion behaves as a **very weak reducing agent**;

(*ii*) **Reduction potential for $Zn^{2+} + 2e^- \rightleftharpoons Zn$:** The reduction potential for this system is **extremely negative**; and, therefore, Zn^{2+} ion designates a very weak oxidizing agent, whereas, Zn (metallic) serves as a **very strong reducing agent.**

In general, one may conclude that Ce^{4+} (ceric) ion is found to be an excellent oxidizing agent by virtue of the high reduction potential [incidentally, the Ce^{3+} (cerous) ion is regarded as a poor reducing agent]. Likewise, Zn (mettalic) is observed to be a good reducing agent on account of the distinctly **low reduction potential** [interestingly, Zn^{2+} ion serves as a considerably poor reducing agent].

3.13 TITRATIONS BASED ON REDOX REACTIONS

A good number of **volumetric titrations** that are intimately based upon the **redox reactions** are in common use in the domain of **analytical chemistry** in general, and in **pharmaceutical analyses** in particular. A few typical examples will now be discussed at length in the sections that follows:

3.13.1 Iodimetry and Idometry

In a broader sense, the **redox titrations** are invariably regarded to be one of the most vital and important types of analyses that may be carried out in several divergent areas of application *viz.*, **pharmaceutical analyses** (*e.g.*, analgin, ascorbic acid, benzyl penicillin, thyroid, mannitol etc.), food analyses, and industrial analyses.

Examples: A few typical examples are, namely:

• titration of Vitamin C in citrous fruit juices,

• titration of sulphite in wines,

• assay of ethanol in distilleries.

Interestingly, we may have to understand the cardinal difference between '**iodine (I_2)**' and '**iodide (I^-)**' as given under:

Iodine [I_2]—Serves as **oxidizing agent** which may be employed to titrate sufficiently **strong reducing agents**.

Iodide Ion [I⁻]—Behaves as a mild reducing agent that may be used for the determination of **strong oxidizing agents**.

A. Iodimetry

Iodimetry may be defined as—'**titrations directly with iodine solution.**'

Effect of pH—In **iodimetry**, pH plays a major role in the titration of the analyse. *Two* situations invariably arise:

(a) **Neutral pH or Mildly Alkaline pH (8.0) or Weakly Acidic Solutions**—In all the environments the titrations usually give fairly good results.

(b) **Very Alkaline Solution**—In this particular environment (*i.e.*, too high pH) the iodine (I_2) will eventually disproportionate into *two* fragmented chemical entities *viz*, hypoiodate (IO^-) and iodide (I^-) as shown below:

$$I_2 \quad + \quad 2OH^- \quad \longrightarrow \quad IO^- \quad + \quad I^- \quad + \quad H_2O$$

$$\text{Iodine} \qquad\qquad\qquad\qquad \text{Hypoiodate} \quad \text{Iodine}$$
$$\text{ion} \qquad\quad \text{ion}$$

Reasons for Preventing Solution from Rendering Strongly Acidic:

There are *three* good reasons for strictly maintaining the solution from rendering strongly acidic in nature, namely:

(a) Freshly prepared '**starch solution**' used as in indicator to locate the equivalence point precisely has a tendency to either get decomposed or undergo hydrolysis in an environment of strong acid, thereby affecting the end point determination seriously,

(b) Reducing ability of many reducing agents has been observed to get enhanced significantly in **neutral solution**:

Example: **Interaction between I_2 and As (III):**

$$H_3AsO_3 + I_2 + H_2O \quad \longrightarrow \quad H_2AsO_4 \quad + \quad 2I^- + 2H^+ \qquad\qquad ...(i)$$

$$\text{Arsenic Acid} \qquad\qquad\qquad \text{Arsonic Acid.}$$
$$\text{As (III)} \qquad\qquad\qquad\qquad \text{As (V)}$$

In Eqn. (*i*) the equilibrium is seen to be affected by the critical presence of the H^+ ion concentration. Thus, at relatively low level of H^+ ion concentration one may observe an apparent shift of the equilibrium in Eqn. (*i*) to the right. However, in the acidic solution the said **equilibrium gets oppositely shifted** *i.e.*, to the left.

(c) Iodide ion (I^-) generated in the redox reaction has an obvious tendency to get duly oxidized by the help of the dissolved O_2 in an acid medium. Thus, we may have:

$$4I^- + O_2 + 4H^+ \longrightarrow 2I_2 + 2H_2O \qquad\qquad ...(ii)$$

However, in usual practice one may appropriately maintain a neutral pH for the titration of As (III) with I_2 [Eqn.(*i*)] by the adequate incorporation of **sodium bicarbonate [$NaHCO_3$]**. In this manner, the continuous smooth bubbling evolution of CO_2 gas generated also keeps critically the effective removal of the dissolved oxygen (O_2). Thus, it dully provides a reasonably good blanket of CO_2 upon the entire ensuing titration medium (solution) to check and prevent the corresponding oxidation of the respective **iodide ion (I^-)**.

Limitations of I_2: It is an universal fact I_2 is **not so a strong oxidizing agent**, which eventually limits its utility with regard to its capability of handling a large number of **reducing agents**. Nevertheless, based on certain absolutely specific and typical examples, besides the **inherent moderate oxidizing power of I_2** renders it to serve as a **much more highly selective titrant** in comparison to several other relatively **stronger oxidizing agents.** Table 3.3 duly includes certain frequently determined analyses by **Iodimetry**:

	Table 3.3 Certain Analyses Frequently Determined by Iodimetry		
S.No.	**Analyse Determined**	**Reaction with Iodine (I_2)**	**Experimental Parameters of Solutions**
1	N_2H_4[or $H_2N = NH_2$]	$N_2H_4 + 2I_2 \longrightarrow N_2\uparrow + 4H^+ + 4I^-$	—
2	SO_3^{2-}	$SO_3^{2-} + I_2 + H_2O \longrightarrow SO_4^{2-} + 2H^+ + 2I^-$	—
3	As (III)	$H_2AsO_3^- + I_2 + H_2O \longrightarrow HAsO_4^{2-} + 3H^+ + 2I^-$	pH8 (slightly alkaline)
4	H_2S	$H_2S + I_2 \longrightarrow S + 2I^- + 2H^+$	Acidic Medium
5	Sn^{2+}	$Sn^{2+} + I_2 \longrightarrow Sn^{4+} + 2I^-$	Acidic Medium

Note: Antimony [Sb^{3+}]— behaves very much akin to As^{3+}; and, therefore, the pH is extremely critical. Tartrate [$(C_4H_4O_6)^{2-}$] is carefully introduced to form complexation with Sb^{3+}, thereby strategically maintain it in a solubilized state (in solution) to avoid hydrolysis.

Solubilizing Iodine [I_2]: Actually, iodine (I_2) has an inherent extremely poor (low) solubility in water; however, it may undergo rapid dissolution in the presence of potassium iodide (KI) to result into the formation of the corresponding **triiodide ion [I_3^-]**, as given under:

$$I_2 \quad + \quad I^- \quad \longrightarrow \quad I_3^-$$

(Iodine Insoluble)   Triiodide Ion (**Soluble**)

Therefore, the triiodide ion [I_3^-] is, in fact, the actual species that gets meticulously utilized in the **iodimetric titration** precisely.

Nevertheless, KI interestingly plays a critical '**double role**' such as: (*a*) in **Iodimetry**— as a prevalent 'solubilizing agent' or I_2 in aqueous medium; and (*b*) in **Iodometry**— as a specific '**reducing agent**' whereby the excess of KI aids in the retention of the evolved I_2 in solution *via* adequate reaction with KI.

B. Iodometry

Interestingly, in **iodometry**, the analyte happens to be essentially an **oxidizing agent** which reacts specifically with liberated I_2 is carefully titrated with **standardized sodium thiosulphate**, thereby making use of the disappearance of the starch-iodine (blue) colouration as the desired equivalence point.

It is, however, well known that iodide ion [I^-] behaves as a **weak reducing agent**, and hence capable of reducing corresponding strong oxidizing agents. Because of the non-availability of an appropriate and convenient visual indicator system, speed of the redox reaction etc. the [I^-] fails to be recognized as a viable titrant in analysis.

Methodology: In a particular instance when an 'excess of [I⁻]' is carefully incorporated into a solution an **oxidizing agent** under investigation, then—'iodine (I_2) gets liberated quantitatively in an amount just equivalent to the actual oxidizing agent precisely present.

Alternatively, the said 'liberated I_2' may, therefore, be titrated with a **reducing agent**; and hence, the result shall be almost identical just like the oxidizing agent being titrated directly.

However, in both these instances sodium thiosulphate is employed as the 'titrating agent.'

The specific analysis of an **oxidizing agent** carried out in this fashion is commonly termed as an **iodometry** or an **iodometric method**.

Examples:

1. **Determination of Dichromate:** The qualitative determination of dichromate $[Cr_2O_7^{2-}]$ ion may be accomplished as per the following **ionic reaction**.

$$Cr_2O_7^{2-} + 6I^- + 14H^+ \longrightarrow 2Cr^{3+} + 3I_2 + 7H_2O \qquad ...(i)$$
$$\text{[In Large Excess]}$$

$$I_2 + 2S_2O_3^{2-} \longrightarrow 2I^- + S_4O_6^{2-} \qquad ...(ii)$$
$$\quad (a) \qquad\qquad\qquad (b)$$

In Eqn. (*ii*) each dichromate $[Cr_2O_7^{2-}]$ ion happen to generate three molecules of iodine $[I_2]$, which eventually interacts with six equivalents $[6S_2O_3^{2-}]$ of thiosulphate ion. In other words, the millimoles (mm) dichromate $[Cr_2O_7^{2-}]$ are found to be equivalent to 1/6th mm of thiosulphate $[S_2O_3^{2-}]$ actually consumed in the titration. [In Eqn. (*iii*): (*a*) = thiosulphate ion ; and (*b*) = tetrathionate ion].

2. **Determination of Iodate $[IO_3^-]$:** The iodate $[IO_3^-]$ ion may also be determined quantitatively by the **iodometric method**, as expressed under:

$$IO_3^- + 5I^- + 6H^+ \longrightarrow 3I_2 + 3H_2O \qquad ...(iii)$$

In Eqn. (*iv*), each iodate ion $[IO_3^-]$ gives rise to the formation of three moles of iodine $[3I_2]$, that subsequently reacts with $6S_2O_3^{2-}$ (thiosulphate ion); and ultimately the millimoles the IO_3^- are duly accomplished ion $[S_2O_3^{2-}]$ adequately employed in the titration by 1/6th the quantum.

3.13.2 Permanganate Titrations

Potassium permanganate $[KMnO_4]$ has been employed extensively and intensively as one of the most versatile, reliable, and valuable oxidizing agents in the domain of **redox titrimetry** since more than a century. It acts as a **self-indicator** for the detection of equivalence point, and serves as a very strong oxidizing agent $[E° = 1.51 \text{ V}]$. In fact, the freshly prepared $KMnO_4$ solution is fairly stable provided adequate necessary precautions are taken duly in its preparation.

Autocatalytic Decomposition of KMnO₄ Solution

It has been duly observed that a freshly prepared $KMnO_4$ solution invariably possesses small quantum of '**reducing impurities**' inherently present in the solution that reduce a small amount of the permanganate $[MnO_4^-]$ ion. Importantly, in a '**neutral solution**' the prevailing reduction product of the corresponding permanganate $[MnO_2]$ is **manganese dioxide $[MnO_2]$**; whereas, in an '**acidic environment**' the resulting reduction product is **manganese metallic ion $[Mn^{2+}]$**. It has been established beyond any reasonable doubt that MnO_2, obtained above as a reduction product, emphatically acts as a **'catalyst'** for carrying out further decomposition of the permanganate $[MnO_2^-]$ ion, which in turn gives rise to more MnO_2 and so on so forth. This observed self chain reaction leading to the formation of MnO_2 is termed as **autocatalytic decomposition**.

Stabilization of KMnO₄ Solution

The $KMnO_4$ solution may be stabilized by adopting the following methods:

1. Removal of manganese dioxide $[MnO_2]$ from the solution.
2. The solution is first and foremost boiled for at least 15-20 minutes to enhance the oxidation of most of the impurities, and is kept overnight to cool down. The solid insoluble MnO_2 is duly removed by filtration through a sintered glass funnel under vacuum.

Potassium permanganate $[KMnO_4]$ is usually used as a potential oxidizing agent in an acidic medium [*viz*, H_2SO_4], and the reaction represented by the following equations:

Chemically we have:

$$2KMnO_4 + 3H_2SO_4 \longrightarrow K_2SO_4 + 2MnSO_4 + 3H_2O + 5(O)$$
$$\text{Nescent oxygen}$$

Ionically we have:

$$MnO_4^- + 8H^+ + 5e^- \rightleftharpoons Mn^{2+} + 4H_2O$$

Standardization of KMnO₄ Solution

The $KMnO_4$ solution (say, 0.1 N) can be easily standardized by titrating an aliquot of a **primary standard*** sodium oxalate $[Na_2C_2O_4]$ which when dissolved in acid, yields oxalic acid $[C_2H_2O_4]$. Thus, we have:

$$\underset{\text{Sodium Oxalate}}{Na_2C_2O_4} + \underset{\text{[An Acid]}}{H_2SO_4} \longrightarrow Na_2SO_4 + \underset{\text{Oxalic Acid}}{H_2C_2O_4} \qquad ...(i)$$

$$5H_2C_2O_4 + 2MnO_4^- + 6H^+ \longrightarrow 2Mn^{2+} + 10CO_2 \uparrow + 8H_2O \qquad ...(ii)$$

Precautions

1. Sufficient quantum of acid should always be present, so as to avoid the formation of a **'brown colouration'** in the course of titration.
2. Acidified solution of oxalic acid must be carefully warmed upto $60 \pm 5°C$ before commencing the actual titration with the titrant *i.e.*, $KMnO_4$ solution. If the solution is heated too high *i.e.*, $90 \pm 5°C$, a brown colour is formed.
3. Using a **dirty flask** also causes a brown colouration, which may be safely avoided by rinsing the flask first with a solution of hydrogen peroxide $[H_2O_2]$, and secondly with a diluted H_2SO_4 solution before carrying out the actual titrations.

---

* **Primary Standard:** Sodium Oxalate, **AnalaR Grade**, which is 99.99% is usually used as a **primary standard reagent**.

Applications of Permanganate Oxidimetry

There are several useful applications of **permanganate oxidimetry** in analytical chemistry, namely:

1. **Arsenic Trioxide [As$_2$O$_3$]:** In fact, the oxidation of As$_2$O$_3$ by permanganate fails to take off quickly at an ambient temperature. However, the presence of such chemical entities as: iodide [I$^-$], iodate [IO$_3^-$], or iodine monochloride [ICl] — acting as a **catalyst**, the desired oxidimetric reaction proceeds rather rapidly; and, therefore, the titration is quite feasible even at room temperature (ambient temperature) only. The equivalence point can be duly seen by the vivid appearance of the pink permanganate colour.

> **Note:** **However, one may even accomplish a much more clear cut and sensitive detection (indication), particularly for titrations performed with diluted KMnO$_4$ solutions, is usually attri-buted by the help of the redox indicator* viz., ferroin [or ortho-phenanthroline-ferrous sulphate] (see Table 3.2), whereby a distinct colour change from pink to faint blue is obtained.**

2. **Iodide [I$^-$]:** The iodide [I$^-$] gets quantitatively oxidized to iodine [I$_2$] by permanganate. Because, I$_2$ is also coloured naturally, a simple visual titration is not possible practically.

   However, this critical problem may be circumvented easily by the judicious incorporation of **hydrocyanic acid [HCN]** to the titration mixture. Thus, the oxidation by permanganate eventually comes into play to result into the formation of **iodine cyanide** [ICN], as given under:

   $$I^- + HCN \rightleftharpoons ICN + H^+ + 2e^-$$

   that is absolutely colourless. Hence, one may easily detect the equivalence point using **ferroin as the redox indicator.**

> **Note:** **The 'iodide titration' is sometimes employed to standardiz potassium permanganate solution due to the availability of 'Analak-Grade' tassium iodide [KI].**

3. **Ferrous [Fe^{2+}] Iron:** In the **permanganate oxidimetry** ferrous [Fe^{2+}] is oxidized quantitatively to ferric [Fe^{3+}] iron. The presence of sulphuric acid [H$_2$SO$_4$] usually employed in this titration does not give a definite change in colour at the equivalence point by virtue of the fact that the **yellow colour produced by ferric sulphate [Fe(SO$_4$)$_3$]** rapidly turns the first ever pink **permanganate colour to orange.** However, this serious problem may be carefully overcome by the addition of **phosphoric acid [H$_3$PO$_4$]**, that critically yields an absolutely **colourless complex with ferric [Fe^{3+}] iron**.

Presence of Chloride [Cl$^-$] Ion

The very presence of the chloride [Cl$^-$] ion yet causes a more complicated and serious difficulty with the **ferrous [Fe^{2+}] iron**. It has been duly observed that under certain experimental parameters viz.. (a) **acidity**, and (b) **speed of titration**, a certain definite additional consumption of the permanganate solution takes place by chloride [Cl$^-$] ion. This erroneous result ultimately leads to false Fe^{2+} ions in the

---

* **Redox Indicator.** It refers to a chemical substance whose corresponding oxidized and reduced states have an altogether distinctly different colours. However, the **redox indicators** may be suitably characterized by their respective observed **transition potentials**, and selected suitably such that the said **transition potential** very much coincides with the **equivalence point potential** of the on-going redox titration.

assay. Interestingly, such an error may be safely avoided by the careful incorporation of **manganous [Mn²⁺] ions** to the titrating mixture.

Thus, the Mn^{2+} ion significantly **minimizes** the ensuing **potential of the MnO_4^-/Mn^{2+} couple** thereby almost stopping permanganate to oxidize the prevailing Cl^- ion *i.e.*, the formal observed potential is found to be less than the **observed oxidation potential [E°]**, on account of the large concentration of **Mn^{2+} ion**.

Zimmermann-Reinhardt Reagent [Z-R Reagent]

This specific reagent, after the names of the 'analysts', essentially contains manganous sulphate [$MnSO_4$], phosphoric acid [H_3PO_4], and sulphuric acid [H_2SO_4] as the solvent for the titration of **ferrous [Fe²⁺] iron.** The **Z-R Reagent** usually helps to sharpen the equivalence point.

3.13.3 Potassium Dichromate [$K_2Cr_2O_7$] Titrations

Potassium dichromate is regarded to be a slightly **weaker oxidizing agent** in comparison to the **potassium permanganate**. Thus, in an acidic medium $K_2Cr_2O_7$ releases *three* nescent oxygens as expressed under:

$$K_2Cr_2O_7 \ + \ 4H_2SO_4 \ \longrightarrow \ K_2SO_4 \ + \ Cr_2(SO_4)_3 \ + \ 4H_2O \ + \ 3(O)$$

| Potassium dichromate | | Potassium sulphate | Chromium sulphate | | Nescent oxygen |

Ionically, we have:

$$K_2Cr_2O_7 \ + \ 14H^+ + \ 6e^- \ \longrightarrow \ 2K^+ \ + \ 2Cr^{3+} \ + \ 7H_2O$$

Therefore, the equivalent weight of potassium dichromate is 1/6th of its molecular weight *i.e.*, 294.22/6 or **49.03 g.**

Advantages of $K_2Cr_2O_7$

The cardinal **advantages of dichromate reagent** may be observed evidently from the following salient characteristic features, namely:

1. The reagent (*i.e*, $K_2Cr_2O_7$) is usually available as a '**primary standard**' (*viz*, **as 'AnalaR' Grade Reagent**); and, therefore, the freshly prepared solution need not be duly standardized in most instances (which saves a lot of time and energy).

2. Titration of Fe^{2+} may be easily accomplished by duly standardizing $K_2Cr_2O_7$ solution *Vs* electrolytic iron which is highly preferable*.

> **Note: However, standardization of $K_2Cr_2O_7$ solution is exclusively important and necessary to carry out certain assays that essentially need utmost accuracy and excellent precision.**

3. **Oxidation of Cl^- Ion:** The '**dichromate oxidation**' of the investigative Cl^- ion does not pose any serious problem at all. In fact, the usual formal **potential of the $Cr_2O_7^{2-}/Cr^{3+}$ couple** gets eventually reduced from 1.33 to 1.0 V in 1 M HCl. Besides, phosphoric acid [H_3PO_4] should

---

* It is, however, supported by the fact that the green colouration caused by the Cr^{3+} ion introduces a **small extent of error** at the **equivalence point** (Indicator used: **Diphenylamine sulphonate**).

be incorporated to afford a **cognizable reduction in the potential** of the ensuing Fe^{3+}/Fe^{2+} **couple.***

3.13.4 Ceric Sulphate Titrations [Cerimetry; Oxidation by Ce⁴⁺ Ions]

Importantly, **ammonium ceric sulphate** $[Ce(SO_4)_2\ 2(NH_4)_2SO_4.\ 2H_2O]$ acts as a **strong oxidizing agent** in an acidic medium. The above salt possesses a **bright yellow colouration**, and so its respective solution. However, after undergoing reduction, the resulting cerous $[Ce^{3+}]$ salt is absolutely colourless; and, therefore, relatively strong. Solutions may be regarded as '**self-indicating**'. The oxidation reaction involved may be expressed as follows:

$$Ce^{4+} + e \rightleftharpoons Ce^{3+}$$

Advantages of Ceric Sulphate Titrations *Vs* Permanganate and Dichromate Methods: The most vital, important, and distinct advantages of the **cerric sulphate titrations *vis-a-vis*** the **permanganate and dichromate techniques** are as enumerated under:

1. Freshly prepared solutions invariably remain quite stable even after boiling,

2. Ce^{4+} solutions normally interact quantitatively with either arsenite $[AsO_3^{3-}]$ or oxalate $[(COO)_2]^{2-}$ ion; and therefore, one may use efficaciously either arsenic trioxide $[As_2O_3]$ or sodium oxalate $[Na_2C_2O_4]$ as a **primary standard**,

3. Ce^{3+} ion is found to be absolutely colourless, and hence causes practically little interference with the '**indicator**' equivalence point at all,

4. Cerous $[Ce^{3+}]$ ion exclusively comes into being due to reduction of Ce^{4+} ion, whereas permanganate $[MnO_4^-]$ ion may get reduced to a variety of oxidation forms, such as: manganese dioxide $[MnO_2]$, manganese metallic ion $[Mn^{2+}]$,

5. Ce^{4+} solution unlike $KMnO_4$ solution, could be used most effectively as a prominent oxidizing agent even in the critical presence of relatively higher concentrations of HCl, which predominantly facilitates the assays of ferrous $[Fe^{2+}]$ ion in the very presence of Cl^- ions, and

6. **Ferroin** [*i.e.*, **Ferrous phenanthrolone complex ion**] has indeed proved to be an extremely useful and successful indicator in the titration with the Ce^{4+} salts. Thus, we may have the following expression:

$$\underset{\substack{\text{Orthophenanthroline}\\ \text{[Colourless]}\\ \text{(Base)}}}{C_{12}H_8N_2}\ +\ Fe^{2+}\ \longrightarrow\ \underset{\substack{\text{Ferroin}\\ \text{[Ferrous Complex]}\\ \text{(Red)}}}{Fe(C_{12}H_8N_2)_3^{2+}}\ \rightleftharpoons\ \underset{\substack{\text{Ferric Complex}\\ \text{(Blue)}}}{Fe(C_{12}H_8N_2)_3^{3+}}\ +\ e^-$$

Consequently, we may evidently observe that the orthophenanthroline (base) undergoes dissolution quite readily in an aqueous medium of ferrous $[Fe^{2+}]$ salts whereby three moles get duly combined with *one* Fe^{2+} ion to give rise to the formation of a complex termed as '**ferroin**' with an intense red colour. Further, any **strong oxidizing agent** adequately converts the **ferrous $[Fe^{2+}]$** to a corresponding **ferric $[Fe^{3+}]$ complex** with a **slight blue colouration**.

---

* This kind of addition is found to extremely vital and necessary due to the fact that it critically **lowers the equivalence point-potential** to almost very close to the **standard potential**, assigned to the **diphenylamine sulphonate** indicator (0.84V) ; otherwise, the end-point may strike very soon.

Standard Solution

The solutions of **Ce^{4+}** [or **Cerium (IV)**] to be standardized are invariably prepared from the following pure reagents, namely:

- Ammonium sulphatocetate: $(NH_4)_4 Ce(SO_4)_4.2H_2O$;
- Ammonium nitratocetate: $(NH_4)_2Ce(NO_3)_6$;
- Hydrous ceric oxide: $CeO_2.4H_2O$;

> **Note: Ammonium nitratocetate may be employed as a primary standard only in such a situation when the solution does not require to be standardized, perhaps due to its rather increased costs involved.**

A number of pharmaceutical substances and corresponding secondary pharmaceuticals (*i.e.*, dosage forms) may be assayed by the help of **ceric sulphate titrations**, such as: **Ferrous gluconate; Ferrous sulphate; Iron Dextran Injection; Menadione; Paracetamol; Tocopherol Acetate** etc.

3.13.5 Titrations with Potassium Bromate [KBrO$_3$]

The specific titrations with potassium bromate, also referred to as '**bromatometry**' may also be exploited as an effective and useful oxidizing agent in the qualitative determination (assay) of a plethora of pharmaceutical substances, for instance: **mephenesin, phenol,** and **sodium salicylate**.

Principle: The fundamental underlying principle of '**bromatometry**' exclusively and predominantly depends upon the formation of **iodine monobromide [IBr]** in relatively higher actual strength of HCl solution.

Theory: Potassium bromate [KBrO$_3$] may be assayed by the addition of **potassium iodide [KI]** and diluted **hydrochloric acid [HCl]** and the chemical reactions involved may be expressed as given below:

$$KBrO_3 + HI \longrightarrow HIO_3 + KBr$$
$$IO_3^- + 5I^- + 6H^+ \longrightarrow 3I_2 + 3H_2O$$

Standardization of $KBrO_3$ solution (say, 0.1N $KBrO_3$) may be accomplished by taking an aliquot of the $KBrO_3$ solution, adding 3 g of KI plus 3 mL of 11.5 N HCl (*i.e.*, conc. HCl). The contents of the **Iodine Flask** are shaken well and allowed to stand for 5–10 minutes so as to complete the liberation of I_2 from the reaction mixture. The liberated I_2 is duly titrated with previously standardized 0.1 N. sodium thiosulphate [$Na_2S_2O_3$] solution using freshly prepared starch solution as an indicate towards the end-point.

3.13.5.1 Assay of Mephenesin

Mephenesin, a muscle relaxant, undergoes oxidation with bromine (**bromatometry**) to give rise to the formation of a '**dibromo analogue**' as given under:

$$BrO_3^- + 6e^- + 6H^+ \longrightarrow Br^- + 3H_2O$$
$$2BrO_3^- + 10e^- + 12H^+ \longrightarrow Br_2 + 6H_2O$$

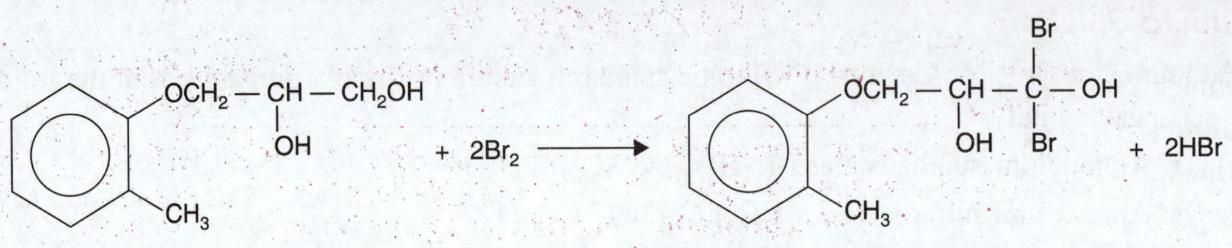

Mephenesin   Dibromo analogue of Mephenesin

From the aforesaid reactions, the unreacted excess of bromate $[BrO_3^-]$ and bromine $[Br_2]$ are duly estimated bromometrically. Thus, we have:

$$C_{10}H_{14}O_3 \equiv Br_2 \equiv 2e$$

or 182.22 g $C_{10}H_{14}O_3 \equiv 2000$ mL N $KBrO_3$

or 91.11 g $C_{10}H_{14}O_3 \equiv 1000$ mL N $KBrO_3$

or 0.00911 g $C_{10}H_{14}O_3 \equiv 1$ mL of 0.1 N $KBrO_3$.

In this way, one may determine the exact quantum of **mephenesin** in the sample.

3.13.5.2 Phenol

Phenol reacts with bromine to produce readily a water-soluble **2, 4, 6-tribromophenol** in an absolute quantitative manner as indicated under:

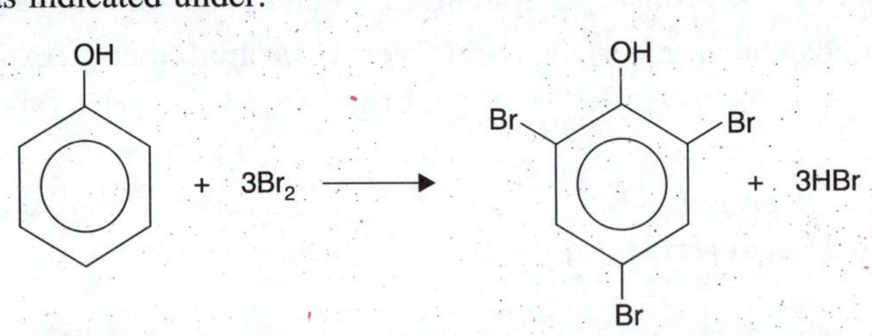

Phenol   2,4,6-Tribromo-Phenol

From the above reaction, we may have:

$$C_6H_6O \equiv 3Br_2 \equiv 6e$$

or 94.11g $C_6H_6O \equiv 6000$ mL N $KBrO_3$

or 15.685 g $C_6H_6O \equiv 1000$ mL N $KBrO_3$

or 0.001569 g $C_6H_6O \equiv 1$ mL of 0.1 N.$KBrO_3$

Assay of **phenol** may be carried out by treating an aliquot of the sample with a known excess volume of standardized $KBrO_3$ solution, adding 1 g of KI, and 10 mL of dilute HCl [10% (u/v)]. The iodine flask is duly stoppered and set aside for about 20 minutes; and finally the excess of $KBrO_3$ solution titrated with previously standardized sodium thiosulphate $[Na_2SO_3]$ solution using starch solution as an indicator towards the end point (from deep blue to colourless).

3.13.6 Titrations with Potassium Iodate [KIO_3]

Potassium iodate [KIO_3] is regarded to be a reasonably strong oxidizing agent which may be employed extensively in the assay of an appreciable number of **pharmaceutical substances**, such as: **benzalkonium chloride, cetrimide, hydrolazine hydrochloride, potassium iodide, phenylhydrazine hydrochloride, semicarbazide hydrochloride** etc.

Principle

The underlying principle of titrations with potassium iodate [KIO_3] is that under suitable experimental conditions the **'iodate'** reacts almost quantitatively with both **iodides [I^-]** and **iodine [I_2]**. It is, however, pertinent to state here that the respective **'iodate titrations'** may be accomplished efficaciously in the presence of **saturated organic acids, alcohols** and a plethora of **several other organic substances**.

The oxidation-reduction methods with KIO_3 usually based on the production of iodine monochloride [ICl] in a medium of strong HCl.

Theory: It has been duly observed that the **'normality'** of KIO_3 solution changes appreciably depending on the nature of the reaction; and, therefore, in actual common practice the **standard iodate solutions having known molarity are used**.

Important Points

There are as follows:

1. In a direct **titrimetric** technique (unlike the reduction of $KBrO_3$ to Br^-) the expected reduction of KIO_3 to I^- is practically not feasible to all; and, therefore, bears no viable utility in the **pharmacopeal procedures**:

$$IO_3^- + 6e^- + 6H^+ \longrightarrow I^- + 3H_2O \qquad ...(i)$$

    Hence, in this kind of a reaction, 1 mol of KIO_3 is 6 equivalent, and a 0.05 M solution would be 0.3 M.

2. In a specific instance, using a large excess of KIO_3 the liberated I_2 may be duly estimated by the **'iodometric procedure'**. Hence, the reduction of **iodate** to **iodine** may be given by the following expression:

$$\underset{\text{Iodate}}{2IO_3^-} + 10e^- + 12H^+ \longrightarrow \underset{\text{Iodine}}{I_2} + 6H_2O \qquad ...(ii)$$

    Thus, in Eqn. (*ii*), 1 mol of KIO_3 is 5 equivalent; and, therefore, a **0.05 M solution** would be equivalent to **0.25 M**. Again, this very reaction of iodate is never used in the **pharmacopeal assay methods**.

3. **Higher concentrations of HCl:** Interestingly, at a definite and distinct higher concentrations of HCl, both the **iodide [I^-]** and the **iodine [I_2]** duly obtained as the reduction products of **iodate [IO_3^-]** [Eqn. (*i*) and (*ii*)] are quantitatively converted to I^+ [**iodine cation**]. It, therefore, precisely forms the fundamental basis of most of the **'official procedures'** for carrying out **iodate titrations** successfully.

    From Eqn. (*ii*), the initial liberated iodine [I_2] caused by the reduction of iodate [IO_3^-] remarkably undergoes **'Solvolysis' in a polar solvent**, as given by the following reaction:

$$\underset{\text{Iodine}}{I_2} \rightleftharpoons \underset{\substack{\text{Iodine} \\ \text{cation}}}{I^+} + \underset{\substack{\text{Iodide} \\ \text{ion}}}{I^-} \qquad ...(iii)$$

    From Eqn. (*iii*), the iodine cation [I^+] forms the respective iodine monochloride [ICl] in a medium containing higher concentration of HCl. Consequently, the **ICl** is adequately stabilized by the subsequent formation of the **'complex ion'**. Thus, we may have the following reactions:

$$I^+ + HCl \rightleftharpoons ICl + H^+ \qquad ...(iv)$$
$$ICl + HCl \rightleftharpoons ICl_2 + H^+ \qquad ...(v)$$

Adding Eqns. (iv) and (v), we may have:

$$I^+ + 2HCl \rightleftharpoons ICl_2 + 2H^+$$

In actual practice, the following steps are taken in a sequential manner:

- Usually carbon tetrachloride [CCl_4] or Chloroform [$CHCl_3$] is incorporated so that the **equivalence point** is visible distinctly.
- Initial liberation of I_2 during titration renders the $CHCl_3$ coloured.
- When almost all the reducing agents under estimation have been duly oxidized, the **iodate predominantly completes** the oxidation of I_2 and I^- to I^+ ; and ultimately, the colour from the $CHCl_3$-layer gets discharged.

A few typical examples of pharmaceutical substances that may be assayed by the **'potassium iodate'** method, shall now be discussed briefly as under:

3.13.6.1 Assay of Benzalkonium Chloride

Benzalkonium chloride, a topical antiseptic, may be assayed by taking an aliquot of the sample, make it alkaline (with 0.1 N NaOH), add KI solution [5% (w/v) in water], and extract the active ingredient successively with at least 4 quantities of chloroform in separating funnel (each of 30 mL $CHCl_3$). The aqueous layer is treated adequately with HCl ($\simeq$ 12 N) and titrate with 0.05 M KIO_3 solution till it becomes pale brown. Add 2 mL of $CHCl_3$, and continue the titration until the $CHCl_3$-layer becomes colourless. Carry out a blank, titration under the same experimental conditions (i.e., except the sample).

Thus, we have:

$$2\ C_{22}H_{40}ClN^* \equiv 2KI \equiv KIO_3$$

or $$354\ g\ C_{22}H_{40}ClN \equiv 2000\ mL\ 1\ M\ KIO_3$$

or $$354\ g\ C_{22}H_{40}ClN \equiv 1000\ mL\ 0.5\ M\ KIO_3$$

or $$35.4\ g\ C_{22}H_{40}ClN \equiv 1000\ mL\ 0.05\ M\ KIO_3$$

or $$0.0354\ g\ C_{22}H_{40}ClN \equiv 1\ mL\ of\ 0.05\ M\ KIO_3$$

$$\text{Each mL of } 0.05\ M\ KIO_3 \equiv 0.0354\ g\ of\ C_{22}H_{40}ClN$$

3.13.6.2 Assay of Potassium Iodide [KI]

The iodine-monochloride [ICl] method, as discussed above, using previously standardized KIO_3 solution is the fundamental basis for the official assay of potassium iodide [KI].

Theory: Based on the above statement of facts, it is absolutely necessary to affect **thorough and vigorous shaking in the vicinity of the equivalence point.**** However, the reaction that involves the above assay may be represented as stated under:

$$2KI + KIO_3 + 6HCl \longrightarrow 3ICl + KCl + 3H_2O$$
$$2(166.0)$$

The reduction of KIO_3 may be expressed as follows:

$$IO_3^- + 4e + 6H^+ \longrightarrow I^+ + 3H_2O$$

---

* Mol.Wt. of Benzalkonium chloride = 354 g.

** Because, both iodine (I_2) and iodate (IO_3^-) in different phases essentially attribute an **obvious heterogeneous medium.**

Thus, we have:

$$2KI \equiv IO_3^- \equiv 4e$$

or $$166 \text{ g KI} \equiv 2e \equiv 2000 \text{ mL N KIO}_3$$
or $$83 \text{ g KI} \equiv 1000 \text{ mL N KIO}_3$$
or $$16.6 \text{ g KI} \equiv 1000 \text{ mL } 0.2 \text{ N KIO}_3 \equiv 1000 \text{ mL } 0.05 \text{ m KIO}_3$$
or $$0.01660 \text{ g KI} \equiv 1 \text{ mL } 0.05 \text{ M KIO}_3$$

i.e., Each mL of 0.05 M KIO_3 is equivalent to 0.0166 g of KI.

3.13.7 Reduction By Ti³⁺ Ions [Titanometry]

Titanometry *i.e.*, reduction by Ti^{3+} ions may be accomplished in *two* ways, namely:

(*a*) Direct titration with Titanium Trichloride [$TiCl_3$]; and

(*b*) Residual titration with Titanium Trichloride [$TiCl_3$].

3.13.7.1 Direct Titration with TiCl₃

In actual practice, these titration exclusively depend upon the reduction of the coloured sample and subsequent discharge of the 'colour' at the **equivalence point**.

3.13.7.2 Residual Titration with TiCl₃

In this instance, the desired sample is heated with an excess of standardized $TiCl_3$ solution in an absolutely inert atmosphere (or environment)*. Thus, the excess reagent is invariably determined by titration with **ferric ammonium sulphate** [$NH_4 Fe(SO_4)_2 . 12H_2$] as the indicator; and the thiocyanate ion gives a distinct red **equivalence point**.

0.1 N Titanous Chloride [$TiCl_3$]: In fact, titanous chloride [$TiCl_3$], is a strong reducing agent, and hence finds a plethora of useful application in **titrimetric analysis**. It is usually employed more specifically for the direct titration of the ferric [Fe^{3+}] salts quantitatively. The reaction with ferric chloride [$FeCl_3$] is as given below:

$$\underset{\text{Titanous chloride}}{TiCl_3} + \underset{\text{Ferric chloride}}{FeCl_3} \longrightarrow \underset{\text{Titanic chloride}}{TiCl_4} + \underset{\text{Ferrous chloride}}{FeCl_2}$$

A '**decinormal solution**', therefore, comprises of 1/10 $TiCl_3.L^{-1}$.

Pharmacopoeal Applications: The most vital and important applications of $TiCl_3$, as a volumetric reagent in the **Official Compendia**, are in the assay of several **dyes**, such as: **Indigo Carmine**; **Methylene Blue, Brilliant Green**, and **Crystal Violet**, besides: **menadione** and its corresponding **bisulphite compound**.

Menadione
[Menaphthone]

---

* **Inert Atmosphere:** It may be duly achieved by passing slowly pure N_2-gas through the reaction (titration) vessel.

The titanous chloride solution rapidly gets oxidized on being exposed to air. Therefore, it is always recommended to be stored in an absolute inert atmosphere; and further be standardized immediately before use.

Note: Necessary and adequate precautionary measures must always be taken to prevent atmospheric oxidation as far as possible during the actual run of the ensuing titrations.

Methodology

The various steps that are intimately involved in the reduction by Ti^{3+} ions [*i.e.*, **Titanometry**] is described as under:

1. **Titanous chloride solution*** is first mixed with an equal volume of conc. HCl, boiled for a minute or so, and diluted with water to almost 10 times the original valence of titanous chloride solution. It ultimately provides a solution which is nearly 0.1 N, and that must be quickly transferred to the following apparatus, known as **'titanous chloride apparatus'** depicted in Figure 3.3, in such quantity as to fill up the bottle right up to the neek.

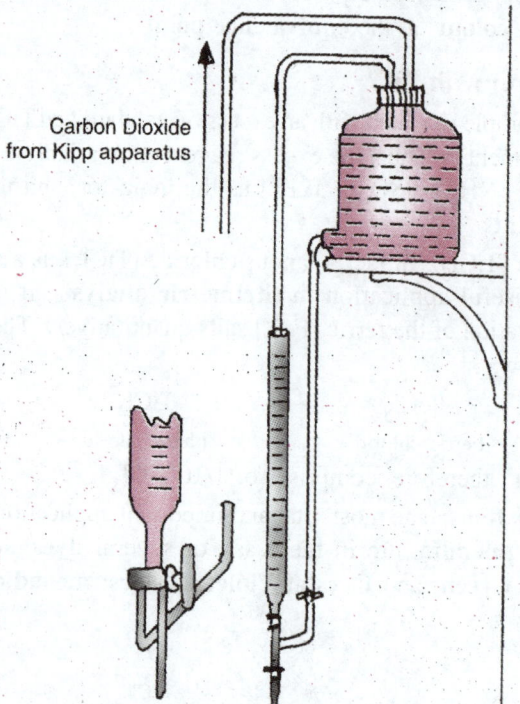

Carbon Dioxide from Kipp apparatus

Fig. 3.3 Titanous Chloride Apparatus

2. The **'Burette'** may be filled as required by duly releasing the upper of the two clips; and as solution is aptly drawn from the bottle, its **'void space'** is dully taken **automatically** by CO_2-gas sucked in instantly from a **Kipp Apparatus** charged with marble and HCl.

---

* Titanous chloride is available as an **'Analytical Reagent'** in the form of 15% solution.

3. The 'first burette full of titanous chloride solution' must be rejected, and a 'free *ad libitum*' flow of CO_2-gas should then be permitted to pass through the 'apparatus'—having the lower clip open for almost 120 seconds so as to ensure that practically all O_2 has been placed.

   [**Instead of a simple burette attached with a T-piece, a burette with a 3-way tap can also be employed alternatively (see enlarged 'inset' in Fig. 3.3)**].

4. Official Compendia usually prescribes that **0.1 N $TiCl_3$-solution** may be 'standardized', immediately before use, by the help of **0.1 N $NH_4Fe(SO_4)_2$ (feric ammonium sulphate) solution.**

5. Because, it is rather difficult and cumbersome to, prepare '**accurate solutions of ferric ammonium sulphate,** it is definitely more easy and convenient to make use of ferrous ammonium sulphate $[(NH_4)_2 Fe(SO_4)_2]$ as stated under:

   (*a*) 25 mL of 0.1 N ferrous ammonium sulphate is transferred to a volumetric flask [250 mL], and acidified strongly with diluted H_2SO_4, and 0.1 N $KMnO_4$ is run in from a burette to obtain a faint permanent pink tinge is accomplished, thereby indicating complete oxidation of Fe^{2+} to the Fe^{3+} state.

   (*b*) All this stage, 5 mL of 10% (*w/v*) ammonium thiocyanate [NH_4SCN] is duly incorporated, followed by 0.5 g of $NaHCO_3$ (sodium bicarbonate)*.

   (*c*) **Titanous chloride [$TiCl_3$] solution** is then run into the Fe^{3+} solution unless and until the red colour (caused on account of ferric thiocyanate) disappears completely.

   (*d*) From the result thus obtained, the **factor of the $TiCl_3$ - solution** is calculated duly.

> Note: Importantly, it is rather more satisfactory as well as convenient to carry out these specific type of titrations in an absolute continuous current if CO_2 [obtained adequately from a marble ($CaCO_3$)/HCl: Kipp Apparatus] passed right into the titration flask *via* a glass tubing strategically help with its end just above the surface of the '*liquid level*'.

3.13.8 Sodium-2, 6-dichlorophenolindophenol

It is a dye, and its aqueous solution has deep blue colouration that gets changed to red by acids. It also liberates iodine from KI in acidic solutions.

Sodium-2, 6-dichlorophenolindophenol is decolourized by '**reducing agent**'. It finds its critical and specific usage as an analytical reagent in the **assay of ascorbic acid (Vitamin C) tablets**, which eventually helps to reduce the '**dye**' to a **colourless hydroxy compound** as given below:

Sodium-2, 6-dichloroindophenolindophenol
[Coloured]

Hydroxy derivative.
[Colourless]

---

* To provide essentially an atmosphere of CO_2 in the titration flask.

i.e., the *'dye'* undergoes *'keto-enol'* **tautomerism** at C1 to produce the colourless hydroxy derivative.

Assay of Ascorbic Acid Tablets

The assay of **'ascorbic acid tablets'** is usually accomplished by an application of the method of **Tillmans***

1. A weighed amount of the tablets is dissolved duly in metaphosphoric acid solution, diluted, and then titrated with a standardized solution of **2, 6-dichlorophenolindophenol**.

2. Dye changes its colour from blue to pale red between pH 5 and pH 4; and subsequently, gets converted into a colourless substance by reducing agent (*viz.*, **ascorbic acid**).

3. Continue the above titration very carefully until a distinct pink colour persists.

> **Note:** The 2, 6-dichlorophenolindophenol solution must be standardized in terms of 'ascorbic acid' immediately before use.

RECOMMENDED READINGS

Alexeyev V: **Quantitative Analysis**, (Mir Publishers-Moscow), CBS-Publishers and Distributors, New Delhi, 2005.

Carter KN and Huff RB: **Second Derivative Curves and End-Point Determinations**, *J-Chem.Ed.*, **56**,: 26, 1979.

De Levie R: **Aqueous Acid-Base Equilibria and Titrations**, Oxford Chemistry Primers, Oxford University Press, London, (UK), 1999.

Hulanicki A: **Reactions of Acids and Bases in Analytical Chemistry**, Ellis Horwood Series in Analytical Chemistry, Ellis Horwood, Chichester, (UK), 1987.

Oxlade C: **Chemical in Action: Acids and Bases** Heinemann Library, 2002.

Rolla E *et al.*:**Kinetics of Decomposition of Tetrathionate, Trithionate and Thiosulphate, and in Alkaline Media**, *Enrion Sci. Technol*, **16**: 852, 1982.

Skoog DA *et al.*: **Principles of Instrumental Analysis**, Thomson (Brooks/Cole), UK, 5th edn, 2005.

Vanderhoff CA: A **Consistent Treatment of Oxidation-Reduction**, *J.Chem. Ed.*, **25**: 547, 1948.

Wagner W and Hull CJ. **Inorganic Titrimetric Analysis**, Marcel Dekker Inc, New York, 1971.

Yolman RG: **Writing Oxidation-Reduction Equations**, *J.Chem. Ed.*, **36**: 215, 1959.

PROBABLE QUESTIONS

1. Discuss the following *two* aspects related to **Oxidation-Reduction Titrations:**
   (*a*) Concepts of Oxidation and Reduction.
   (*b*) Redox-Reactions.

2. (*a*) What is the importance of the **'Standard Oxidation Potential'**? Discuss.
   (*b*) Describe the effects of concentrations on potentials [*i.e.*, **Nernst Equation**].

3. Give a comprehensive account on the **'Strengths and Equivalent Weights of Oxidizing and Reducing Agents'**.

4. Explain the **'Theory of Redox Titrations'** with appropriate typical examples.

5. Discuss any **two** of the following aspects:
   (*a*) Equilibrium Constants of Oxidation Reduction Reactions.

---

* Tilmans, Hirsch, and Reinshagen: *Zeitschrift fur Untersuchung der Lebbensmittel*, **56**: 272, 1928; Tilmans *et at . ibid*; **63**; 1, 1932.

(*b*) Side-Reactions in Redox Titrations.

(*c*) Redox-Titrations Curves.

6. What do you understand by **Redox Indicators**? Explain the following aspects in this aspect:

(*a*) Redox-Indicator Variants

(*b*) Typical Redox Indicators

7. Write comprehensive accounts on:

(*a*) Redox-cell Representations [**Electrochemical Cells**]

(*b*) Measurement of Electrode Potentials [**Half-Reaction Potentials**].

8. Describe in details the theory, application of the *Iodimetric* and *Iodometric titrations* in **Pharmaceutical Analysis.**

9. '**Permanganate Titrations** represent the most reliable, versatile, and valuable oxidizing titrations in the domain of *Redox Titrimetry*'. Explain and justify the statement exhaustively.

10. (*a*) Discuss the '**Potassium Dichromate Titrations**' with their theoretical and applications.

(*b*) Give a comprehensive account of the '**Ceric Sulphate Titrations**'.

11. Attempt any *three* of the following:

(*a*) Titrations with Potassium Bromote [Bromatometry].

(*b*) Titration with Potassium Iodate.

(*c*) Assay of Benzalkonium Chloride'

(*d*) Assay of Potassium Iodide

(*e*) Reduction by Ti^{3+} ions [Titanometry].

Contains

Precipitation Titrations

4.1 INTRODUCTION

In the vast kingdom of **'analytical chemistry'** the typical titrations carried out with a wide spectrum of an array of **'precipitating reagents'** are found to be extremely useful in the particular assay of certain **analytes** (including drug substances). It is, however, pertinent to state here that such type of **precipitation titrations** are duly attainable and hence accomplished with utmost success provided the **'equilibria'** are rapid. Besides, an appropriate means of detecting the **equivalence point** (*i.e.* **end-point**) is available profusely.

Nevertheless, an in-depth of wisdom, knowledge, and consideration of **titration curves** will tremendously enhance our understanding of such vital aspects as: **indictor selection**, **precision**, and **titration of mixture of analytes.**

4.2 PRINCIPLE OF PRECIPITATION TITRATIONS

The fundamental basis for a viable, effective, and reproducible **'titrimetric analysis'** being a definite **chemical reaction** that should take place almost **"quantitatively"** *i.e.* it must always proceed completely to give rise to the formation of **desired products.** In reality and actual practice the kind of reaction which intimately fulfil this specific requirement is the combination of **two ionic species** to yield a **highly insoluble product.** Therefore, the **'phenomenon of precipitation'** of the resulting product subsequently exerts enough force towards completion of the reaction. Titrations that are exclusively based on this typical type of reactions are invariably termed as **'precipitation titrations'.**

Nevertheless, the underlying theoretical approach to the respective **precipitation titrations** may be readily accomplished *via* actual consideration of the **'solubility of the product of reaction',** because it would be duly recognized that the particular **titration reaction** is nothing but the reverse of the dissolution of the respective salt. Importantly, these factual evidences, observations, and considerations are almost closely and intimately applicable to the so called **'classical gravimetric analysis'.**

Dissolution Phenomenon

It has been duly observed that the degree to which an **'analyte'** gets dissolved is duly specified by its prevailing **molar equilibrium solubility,** that critically designates the precise concentration of the

dissolved solute (*i.e.*, **analyte**), usually expressed in moles. L^{-1} in an observed situation when the **solution is in equilibrium with a solid analyte.** Conclusively, the solubility of a compound (analyte) is solely dependent upon the **solvent,** the **pH of the medium,** and the temperature—that should be explicitly stipulated.

Ionic and Nonionic Analytes

In usual practice, one may come across the **'crystalline'** solid state of the ensuing analyte *i.e.*, the *analyte molecules* predominantly occupy certain quantum (volume) of space that exclusively rests on the inherent structure of the **analyte.** Generally, we would encounter with *two* distinct types of substances, namely: **(a) ionic analytes** *viz.*, **sodium chloride (NaCl), phenol (C_6H_5-OH)** etc., and **(b) nonionic analytes** *viz.*, **benzoic acid (C_6H_5-COOH), glucose ($C_6H_{12}O_6$)** etc., that may conveniently assume respective **crystalline well-defined states in the solid form.** The ensuing **'crystalline structure'** thus obtained and maintained by the well deserved support in terms of **'intramolecular forces of attraction'.** Normally, there are *three* distinct types of forces come into play, namely:

(*a*) **electrostatic** *viz.*, crystals of salts (NaCl),

(*b*) **hydrogen-bonding,** and

(*c*) **dipole-dipole interactions.**

Dissolution of a Solid Analyte

In the case of the **dissolution of a solid analyte,** the various, targetted forces of attraction which specifically place in position the molecules together in the environment of a crystal should be overcome at any cost. Interestingly, this particular aspect is adequately obtainable by the solvent. Nevertheless, the **solute-solute attraction** prevailing very much within the crystal is adequately **interchanged** by a **solute-solvent attraction;** and, therefore, the **'analyte'** gets dissolved ultimately.

Molar Solubility may be determined by establishing the **'relative strengths'** of the **solute-solvent/solute-solute interactions.** Importantly, based upon this ensuing specific competition existing between the **solute-solute/solute-solvent interactions,** a solvent would be markedly effective in the dissolution of an analyte provided it is capable of competing with the **'crystal forces'** sufficiently. In other, words, the ensuing **environment of the solvent** should be almost identical, to that usually put forth by the respective **'crystal structure'** so as to enable the **'solvent'** to be effective. Therefore, one may infer legitimately that an **'ionic analyte'** is generally observed to **exhibit a far greater degree of solubility** in a **polar solvent** (*viz,* water, ethanol, acid) *vis-a vis* in a **nonpolar hydrocarbon solvent** (*viz.*, *n*-hexane, benzene. Perhaps it could be the most plausible explanation for the well-known adage **'like-dissolves-like'** *i.e..*, a **'solvent** shall most easily and rapidly dissolve such **'analytes'** that essentially bears an **extremely close resemblance chemically.**

Equilibrium Solubility

The **equilibrium solubility** refers to either the **rate of dissolution** or the **velocity that ultimately establishes the very equilibrium condition.** However, the prevailing **'rate of dissolution'** is virtually governed by several cardinal factors, such as:

- Temperature,
- Rate of stirring the mixture, and
- Surface area of solid phase.

4.3 PRECIPITATION REACTION CHEMISTRIES

In actual practice, the **precipitation reaction chemistries** that are intimately involved in practically all instances should be more or less extremely selective and hence must proceed to completion by all means. In other words, one would like to emphasize upon the following *two* vital and important criteria, namely:

(a) Total absence of **competing reaction chemistries'** which could give rise, to '**unwanted products'** and subsequently, to the **analyte forming soluble products,** and

(b) Precise quantum of '**additional reagents'** that are invariably being taken up to the undesired/unwanted chemical reactions.

> **Note: However, the quantitative aspect of the analysis critically assumes that almost all of the 'analyte' completely reacts to produce the same products, that could be conveniently collected to a 100% efficiency.**

From the aforesaid statement of facts it is quite evident that if one aims at collecting the end product at almost absolute total efficiency, it (*i.e.* **end-product**) should be virtually **insoluble totally.** Importantly, the exact solubility of the product is adequately and expatiately described under the '**solubility product'** (see Section. 4.4.), and that happens to be at its lowest attainable ebb in this particular instance.

Let us duly take into consideration an **equation** that specifically describes either the '**dissolution'** or the '**precipitation'** of a certain complex X – Y, we may have the following expression:

$$aX - bY \longrightarrow aX_{(aq)} + bY_{(aq)} \qquad \qquad ...(i)$$

thus, the **solubility product** (K_{sp}) may be defined as:

$$K_{sp} = [X]^a [Y]^b \qquad \qquad ...(ii)$$

Interestingly, the **precipitation reaction chemistries** are found to be dependent upon several factors, namely:

- pH,
- temperature, and
- stability of the '**precipitate'**.

In a rather broader perspective one may assume that all of the precipitates are ultimately obtained as the '**crystalline solids'**. In case, the solubility of this product happen to be extremely small, the resulting '**relative supersaturation'** shall invariably be fairly large in the actual course of the '**precipitation phenomenon'**. Thus, it is most likely that the solid obtainable would be in the actual state of **non-crystalline colloidal suspension.** In actual practice, one may observe that the colloids will neither **settle down** nor **undergo filtration.** Fortunately, it is quite feasible to either **agglomerate** or **coagulate** the residual obtainable solid easily into a **non-crystalline mass** that could be eventually separated by means of filtration.

4.4 SOLUBILITY PRODUCT [K$_{SP}$]

Assuming the equilibrium in an adequately saturated solution of silver chloride [AgCl], we may have:

$$\underbrace{AgCl}_{\text{Solid}} \rightleftharpoons \underbrace{Ag^+ + Cl^-}_{\text{Dissolved}}$$

Now, at this point in time if one considers the applicability of the **Law of Mass Action** to such an 'equilibrium', as in (a) above, one day obtain the following expression:

$$K = \frac{\left[Ag^+\right]\left[Cl^-\right]}{(AgCl)} \qquad \text{....}(b)$$

Where, K = Equilibrium constant

$$\left[Ag^+\right] = \text{Ionic concentration of Ag.}$$

$$\left[Cl^-\right] = \text{Ionic concentration of Cl.}$$

It has been duly observed that in a 'heterogeneous system' the prevailing actual concentration of a solid (*i.e.*, in this particular instance, AgCl) can be virtually regarded as a constant; therefore, we may have:

$$\left[Ag^+\right]\left[Cl^-\right] = S \qquad \text{...}(c)$$

where, 'S', is a constant, and is termed as the **Solubility Product**.

Example: **Solubility Product of AgCl:** In fact, the solubility of silver chloride [AgCl] in water 25°C is **0.000014 or 1.4×10^{-5} gramme-moles. L^{-1}** *i.e.*, the saturated solution of AgCl invariably comprises of **1.4×10^{-5} grammes-ions of both Ag^+ and Cl^- per litre.** Therefore, we may have:

$$\left[Ag^+\right]\left[Cl^-\right] = (1.4 \times 10^{-5})(1.4 \times 10^{-5})$$

or

$$= \mathbf{1.96 \times 10^{-10}}$$

In other words, **1.96×10^{-10}** designates the **solubility product of AgCl,** that may be considered as a **'constant'** at that specific **temperature.** Now, at this point in time if one introduces either **HCl** or a **soluble (plus ionizable) chloride (common-ion effect)** to the existing saturated solution of AgCl, one would observe that sufficient AgCl shall be duly precipitated for the **product of the ionic concentrations to remain very much at 1.96×10^{-10}.**

Addition of NaCl Solution: Interestingly, if we may incorporate a **solution of NaCl** in a substantial quantum to render the solution **'normal'** with respect to the corresponding chloride ions $\left[Cl^-\right]$, we may have:

$$\left[Ag^+\right] = \frac{1.96 \times 10^{-10}}{\left[Cl^-\right]}$$

or

$$= \frac{1.96 \times 10^{-10}}{10^\circ}$$

or

$$= \mathbf{1.96 \times 10^{-10}}$$

i.e., in such an instance the **solubility** of AgCl becomes so largely and significantly minimized that only **1.96×10^{-10} grammes-molecules per litre** would ultimately remain in solution:

Exactly in a similar manner, the solubility of the **silver chloride [AgCl]** is significantly diminished (lowered) by the careful addition of a **soluble silver salt** [*viz.,* **silver carbonate** (soluble in 30,000 parts cold water)]

Salient Features

The various **salient features** of the **solubility product** are as enumerated under:

1. Theory of **'solubility products'** provides an excellent qualitative concept and idea with regard to the overall ensuing effect upon the **solubility of an electrolyte** *vis-a-vis* the addition of a **common ion**.

2. Obviously, from an absolute **'quantitative aspect'**, the final outcome of results are not so very encouraging and satisfactory; however, the **stark, discrepancies** may be duly expatiated and adequately explained based entirely upon the so called **'modern theory'**, that invariably supposes that a good segment of the **'metallic salts'** get ionized almost completely, even if they are present, in the **'solid state'**.

3. An apt consideration of **'solubility products'** definitely takes care of the **importance in quantitative analysis.** Thus, the actual precipitation of such sparingly soluble substances as: **barium sulphate [BaSO$_4$]; calcium oxalate [Ca(COO)$_2$]; ferric hydroxide [Fe(OH)$_3$]; and silver chloride [AgCl]** only moves towards completion precisely in the presence of certain considerable excess of the **'precipitant'**.

4. **Gravimetric Assays:** The ultimate precipitates finally accomplished in **gravimetric assays** invariably exhibit a lot of variance in character from the **gelatinous ones** *viz.,* **ferric hydroxide [Fe(OH)$_3$], aluminium hydroxide [Al(OH)$_3$]** to the **crystalline ones** *viz.,* **magnesium ammonium phosphate [MgNH$_4$PO$_4$.6H$_2$O].** For this specific experimental parameters with respect to **concentrations** and **temperature** must be duly adjusted to give rise to the formation of a reasonably substantial amount of the precipitate that could be easily and conveniently **collected, washed,** and **dried**.

   Examples: **Barium Sulphate [BaSO$_4$]; Lead Carbonate** [Pb(CO$_3$)$_2$]; and **Magnesium Ammonium Phosphate [Mg NH$_4$ PO$_4$. 6H$_2$O]**—are mostly best precipitated from the **boiling solutions.** Such precipitates must be allowed to stand at the ambient temperature from a period varying between 60–120 minutes so as to cause **agglomeration of precipitation** to ease collection, washing and weighing respectively.

5. **Ferric Hydroxide [Fe(OH)$_3$] and Aluminium Hydroxide [Al(OH)$_3$]:** In Actual practice, the precipitates of both Fe(OH)$_3$ and Al(OH)$_3$ are best obtained from a solution, which is boiled gently later on, but in no case **prolonged boiling** of the resulting solution comprising of the said precipitates must be avoided at any cost.

Specialized Techniques

There are certain **'specialized techniques'** that are particularly applicable for the **assay** of pharmaceutical substances, such as:

(*a*) **Ferric Sulphate:** In this specific instance, the precipitate of **ferric hydroxide [Fe(OH)$_3$]** obtained duly from **ferric sulphate solutions** by the careful incorporation of ammonia [NH$_4$OH] is likely to contain **basic ferric sulphate [Fe$_2$(SO$_4$)$_3$]**. However, the formation of the said **ferric sulphate** may be avoided almost completely by the **usage of an excess amount of ammonia**, added quickly with constant vigorous stirring to the **hot (but not boiling)** ferric sulphate solution.

(b) **Silver Nitrate:** The **silver chloride [AgCl]** from **silver nitrate [AgNO$_3$]** must be precipitated in a **hot (but not boiling)** solution; besides, the liquid should be kept pretty hot together with constant vigorous stirring* for a sufficient length of time to allow the precipitate (of AgCl) to coagulate predominantly. Further more, the contents of the flask (containing AgCl) must be set aside in the **dark**** for at least 10-12 hours before carrying out the titration.

Adsorption of Impurities by Precipitates

It has been duly observed that the precipitates obtained in the course of some titrations do adsorb **'substances'** from the solution. A few typical examples are as cited under:

1. **Barium Sulphate:** Obviously, **barium sulphate [BaSO$_4$]** adsorbs substantiable traces of **barium chloride [BaCl$_2$]**, **sodium sulphate [Na$_2$SO$_4$]**, and other **soluble salts.**

2. **Ferric and Aluminium Hydroxides:** The gelatinous precipitate of **ferric and aluminium hydroxide** do adsorb certain impurities which cannot be removed by simple washing and hence pose a rather serious and troublesome problem. However, there are hardly any plausible solution that may minimize such entrapped unavoidable impurities.

3. **Official Quantitative Test for Iron as Impurity in Copper Sulphate (CuSO$_4$):** In this specific instance, one may circumvent the ensuing problem usually encountered by precipitating **iron** first as **ferric hydroxide [Fe(OH)$_3$]** with ammonia, that eventually leaves behind the **copper very much in solution**. The precipitate [Fe(OH)$_3$] thus obtained is adequately **dissolved in acid** and subsequently **reprecipitated**; whereas, the **second precipitation** performed in a **solution having traces a copper exclusively**, would exhibit fairly **negligible adsorption.**

4.5 INFLUENCE OF ACIDS (pH), STOICHIOMETRY, STABILITY AND COMMON-ION EFFECT *vis-a-vis* SOLUBILITY OF PRECIPITATE

In a broader perspective, the **precipitation reaction chemistries** may be solely dependent on such cardinal factors, such as: influence of acids (pH), stoichiometry, stability, and common-ion effect *vis-a-vis* the solubility of the precipitate. All these aspects shall now be discussed individually in the sections that follows:

4.5.1 Influence of Acids (pH) on Solubility of Salts

In a situation when the **'anion'** of a slightly soluble salt represents the **'conjugate base of a weak acid'**, it has been predominantly observed that the solubility of the salt will be duly affected by the pH of the medium.

Example: **Silver Acetate [CH$_3$COOAg]:** It is quite feasible and possible to correlate effectively and meaningfully the solubility of the salt [silver acetate] to the corresponding **H$^+$ ion concentration** of the solution.

---

* Preferably on a **Hot-Plate-cum-Magnetic Stirrer.**

** Because it gets decomposed in **'light'** along with **darkening** and loss of **chlorine.**

Thus, if **YX** designates the **'slightly soluble salt'** , at the *equilibrium* its equation may be expressed as follows:

$$YX(s) \rightleftharpoons Y^+ + X^- \qquad ...(a)$$

Because, **A⁻ represents the conjugate base of a weak acid**, the **acid-base equilibrium** should get duly satisfied simultaneously as given under:

$$HX \rightleftharpoons H^+ + X^- \qquad ...(b)$$

In actual practice, the operation of this particular equilibrium enhances the solubility of **YX** appreciably by adequately driving the Eqn. (*a*) to the right-hand side. However, the molar solubility of **YX** is equal to the concentration of Y^+, which happens to be almost equal to the total concentration of Y; *i.e.*:

$$s = [Y^+] = [X^-] + [HX] \qquad ...(c)$$

Therefore, the equilibrium expressions are duly designated as:

$$K_{sp} = [Y^+] [X^-]$$

and,
$$K_a = [H^+] [X^-]/[HX]$$

Now, substituting these values correctly in Eqn. (*c*) we have:

$$[Y^+] = \frac{K_{sp}}{[Y^+]} \left(1 + \frac{[H^+]}{K_a} \right)$$

or
$$s = \sqrt{K_{sp}(1 + [H^+]/K_a)} \qquad ...(d)$$

Thus, one may notice critically that Eqn. (*d*) sharply relates the molar solubility to K_{sp} , K_a and **H⁺ ion** concentration.

Important Observations

A few important and vital observations are as given under:

1. When [H⁺] is extremely low in comparison to *Ka*, the overall solubility almost gets near to $K_{sp}^{1/2}$, that usually designates the value for a **'slightly soluble salt'** whose ultimate integral component ions are neither **acids** nor **bases**.

2. With the apparent enhancement in the H⁺ ion concentration the observed solubility also increases proportionately.

3. However, in the specific critical instance when [H⁺] = K_a *i.e.*, pH = pK_a , the Eqn. (*d*) almost turns out to be:

$$s = 1.41 \, K_{sp}^{1/2} \qquad ...(e)$$

Thus, Eqn, (*e*) helps to predict that when **pH** would be equivalent to **pK_a**. It has been duly observed that the solubility of YX is almost equal to 41% greater in comparison to the particular status when the H⁺ ion concentration is almost negligible.

> **Note: An identical equation may also be accomplished for a 'specific salt' whose cation happens to be the conjugate acid of a weak base. Evidently, the solubility would increase as the H⁺ ion concentration gets duly minimized for this type of a salt.**

4.5.2 Stoichiometry *vis-a-vis* Solubility

The following Table 4.1 records certain **solubility products** $[K_{sp}]$ together with the corresponding **calculated molar solubilities** [s (mol.L^{-1})] for a few slightly soluble salts. It is, however, pertinent to state here that the **molar solubility** as determined may not necessarily be directly proportional to the corresponding K_{sp} value, because it exclusively depends on stoichiometry* of the salt.

(1) **Silver Iodide [AgI]:**

Examples: K_{sp} of **silver iodide [AgI]** is 5×10^5 greater in comparison to that of Al $(OH)_3$; however, its **molar solubility** [s (mol . L^{-1})] is observed to be *two* folds only to that of **aluminium hydroxide [Al(OH)$_3$]**. In other words, a 1: 1 salt invariably gives rise to a rather much lower solubility in comparison to a **nonsymmetric salt** for a known K_{sp} .

(2) **Mercuric Sulphide [HgS]:** Mercuric Sulphide [HgS] exhibits a **solubility product** $[K_{sp}]$ of merely 4×10^{-53}, having a **molar solubility of 6×10^{-27} M.** Interestingly, it actually corresponds to less than **one ion of each Hg^{2+} and S^{2-}** in 1 L at equilibrium with the ensuing precipitate (which is just like the **two ions** looking for each other in a normal bath tub).

	Table 4.1 Solubility Product Constant [K_{sp}] of some Selected Slightly Soluble Salts		
S. No.	**Selected Slightly Soluble Salts**	**Solubility Product Constant [K_{sp}]**	**Molar Solubility S [mol. L^{-1}]**
1	Pb SO_4	1.6×10^{-8}	1.3×10^{-4}
2	AgCl	1.9×10^{-6}	1.0×10^{-5}
3	AgBr	4×10^{-13}	6×10^{-7}
4	AgI	1×10^{-16}	1×10^{-8}
5	Al $(OH)_3$	2×10^{-32}	5×10^{-9}
6	Fe $(OH)_3$	4×10^{-38}	2×10^{-10}
7	Ag_2S	2×10^{-49}	4×10^{-17}
8	HgS	4×10^{-53}	6×10^{-27}

4.5.3 Stability

The **precipitation reaction chemistries** is also dependent on the **stability of the precipitate**. Evidently, the importance of **'stability'** must not be either forgotten or ignored at all, and it is invariably essential that the precipitate is capable of tolerating the **'required heating'** absolutely necessary to get rid of the residual amount of water.

4.5.4 Common-Ion Effect

In a situation, where there exists an excess of one specific ion over the other, the concentration of the other is duly suppressed (**common-ion-effect**); and, therefore, the prevailing solubility of the precipitate is reduced. Ultimately, one may still be able to calculate the concentration from the **solubility product**.

---

* The study of the **mathematics of chemistry** and **chemical reactions; chemical calculations** as well.

4.6 PROFILE OF PRECIPITATION TITRATIONS: INVOLVING

(*a*) Silver nitrate,

(*b*) Ammonium or potassium thiocyanate,

(*c*) Mercuric nitrate, and

(*d*) Barium sulphate.

4.6.1 Silver Nitrate

In the specific precipitation reaction that essentially involves **chloride ion [Cl⁻]** and **silver nitrate [AgNO₃]**, the careful incorporation of even a small quantum of the latter will prominently influence the precipitation of **AgCl** only if the K_{sp} has been increased appreciably. Hence at this point in time, the concentrations of both Ag^+ and Cl^- are directly related by the **solubility product equilibrium constant**. Thus, we may have:

$$Ag^+ \text{ (titrant)} + Cl^- \text{ (analyte)} \rightleftharpoons AgCl\ (s)$$

The '**chromate ion concentration**' predominantly needed to initiate the actual precipitation of Ag_2CrO_4 starts at the **equivalence point** (*i.e.*, **end point**), and may be easily calculated with the solubility products for **AgCl** and **Ag₂CrO₄** :

Solubility Product (K_{sp}) of AgCl = 1.8×10^{-10} = $[Ag^+]\ [Cl^-]$

Solubility Product (K_{sp}) of Ag₂CrO₄ = 1.2×10^{-12} = $[Ag^+]^2\ [CrO_4{}^{2-}]$

Let us consider that at the Equivalence point:

$$[Ag^+] = 1.3 \times 10^{-5}\ M$$

the ensuing chromate ion concentration should be:

$$[CrO_4{}^{2-}] = \frac{[AgCrO_4]}{[Ag^+]^2}$$

or

$$= \frac{1.2 \times 10^{-12}}{[1.3 \times 10^{-5}]^2}$$

or

$$= 6.7 \times 10^{-3}\ M$$

Importantly, one may normally make use of concentration of 5×10^{-3} M for chromate suggests that $[Ag^+]$ would be definitely more than **1.3 × 10⁻⁵ M** at the equivalence point thereby inducting a **positive determinate error**. It has also been proved beyond any reasonable doubt that even with concentrations as low as 2×10^{-3} M the degree of error actually caused is negligibly small.

4.6.2 Ammonium or Potassium Thiocyanate

The ammonium thiocyanate [NH₄CN] *Vs* silver nitrate [AgNO₃] titrations is commonly termed as the **Volhard's Method**, which is based upon *two* major aspects, such as:

(*a*) **Precipitation of insoluble silver salts** to near completion from the nitric acid (NHO₃) solution by adding an excess of silver nitrate (AgNO₃) solution to a corresponding **soluble salt**, and

(*b*) Assay of excess of silver nitrate (AgNO₃) solution by performing the residual titration with previously standardized ammonium thiocyanate solution, using the **ferric ammonium sulphate** as an indicator (end-point: first appearance of a red-brown colour).

In this way, ammonium thiocyanate (NH_4SCN) reacts rapidly with silver nitrate (in HNO_3) as stated under:

$$NH_4SCN + AgNO_3 \longrightarrow AgSCN \downarrow + NH_4NO_3$$

Methodology

In fact, the thiocyanate solution is normally taken in the burette, and is almost run directly into the silver nitrate solution taken in the conical flask which has been adequately acidified with HNO_3. Ferric ammonium sulphate being the **choicest indicator** by virtue of the fact that the equivalence point is clearly detected by the appearance of a deep-red colouration (due to **ferric thiocyanate**) on account of the interaction of Fe^{2+} **ion** and a trace of SCN^- **ion**.

Precautionary Measures

Following are the *two* vital and important **precaution measures** in this precipitation titration, such as:

1. **Nitric acid** should be free from **nitrous acid** (HNO_2), otherwise **thiocyanic acid (HSCN)** may give rise to an intense-red colour, and

2. **Temperature** of the titrating solution must be maintained below 25°C throughout the titration due to the fact that at an elevated temperature the red colouration of the **ferric thiocyanate complex** invariably fades away quite fast.

4.6.3 Mercuric Nitrate

In contrast to the aforesaid '**thiocyanate method**' as described under Section: 4.6.2, the titration of **mercuric nitrate [Hg(NO$_3$)$_2$]** may also be accomplished in the presence of the **peptizing agents.*** It has been duly observed that even **hydrogen peroxide (H_2O_2)**, at a concentration level of **5 M**, fails to interfere either. Therefore, in this manner it is quite feasible as well as possible to carry out the estimation of **chlorides [Cl⁻]** in two typical situations, such as:

(*a*) In the presence of a number of **reducing agents**, and

(*b*) In the presence of certain **oxidizing agents** *viz.*, sulphite [SO_3^{2-}], sulphide [S^{2-}], nitrite [NO_2^-], chromate [CrO_4^{2-}], and permanganate [MnO_4^-]; that are ultimately decomposed by the action an excess of hydrogen peroxide (H_2O_2) in an acidic medium.

Methodology

The various steps involved are as follows:

1. The '**analyte**' solution is first acidified with nitric acid [**AnalaR Grade** *i.e.*, free from chlorides] so that the concentration of the acid lies within the range of 0.2 to 5.0 N.

2. **Indicator** is introduced and a first rough titration is performed to an accuracy of almost 1 mL.

3. As we add the **mercuric nitrate [Hg(NO$_3$)$_2$]** solution, the liquid in the flask turns blue gradually.

4. At the '**equivalence point**' the colour of the resulting solution at once gets changed to **blue-violet**.

---

* **Peptizing Agents:** Such agents that specifically help the process making a colloidal solution rather stable due to the conversion of a gel to a solution.

Important Precautions

The two important precautions in the titration are as follows under:

1. The titration must always be carried out in the absence of '**direct sunlight**' (*i.e.*, UV-light).

2. In order that the '**pale blue colour**' must not interfere with the estimation of the '**equivalence point**', one must add the said '**indicator**' in the **replicate titrations** only when 1 to 2 mL of the titrant remains to be added to arrive at the exact end-point. Therefore, in this particular instance the need for an '**indicator correction**' is almost avoided safely.

4.6.4 Barium Sulphate

Barium sulphate* is invariably not so easily obtained in the purified form. Hence, for pharmaceutical and other purposes the pure substance is duly prepared by the careful precipitation from a solution of barium chloride [$BaCl_2$] by the incorporation of a **soluble sulphate** *e.g.*, **sodium sulphate** [Na_2SO_4]. Thus, we may have:

$$BaCl_2 + Na_2SO_4 \rightleftharpoons BaSO_4 \downarrow + 2\,NaCl$$

The white precipitate is duly collected, thoroughly washed, and carefully dried **preferably in a steam-oven**.

Official Tests for Purity

The **official tests** for the purity of **Barium Sulphate** are mostly those recommended duly by cocking**. The particular attention has been focused upon the importance of the purity of barium sulphate meant exclusively for the medicinal usage***. In fact, the '**sedimentation test**' was duly incorporated in the 1953 **British Pharmacopoea**, and since then the same has been adequately modified at length.

4.7 SPECIFICALLY NAMED PRECIPITATION TITRATIONS

The following are some of the most vital and important specifically '**named precipitation titrations**' namely:

(*a*) Gay-Lussacs Method,

(*b*) Mohr's Method,

(*c*) Volhard's Method, and

(*d*) Fajan's Method.

The aforesaid **named precipitation titrations** shall now be described in details in the sections that follows:

4.7.1 Gay-Lussac's Method

The **Gay-Lussac's method** is one of the most reliable means for determining the equivalence point in titration by the **precipitation technique**.

---

* **Barium Sulphate:** It is usually obtained in the form of barytes *i.e.*, one of the major sources of **barium compounds**.

** Cocking: *Quarterly Jr. of Pharmacy*, **1**: 363, 1928.

*** **Medicinal Usage of BaSO$_4$:** Large doses of '**barium meal**' are orally administered to the patients before the **thorough** examinations of the damages caused in the **alimentary canal (tract)**.

It may be explicitly exemplified by the reaction that occurs when **sodium bromide (NaBr)** solution is being titrated with silver nitrate (AgNO$_3$) solution or *vice-versa*.

Thus, we may have:

$$NaBr + AgNO_3 \longrightarrow AgBr \downarrow + NaNO_3$$

From the above reaction one may observe critically that eventually precipitation of **silver bromide (AgBr)** continues as long as an excess of the **bromide (Br$^-$) ion** is present in the reaction mixture. Therefore, one may precisely detect the point at which the precipitation caused virtually comes to a stand-still by taking carefully small amounts of the titrated solution towards the end of the titration, and adding to each of them one drop of the AgNO$_3$-solution previously diluted to ten times. In this particular case, obviously the actual detection of the end point is rendered much easier and convenient by the fact that almost at the vicinity of the end-point the precipitate of AgBr gets coagulated and duly collected at the bottom of the vessel usually in the shape of '**large curdy flakes**'. At this point in time, the solution gets cleared rapidly which eventually is facilitated either by vigorous shaking or stirring.

> **Note: As the above procedure does not make use of any 'indicator' whatsoever, hence this method is also called the 'non-indicator method'.**

AgCl Vs AgBr Method: In the specific instance of **silver chloride (AgCl)**, which distinctly exhibits the solubility product, $K_{sp} = 1.56 \times 10^{-10}$, is clearly **not** as low as that of **silver bromide (AgBr)**, which stands at $K_{sp} = 7.7 \times 10^{-13}$, suggests profusely that the ensuing methodology is certainly some what more complicated.

The possible logical explanation for the above variation in the **solubility product** by almost 5000 folds is solely due to the fact that the **saturated AgCl solution** produced at the end-point yields a **distinct turbidity** with both AgNO$_3$ and NaCl solutions.*

Interestingly, the obviously turbidity in the above *two* instances is exactly the same at the prevailing **equivalence point**.

Salient Features

The salient features of the AgNO$_3$/NaCl **precipitation titrations** are as enumerated under:

1. In case, the resulting solution is not fully titrated and leaves behind a small excess of the **chloride (Cl$^-$) ions**, the overall turbidity caused by the addition of AgNO$_3$ should obviously be greater than that produced by sodium chloride (NaCl).

2. Conversely, in a situation whereby the resulting solution is over-titrated to a small extent, the present NaCl definitely gives rise to more turbidity in comparison to AgNO$_3$. Hence, to carry out the determination of the **equivalence point** one should always take two identical **samples** of the solution just prior to the end of the titration and treat them separately as indicated under precisely:

    (*a*) Treat *one* with a drop of **AgNO$_3$ solution**, and

    (*b*) Treat **second** with a drop of **NaCl solution** having the **same concentration**.

    Thus, the '**titration**' is virtually stopped at a stage when both the samples practically afford an '**equal turbidity**'.

---

* Due to decrease of the solubility of AgCl by the introduction of a **common ion**.

3. Though in this particular method a 'certain proportion' of the titrated solution should be removed periodically for 'sampling' the prevailing 'method of equal turbidity' is still regarded to be one of the most **reliable**, trustworthy and precise methods in the domain of **volumetric precipitation analysis**.

In fact, it does require a lot of skill besides being time consuming and equally laborious. Hence, in actual practice the 'indicator methods' are overwhelmingly popular and used in the **argentometric titrations**.

4.7.2 Mohr's Method [or Indicator Method]

Mohr's method exclusively makes use of the **potassium chromate [K$_2$CrO$_4$]** solution as an **indicator** in **argenometric titrations**.

Theory: The underlying principle is the use of **potassium chromate [K$_2$CrO$_4$]** as an **indicator**, whereby it gives rise to the formation of a **brick red precipitate** of silver chromate [Ag$_2$CrO$_4$] by the interaction of **chromate ion [CrO$_4$$^{2-}$]** upon the **silver ion [Ag$^+$]**. In actual practice, one may distinctly observe that the precipitated of Ag$_2$CrO$_4$ only begins to generate after the **Cl$^-$ ions** have been precipitated almost completely as silver chloride [AgCl].

Explanation: The most plausible explanation of the above facts almost rests upon the prevailing difference between the K_{sp} of **AgCl** and **Ag$_2$CrO$_4$**.

At this juncture, let us consider that a 0.1 N NaCl solution previously charged with the indicator potassium chromate [K$_2$CrO$_4$] at a concentration of 10^{-2} M, is carefully titrated with AgNO$_3$ **solution**. However, it may be observed critically that the *two* individual precipitates, namely: **AgCl** and **Ag$_2$CrO$_4$** start production only after its **solubility product** has been duly and distinctly exceeded.

As the **solubility product of AgCl** is nearly equal to 10^{-10} *i.e.*, SP$_{AgCl}$ $\approx 10^{-10}$, the expected and desired value of the Ag$^+$ ion concentration prevailing in the solution required to reach almost the 'said value' is:

$$[Ag^+] = \frac{SP_{AgCl}}{[Cl^-]} = \frac{10^{-10}}{10^{-1}} = 10^{-9} \text{ g ion. L}^{-1}$$

Let us now attempt to calculate the actual concentration of the **silver ions [Ag$^+$]** at a point where the precipitation of **Ag$_2$CrO$_4$** just commences. Therefore, the solubility product of **silver chromate [Ag$_2$CrO$_4$]** may be given by the following expression:

$$[Ag^+] [CrO_4{}^{2-}] = SP_{Ag_2CrO_4} = 1.1 \times 10^{-12}$$

Hence,

$$[Ag^+] = \sqrt{\frac{SP_{Ag2CrO4}}{[CrO_4{}^{2-}]}} = \sqrt{\frac{1.1 \times 10^{-12}}{10^{-2}}} = \sqrt{1.1 \times 10^{-10}}$$

or
$$[Ag^+] = 1.05 \times 10^{-5} \text{ g ion. L}^{-1}$$

Evidently, the **solubility product** of AgCl is duly accomplished relatively much earlier *i.e.*, at a lower concentration of **Ag$^+$ ions** (*viz.*, 10^{-9} g ion. L^{-1}) in comparison to that of **Ag$_2$CrO$_4$** (*viz.*, 1.05 $\times$ 10^{-5} g ion . L^{-1}).

From the aforesaid statement of facts one may infer that **AgCl** must be precipitated as a '**first-step**'. Nevertheless, the resulting product $[Ag^+]$ $[Cl^-]$ invariably remains constant always, by virtue of the fact that the **Cl$^-$ ions** get duly precipitated as **AgCl**, whereby the Ag^+ ion concentration in the solution should enhance slowly. Ultimately, the concentration of the **Ag$^+$ ion** in relation to the solubility product of Ag_2CrO_4 is duly accomplished as given by the following expression:

$$[Ag^+] = \sqrt{\frac{SP_{Ag_2CrO_4}}{[CrO_4^{2-}]}} = 1.05 \times 10^{-5} \text{ g ion. L}^{-1}$$

Interestingly, at this juncture Ag_2CrO_4 starts getting precipitated along with **AgCl**. Thus, the precipitate suspended in the liquid attains a reddish-brown colouration, which directly suggests the actual **equivalence point**. Therefore, based on the following equation:

$$[Ag^+] \, [Cl^-] = SP_{AgCl}$$

one may easily and conveniently calculate the **Cl$^-$ ion concentration** in the resulting solution at this material point:

$$[Cl^-] = \frac{SP_{AgCl}}{[Ag^+]} = \frac{1 \times 10^{-10}}{1.05 \times 10^{-5}} \approx 9.524 \times 10^{-6} \text{ g ion. L}^{-1} \qquad ...(a)$$

Important Points

From Eqn. (a) we may observe the following **important points**, namely:

1. **Silver chromate [Ag$_2$CrO$_4$] precipitation** usually commences only after almost all the available chloride ions [Cl$^-$] have been duly precipitated as **silver chloride [AgCl]**.

2. **Concentration of chloride ions [Cl$^-$]** present in the residual solution invariably corresponds to:

$$pCl = - \log 1.05 \times 10^{-6} \approx 5.03 \qquad \text{[pCl = Negative logarithm of the chloride concentration.]}$$

The above value of **pCl $\approx$ 5.03** evidently suggests that this indicator [viz., potassium chromate (K_2CrO_4)] at a prevailing concentration of 10^{-2} **M** renders it absolutely possible to establish and determine the equivalence point with **utmost accuracy and precision**.

4.7.3 Volhard's Method

Another typical example representing precisely the '**indicators reacting with the titrant**' is distinctly illustrated by the **Volhard titration method**. Importantly, it designates an **indirect titration procedure** to specifically '**assay anions**' that critically get precipitated with **silver ion [Ag$^+$]** e.g., SCN$^-$ (thiocyanate ion), Cl$^-$ (Chloride ion), and Br$^-$ (Bromide ion) ; besides, it is invariably carried out in an acidic medium (viz., **HNO$_3$-solution**). In this particular method it is a common practice to incorporate carefully a certain **measured excess quantum of silver nitrate (AgNO$_3$)** to help in the complete precipitation of the anion (i.e., SCN$^-$, Cl$^-$, Br$^-$) ; and subsequently, estimating the '**excess of Ag$^+$**' by carrying out **back-titration with standard potassium thiocyanate** or **ammonium thiocyanate** solution meticulously.

Thus, potassium thiocyanate [KSCN]/ammonium thiocyanate [NH$_4$SCN] reacts quantitatively with silver nitrate [AgNO$_3$] in nitric acid solution as given under:

$$KSCN + AgNO_3 \longrightarrow AgSCN\downarrow + KNO_3$$
$$NH_4SCN + AgNO_3 \longrightarrow SCN\downarrow + NH_4NO_3$$

Eventually, the insoluble precipitate of **silver thiocyanate** [AgSCN] get duly separated, while the soluble salts of **potassium nitrate** [KNO_3] and **ammonium nitrate** [NH_4NO_3] remain very much in the residual clear solution. Thus, we have:

$$\left. \begin{array}{l} X^- + Ag^+ \longrightarrow AgX^- + \text{excess Ag} \\ \text{excess } Ag^+ + SCN^- \longrightarrow AgSCN^- \end{array} \right\} \quad [X = Cl^- \text{ or } Br^-] \quad ...(a)$$

Detection of End-Point

The end-point may be accomplished accurately by the addition of Fe (III) as a **ferric alum** or **ferric ammonium sulphate** [$NH_4Fe(SO_4)_2$], that essentially gives rise to a specific **soluble red complex** critically with the first excess of the **titrant** (thiocyanate solution in Burette):

$$Fe^{3+} + SCN^- \longrightarrow Fe(SCN)^{2+} \quad ...(b)$$

Explanation: In Eqn. (a) assuming that the ensuing precipitate, **AgX**, is found to be less soluble in comparison to that of **AgSCN**, one may avoid safely the removal of the precipitate before performing the actual titration, as may be seen in the instance of I^-, Br^-, and SCN^- anions.

Special Points: There are *two* **special points** with respect to this particular kind of **precipitation titrations**, such as:

(a) **Typical instance of I^-:** Here, one may not add at all the **requisite indicator** unless and until all the **iodide ion** [I^-] gets duly precipitated, due to the underlying fact that the same will be adequately oxidized by the **ferric ion Fe^{3+}**, and

(b) **Precipitate being more soluble than AgSCN:** In such a situation, it may react with the **titrant** to produce a **significantly high** and **apparently diffuse end-point**, as may be observed in the case of AgCl:

$$AgCl\downarrow + SCN^- \longrightarrow AgSCN\downarrow + Cl^- \quad ...(c)$$

From Eqn. (c) it is quite evident to justify explicitly the cause for the removal of the precipitate [AgSCN] by the help of filtration before carrying out the actual titration.

> **Note: 1. Indicators employed should not give rise to a compound by interaction with the titrant which happens to be more stable in comparison to the ensuing precipitate.**
> **2. Colour reaction shall precisely take place soon after the very first drop of the 'titrant' being added.**

Precautions: The following *two* vital and important **precautions** must be adhered to strictly as stated under:

1. **Nitric acid (HNO$_3$)** should be absolutely **free** from any **nitrous acid (HNO$_2$)**, otherwise the resulting **thiocyanic acid [HSCN]** will render an almost **instant red colouration**, and

2. **Temperature (25 °C)** — The temperature of the reacting solution must be maintained usually below 25°C by virtue of the fact that at an '**elevated temperature**' the **red colour of the ferric thiocyanate complex** [$Fe(SCN)_3$] invariably fades away rapidly.

4.7.4 Fajan's Method

In order to understand Fajan's method in the right sense and perspective we may have to take a close look at the so called **Adsorption Indicators**.

Adsorption Indicators

In this particular instance, the 'indicator reaction' actually occurs just on the outer surface of the ensuing precipitate. Usually, the 'adsorption indicator'—which happens to a **dye** and exists predominantly in the solution as its **typical ionized** status *viz.*, **an anion** designated as **In⁻**.

Table 4.2 records the list of certain commonly employed 'adsorption indicators', the **specific titration involved**, and the **criteria of solution**:

S.No.	Name of Indicators	Specific Titration	Solution Criteria
	Table 4.2 Some Important Adsorption Indicators		
1	Bromocresol Green	SCN^- with Ag^+	pH 4 to 5.
2	Bromocresol Blue	Hg^{2+} with Cl^-	0.1 M solution
3	Dichloro fluoroscein	Cl^- with Ag^+	pH 4
4	Eosin [Tetrabromo Fluorescein]	Br^-, I^-, SCN^- with Ag^+	pH 2
5	Fluorescein	Cl^- with Ag^+	pH 7 to 8
6	Methyl Violet	Ag^+ with Cl^-	Acidic medium
7	Orthochrome T	Pb^{2+} with CrO_4^{2-}	Neutral; 0.02 M solution.
8	Rhodamine 6G	Ag^+ with Br^-	HNO_3 [≤ 0.3 M]
9	Thorin	SO_4^{2-} with Ba^{2+}	pH 1.5 to 3.5.

It has been duly established that **fluorescein** may be used as an **adsorption indicator** for any of the halides (*e.g.*, Cl^-, Br^-, I^-) at pH 7 due to the fact that it will not displace any of these halides at all. However, the corresponding derivative **dichlorofluorescein** will definitely displace the **chloride ion (Cl^-) at pH 7** but **fails to do so at pH 4**. Consequently, the results ultimately tend to be quite low when these titrations are duly carried out at pH 7.

Fajan's Method is nothing but the actual titration of chloride ion [Cl^-] employing these highly specific adsorption indicators.

Interestingly, fluorescein was discovered to be the very first original indicator described meticulously by Fajan; however, the advent of intensive and extensive research has virtually replaced the same with **dichlorofluorescein**.

> **Note:** Eosin, the corresponding tetrabromoderivative of fluorescein cannot be employed effectively for the titration of chloride at any pH by virtue of the fact that it usually gets adsorbed too strongly by the precipitates.

Standardization to Titrant

It has been duly observed and concluded that as a good number of these **end-points** fail to coincide with the **equivalence point**–'the titrant must be duly standardized by the same titration as employed

for the sample.' Therefore, one may get rid of the '**errors**' that will virtually cancel provided almost the same quantum of the titrant being consumed for the **standardization** as well as the on-going **analysis**.

Example: **Photodecomposition of Silver Halide [AgX]:**

As a typical example of the major culprit (error) in the titrations with silver [Ag^+] being the **photodecomposition of silver halide [AgX]**, which in turn is adequately catalyzed by the '**adsorption indicator**'. Thus, one may even accomplish accuracies and precisions upto **one part for thousand** by duly carrying out the **proper standardization**.

RECOMMENDED READINGS

Coetzee JF: In-**Treatize in Analytical Chemistry,** Kolthoff 1M and Elving PJ (eds): Interscience, New York, Part 1, Vol. 1. 1959.

Duval C: **Inorganic Thermogravimetric Analysis,** Elsevier, Amsterdam, 1963.

Erdey L: **Gravimetric Analysis: International Series of Monographs in Analytical Chemistry,** Vol. 7, Pergamon Press, London, 1965.

Gordon L *et al.*: **Precipitation from Homogeneous Solution,** John Wiley, New York, 1959.

Hawkins MD: **Calculations in Volumetric and Gravimetric Analysis,** Butterworth, London, 1970.

Laitinen HH and Harris WE: **Chemical Analysis,** Mc Graw-Hill, New York, 2nd edn, 1975.

Lewin S: **Solubility Product Principle,** Interscience, New York, 1960.

Mendham J *et al.*: **Classical Methods of Chemical Analysis,** Vol. II, ACOL-Wiley, Chichester (UK), 1987.

Rattenbury EM: **Introduction to Titrimetric and Gravimetric Analysis,** Pergamon Press, London, 1966.

Schales O: '**Chloride**': In: Reiner M (ed.): **Standard Methods of Clinical Chemistry,** Vol. 1., Academic, New York, 1953.

Smith WF: **Analytical Chemistry of Complex Matrices,** John Wiley, Chichester (UK), 1996.

Tyson J: **Analysis,** Royal Society of Chemistry, London, 1994.

PROBABLE QUESTIONS

1. Discuss the underlying principle of '**Precipitation Titrations**' with reference to the following cardinal aspects:
    (*a*) Dissolution Phenomenon
    (*b*) Ionic and non-ionic analytes
    (*c*) Dissolution of a solid analyte
    (*d*) Equilibrium solubility

2. Elaborate explicitly the importance of **Solubility Product [$K_{sp\backslash}$]** on the Precipitation Titrations. Give suitable examples.

3. Describe in details the influence of:
    (*i*) pH
    (*ii*) Stoichiometry
    (*iii*) Stability, and
    (*iv*) Common-Ion Effect
    upon the over-all **solubility of precipitate.**

4. How would you carry out the **precipitation titrations** involving:
    (*i*) Silver Nitrate
    (*ii*) Ammonium or Potassium Thiocyanate
    (*iii*) Mercuric Nitrate
    (*iv*) Barium Sulphate

5. Give a comprehensive account of any **THREE** of the following **named-precipitation reactions,** namely:
    (*a*) Gay-Lussac's method
    (*b*) Mohr's Method
    (*c*) Volhard's Method
    (*d*) Fajan's Method.

Contains

5

Gravimetric Analysis

5.1 INTRODUCTION

The **Gravimetric** (or **mass based**) **analyses** represents an excellent and unique method whereby either an element or a compound is duly accomplished in its purest form *via* careful and articulated isolation, and subsequent final weighing. It may also be regarded as one of the most recognized, widely accepted accurate and precise methods of **micro-quantitative analysis.** Importantly, the so called **gravimetric analysis** has been further categorized predominantly into *two* well-developed techniques, namely:

(*a*) Electrogravimetric analysis, and

(*b*) Thermoanalytical analysis.

Nevertheless, the **traditional gravimetric assays** essentially include the following vital and important steps, such as:

1. Selective conversion of the analyte to an insoluble form.

2. Transformation of the element, ion or radical to be estimated into a pure stable compound.

3. Separated precipitate is carefully dried or ignited, possibly to another form, and is weighed accurately using a fairly sensitive single-pan electric balance.

4. Mass of the element, ion or radical in the original substance (analyte) may now be calculated based upon the knowledge of its **'chemical composition'** *vis-a-vis* the corresponding relative atomic masses of the constituent elements.

The copious volumes of evidences from the literature one may legitimately conclude that the **'actual gravimetric analysis'** do make use of the final weight (mass) of the product which is invariably obtained by adopting either of the following **standard procedures** for instance:

(*i*) Solvent extraction,

(*ii*) Volatilization or ignition, and

(*iii*) Precipitation from solution.

It has been broadly observed that the **'gravimetric techniques'** are heavily dependent upon the **quantitative absolute** precipitation of the corresponding **cation** or **anion** from a given solution by *two* different means:

(*i*) As an **insoluble compound** which yields a residue with a particular composition after ignition, and

(*ii*) As an **insoluble compound** with a definite known composition.

Advantages

The various **advantages** accomplished duly by the **gravimetric analysis** are as enumerated under:

1. Proves to be an accurate and precise when making use of modern analytical balances (*viz,* Mettler, Anamed, Dhona).

2. Possible sources of error are instantly checked, because the filtrates may be ascertained towards completeness of precipitation, besides, the resulting precipitates may be adequately screened for the presence of undesired impurities.

3. Distinctly designates an **'absolute method of analysis'**. In other words, it essentially involves **direct measurement** within any form of calibration invariably required.

4. All estimations (assays) may be performed with rather **inexpensive apparatus.** However, the most expensive items being the **'Muffle Furnace'** and the **'Platinum Crucibles'**.

5. Being classified as a **microscopic method** normally using relatively **large sample sizes** *vis-a-vis* several other **quantitative analytical procedures.**

6. Possible to accomplish an extremely high degree of accuracy even at ordinary laboratory parameters, thereby providing the extent of repeatability of results between the range 0.3 to 0.5%.

In short, one may rightly add that the **'gravimetric analysis'** in many instances provides a **product having known composition** which gets precipitated almost quantitatively as an **absolute insoluble product** duly emerged from a **reaction mixture.**

5.2 THEORY [or FUNDAMENTALS]

Mackenzie (1979)* opined that **gravimetric analysis** is exclusively concerned with the weighing of a substance which has been either scientifically precipitated from a solution (through typical chemical reactions) or duly volatilized and absorbed.

However, it is pertinent to state here that it is absolutely essential for the **'selected method'** to precipitate the respective **ion** or **element** being assayed in a specific state so as to render it not only **slightly soluble** but also to **prevent appreciable loss** taking place when the desired precipitate is adequately separated by filtration and weighed ultimately.

The above statement of facts may be further expatiated by the help of the following *two* typical examples:

Examples:

(*a*) **Estimation of Ag$^+$:** A requisite volume of the solution of **'analyte'** is carefully treated with an excess of NaCl or KCl solution, and the following steps are taken in a sequential manner, namely:

---

* Mackenzie RC: *Thermochim Acta,* **28**: 1, 1979.

- precipitate obtained is filtered off,
- resulting precipitate washed thoroughly to get rid of soluble salts,
- recovered precipitate dried duly between 130–135°C and
- dried precipitate weighed as AgCl.

(b) **Estimation of Mg^{2+}:** In this particular instance the Mg^{2+} ion being assayed is finally weighed in a *state* which is entirely different from its original form. Hence Mg^{2+} is duly precipitated as a complex salt known as **ammonium magnesium phosphate $[Mg(NH_4)PO_4 . 6H_2O]$**; however, it is duly weighed after careful inceneration (ignition) as its pyrophosphate salt *i.e.,* **magnesium pyrophosphate $[Mg_2P_2O_7]$**.

There are, in fact, *there* cardinal factors whch have gained cognizance to accomplish a successful assay by precipitation, such as:

(a) **Absolutely Optimized Precipitation** *i.e.,* the **ultimate precipitate** should be **insoluble** to such an extent that it affords practically no significant loss, when the same is duly collected by filtration.

Example: In actual practice, the '*left over*' amount of precipitate available in the solution **must not exceed more than 0.1 mg** *i.e.,* the minimum detectable amount by an ordinary analytical balance.

(b) **Typical and Distinct Physical Status of Precipitate** *i.e.,* the ultimate **'a physical status'** should be of such a nature that it may be completely any rapidly separated from the enusing solution (reaction mixture) by the help of normal filtration procedure adopted. Besides, the resulting precipitate can be washed effectively free of the usual soluble impurities encountered in the **gravimetric analysis.** For this, one may have to consider the following *two* important experimental parameters such as:

(i) Particles should not be able to get across the filtering medium *viz.,* filter paper, sintered glass filters, and

(ii) Particle size is almost unaffected by the prescribed, washing process.

(c) **Convertibility of Precipitate into a Pure Product (with Definite Chemical Composition)** *i.e.,* the precipitate under investigation should be aplty convertible into a pure substance having a specific definite chemical composition, and it may be judiciously achieved either by inceneration (ignition) or by a simple chemical mean *e.g.,* effective evaporation with an appropriate liquid (solvent).

Supersaturation

In true sense, the phenomenon of supersaturation invariable poses another serious difficulty that may take place in **gravimetric analysis.** It is quite well-known that a **supersaturated solution** usually comprise of a relatively greater concentration of solute as expected for **equilibrium solubility** at the temperature under experimental parameters, Obviously, it represents an **absolute unstable state;** and, therefore, the corresponding form of **'stable equilibrium',** may be easily established by adding crystal of the pure **analyte** (*i.e.,* **solute**)* or by creating various points for initiating the process of crystallization to commence by mechanical scratching the inside of the reaction container with a glass rod.

---

* Known usually as **seeding the solution** for effective crystallization.

Problems Vs Effective Measures in Gravimetric Analysis

The various kinds of problems usually encountered in the **gravimetric analysis** may be overcome by the aid of certain effective measures *i.e.,* well-established techniques as enumerated under:

1. Preferably the process of precipitation must be done in dilute solution to the following aspects meticulously:
   - solubility of the precipitate,
   - time needed for completion of the filtration, and
   - follow up operative measures with the filtrate.

   All these *three* vital aspects would contribute a long way to minimize the undue errors caused on account of the phenomenon of **co-precipitation.**

2. Reagents involved must be mixed gradually and with constant vigorous stirring. Essentially it would certainly help to maintain the extent of actual supersaturation pegged at a low ebb; and hence, will definitely assist the realistic growth of large crystals. One may anyone of the following options, namely:
   - addition of a slight excess of the reagent,
   - addition of a large excess of the reagent in certain exceptional cases,
   - the order of actual moving of the reagents is most important, and
   - experimental parameters most suitable for enhancing solubility of precipitate, thereby lowering the degree of supersaturation.

3. Hot solutions usually affect the **'precipitation'** directly which depends upon the **solubility** and the **stability** of the ensuing precipitate. To accomplish their, either one or both of the solutions must be heated carefully to a desired favourable temperature or just below the boiling point. In fact, **three** critical situations invariably, come into being, namely:
   (*a*) An increase in solubility with a resulting definite lowering of the extent of supersaturation,
   (*b*) An assistance in coagulation with minimized solution formation, and
   (*c*) A definite increase in the **'speed'** of crystallization, that may ultimately lead to **better-formed crystals.**

4. Digestion of **'crystalline precipitates'** must be continued to the maxmium possible duration, preferentiallly overnight, except in such instances where the possibility of **'post-precipitation'** do take place. **Digestion** should be performed always on a steam bath. **Digestion** hardly affects either the **gelatinous or the amorphous precipitates**; whereas, it certainly lowers the degree of co-precipitation, and ultimately yields more readily filterable precipitates.

5. Precipitate must be washed with the **suitable diluted solution of an electrolyte. Peptization*** may usually occur when the precipitate is washed with **'pure water'.**

6. **Reprecipitation** of the so called **'crude precipitate'** from an **appropriate solvent** helps to remove the appreciably contaminated precipitate due to **coprecipitation** or several other causes

---

* **Peptization:** In the chemistry of colloids, the phenomenon of rendering a colloidal solution more stable of conversion of a gel to a solution.

quite affectively. Thus, the quantum of any foreign substance (as an impurity) duly present in the **second precipitation product** shall be very negligible; and, therefore, the amount of actual entrainment by the precipitate will also be quite small.

7. Gordon *et al.* (1959) demonstrated that the precipitation from a homogeneous solution is invariably carried out so as to prevent **supersaturation** to a great extent.

5.3 PRECIPITATION TECHNIQUES

The **precipitation techniques** essentially involve the careful **'precipitation of the product'** that usually takes place following the addition of the reagent(*s*) to the respective **'analyte'**. Obviously, precipitates having **bigger particle sizes** are more prone for easier collection by **'filtration'; and** therefore, inherently comprises of fewer contaminants in comparison to the precipitates with finer particles.

The **precipitation techniques** employed in the **'gravimetric analysis'** generally consist of **seven** distinct and vital steps, namely:

(*i*) Solution preparation,

(*ii*) Precipitation,

(*iii*) Digestion or Ostwald Ripening,

(*iv*) Filtration,

(*v*) Washing,

(*vi*) Ignition or inceneration of drying, and

(*vii*) Weighing to constant weight.

All these steps shall now be treated separately to discuss its pivotal and inportant role in the present context *i.e,* **gravimetric analysis.**

5.3.1 Solution Preparation

The very first step in the **'gravimetric analysis'** is to prepare the **'analyte solution'**. To accomplish this one may have to:

(*i*) cause the preliminary separation to remove the major interfering substances,.

(*ii*) adjust essentially the solution parameters so as to maintain the overall **'low solution'** of the precipitate, and to obtain it in such a state which is absolutely fit for filtration.

(*iii*) extremely careful pre-adjustment of the solution parameters before actual precipitation can also mask, the relevant and potential interferences predominantly.

(*vi*) various governing factors that should be borne in mind are:

- overall effective volume of the solution in the course of precipitation,
- concentration spectrum of the 'analyte',
- concentration and presence of other accompanying constituents,
- prevailing temperature, and
- pH of the solution.

---

* Gordon *et al.: Precipitation from Homogeneous Solution,* John Wiley, New York, 1959

It has been observed commonly that the specific **'precipitation reaction'** is overwhelmingly **'selective for the analyte'**. In fact, the preliminary separation is an absolute must, but in certain other cases the precipitation step occurring in the gravimetric analysis happens to be **'highly selective'** and hence, the other separations may safely be ignored completely. Importantly, the pH of the solution is quite important and significant due to the fact that it invariably influences not only the critical **'solubility of the analytical precipitate,**' but also the apparent possibility of **'interferences caused from other constituents.'**

Examples: Following are *two* classical examples to expatiate the overwhelming impact of pH in the preparation of the solution:

(a) **Calcium oxalate [CaC$_2$O$_4$]:** It is found to be almost **insoluble in a basic medium;** however, at **low pH** the oxalate **[C$_2$O$_4$$^{2-}$] ion** predominantly combines with the **H$^+$ ion** to give rise to the formation of a **weak acid.**

(b) **8-Hydroxy-quinoline [oxine]:** It may be employed mostly to enable the precipitation of a large quantum of elements, of course by strictly controlling the ensuing **pH,** so as to precipitate the **'elements'** very selectively.

Example: Al^{3+} ion can be precipitated conveniently at pH4 as given below:

| Oxine | | Oxine anion | | Oxine anion | | Aluminium oxine complex |

Notes: 1. At pH4 the aluminium ion [Al^{3+}] can be precipitated effectively.

    2. The actual prevailing concentration of the 'Oxine Anion' happens to be very low at pH4 to allow the complete and effective precipitation of magnesium ion [Mg^{2+}].

    3. However, at a higher pH it may be possible to cause the ionization to the right so as to precipitate Mg^{2+}. Importantly, when the pH is too high there is every possibility that magnesium hydroxide [Mg (OH)$_2$] shall also get precipitated duly thereby causing cumbersome interference.

5.3.2 Precipitation

It has been duly observed that **'actual particle size'** depends not only upon on the realistic parameters during the process of precipitation.

Generally, the actual size of the particle may not alter in regular phases *i.e.,* consistently. However, in the **colloidal particles specifically** the range in the size of the particles vary between **10^{-6} to 10^{-4} mm in diameter**; and, therefore, exhibit absolutely little tendency to settle down from the solvent. Thus these particles are beyond the scope of collection by filtration.

Nevertheless, at the other terminal end of the spectrum one may distinctly observe the **'true precipitation'** when the respective particles are duly obtained with sizes very much within the fractions of a millimeter (mm).* Thus, the corresponding particles having **larger dimensions** present in the solvent give rise to definitive crystalline suspensions that spontaneously, settle out thereby enabling them to be collected by filtration without any difficulty at all.

It is, however, pertinent to state here that the size of the precipitation particles are predominantly influenced by *three* cardinal factors, such as:

- temperature,
- concentration of reactants, and
- rate at which reactants mix.

Relative supersaturation refers to the **'single cumulative parameter'** related to the assumed particle size based on the aforesaid variables, which may be duly defined by the following expression:

$$\text{Relative supersaturation} = \frac{Q - S}{S} \qquad \qquad ...(a)$$

where, Q = **Concentration of mixed reagents**** (solutes) before precipitation commences, and

S = **Solubility of precipitate** at equilibrium.

The ratio Q–S/S in Eqn. (*a*) is invariably referred to as the **von Weimann ratio.**

Observations: There are *two* critical observations with respect to the process of **precipitation,** namely:

(*i*) In the course of precipitation, the system gets **supersaturated momentarily**, and a certain relief is achieved by precipitation of the desired **'solid residue'.**

(*ii*) In a situation whereup the **relative supersaturation** is apparently **'small'**, one may come across with the precipitates with **prominent larger particulate dimensions.**

Thus, we may have:

High Relative Supersaturation $\longrightarrow$ Several Tiny Crystals (**more surface area**)

Low Relative Supersaturation $\longrightarrow$ Fewer Large Crystals (**less surface area**)

Targetting Large Crystals by Minimizing Supersaturation

Larger crystals may be duly accomplished by the critical minimization of the **supersaturation phenomenon** *via* the *four* undermentioned sequential steps, such as:

(*a*) Obtain precipitate from significantly dilute solution, thereby keeping **'Q'** at a low ebb *i.e.*, concentration of mixed reagents,

(*b*) Incorporate dilute precipitating reagents **gradually,** with constant stirring, thereby reducing **'Q'.**

---

* **Colloidal Suspension:** In case, colloidal particulate matters are eventually present within a solvent medium, the mixture is usually termed as a **colloidal suspension,** wherein the **particles do remain in suspension** by the **Brownian Movement (or Motion)**

** Represents the **degree of supersaturation.**

(*c*) Precipitation from hot solution, which increases. However, the ensuing solubility must not be two high otherwise the **precipitation** shall not be of a **'quantitative nature'.*** Bulk of the **'percipitation'** can be carried out even in the hot solution. Subsequently, the resulting solution must be chilled adequately to accomplish the so-called **'quantitative precipitation'**.

(*d*) **Precipitation** must be performed at the lowest possible **'pH'** so as to adequately obtain **quantitative precipitation.**

Mechanism of Precipitation

It has been proved and established beyond any reasonable doubt that **'solid particles'** invariably, crystallize and cease to be solvated by the help of *two* distinct **mechanisms of precipitation,** such as:

(*a*) Nucleation, and

(*b*) Particle Growth.

Nucleation: Precipitation is usually initiated by **nucleation,** which refers to the process of nucleus formation in which further growth occurs *e.g.,* **crystalline nucleation** on which a **larger crystal is grown.** In fact, the very first stage of **nucleation** essentially cause to participate the spontaneous association of a few **ions, atoms or molecules** to produce a reasonably **stable second phase:** and it usually comes into being on certain irregularly shaped surface, *viz,* a *suspended dust particulate matter* present within the solvent. Nevertheless, further precipitation may now persistently continue either *via* additional subsequent **spontaneous nucleation reaction** or *via* the critical growth of the existing nuclei.

Particle Growth: The particle growth usually refers to the critical growth of the prevailing nuclei on account of the further persistently continued precipitation. It has been duly observed that in a situation when **nucleation predominates** exclusively, it normally follows that the average particle size would be **mostly small.** Conversely, in an instance when the **particle growth predominates** exclusively, it would give rise to an average particle size which tends to be larger.

In conclusion, one may add that the ensuing **enhanced levels of supersaturation** are believed to increase the **rate of nucleation**; and, therefore, it ultimately leads to the dictum that – **increased levels of supersaturation typically and evidently cause the smaller particles to be generated conspicuously.** Importantly, in the same vein–**the causation of supersaturation occurring at a lower ebb usually tend to favour precipitation *via* particle growth; and this in predominantly leads to the formation of distinctly larger particulate matters very much within the precipitate.**

5.3.3 Digestion

Ostwald Ripening Digestion usually refers to—**'A method of extraction wherein the solute and solvent are heated gently for long specified time period.'**

In other words, the digestion of the precipitate renders to make distinctly bigger and definitely more pure crystals. However, it is an universal truth that relatively **'small crystals'** having' a **larger specific surface area** do exhibit an equally **higher surface energy** plus a **higher apparent solubility (S)** in comparison to the large crystals. In true sense it obviously designates an **universal rate**

---

* That is, with < 1 part per thousand remaining.

phenomenon. Besides, it fails to represent the **equilibrium parameter;** and, therefore, it actually appoints to a position which is nothing but simply **one consequence of the heterogeneous equilibrium.** Let us consider a particular instance when a precipitate is permitted to stand along with the '**mother liquor',** * one may observe critically that the '**big crystals'** shall be growing at the expense of the '**small crystals'.** The said phenomenon is termed as **digestion or Ostwald ripening.**

Figure 5.1 illustrates the phenomenon of **digestion** of the **Ostwald ripening** where by the *'larger crystals'* of **silver chloride [AgCl]** are duly formed from the available Ag^+ and Cl^- ions.

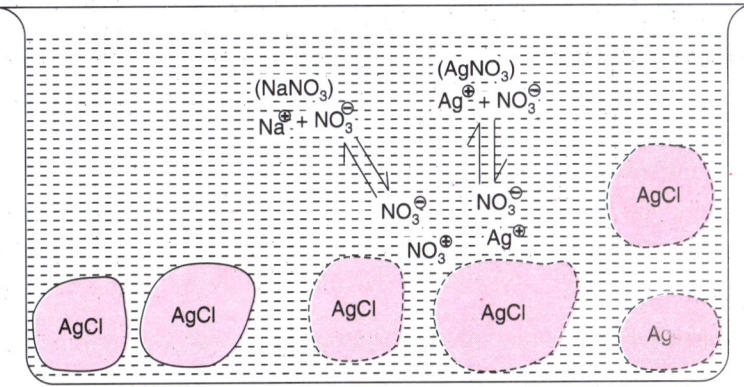

Fig. 5.1 Digestion or Ostwald Ripening of Silver Chloride (AgCl) Crystals.

It is evident from the above Fig. 5.1 that the **small crystals of AgCl** usually have a tendency to get dissolved and reprecipitate upon the surface of the **larger crystals.** Besides, the **individual crystals** also **agglomerate** to share predominantly a '**common counter ion'** layer. Thus, the resulting '**agglomerated crystals'** ultimately **cement** together due to the formation of the apparent '**connecting bridges',** which eventually reduces the **surface area** precisely.

5.3.4 Filtration

The '**precipitate'** once adequately generated is invariably collected by **filtration** employing a **Büchner Flask** along with a suitable **sintered glass crucible**** or **fritted glass crucible.** The **mother liquor** is slowly poured into the crucible, with a gentle suction, so as to collect the **filtrate** and **the solid precipitate. Preparation of sintered glass crucible**: For this the thoroughly cleaned (with *chronic acid*)/washed/ rinsed with double-distilled water sintered glass crucible is duly baked in an electric oven at a temperature of $100 - 120°C$ to get rid of any residual absorbed moisture completely. After the requisite heating the crucible is cooled duly in a desiccator, charged with fused calcium chloride $[CaCl_2]$ along with the desired precipitate, at room temperature. The actual weight must be recorded onto a good analytical balance upto the fourth place of the decimal.

---

* **Mother Liquor:** The solution from which the crystals got duly precipitated.

** **Sintered Glass Crucible.** These are normally available in **three** different grades *viz, fine, medium,* and *coarse.*

Note: It is absolutely necessary that the sintered glass crucible must have truly attained the temperature of its surroundings adequately, because the under thermal convection currents above a warm crucible may certainly cause the disturbing fluctuations in the final observed weight.

Salient Features

The **salient features** of **filtration** are as stated under:

1. The side-arm of the **Büchner-Flask** is carefully attached either to a **centralized vacuum line** or to a localized **individual water vacuum pump attached to laboratory water-tap**.

2. **Mother liquor** *i.e.*, solution from which solid got duly precipitated, must not be thrown out but rather retained.

3. In most cases, it is quite possible to recover a **'second crop'** of crystals/precipitates from the **'mother liquor'** by concentration and sudden chilling (**'thermal stock'-treatment**).

4. Mostly it is not possible to virtually collect all the ensuing filtrate by just one filtration step by virtue of the fact that certain quantum, of the solid particulate matter shall invariable adhere to the sides of the beaker or vessel wherein the actual precipitation was carried out.

Note: It is always preferred that one must collect the solid precipitate to the maximum extent in order to accomplish a perfect reproducible quantitative analysis.

5. **Use of Mother Liquor: Mother liquor** is usually employed to rinse the **'precipitation vessel'** and filtered subsequently to collect the residual precipitate. In actual practice, it is always preferred to utilize the **mother liquor** instead of **fresh distilled water** for the said **'rinsing process'** for *two* vital and important reasons:

   (a) Mother liquor may still contain certain quantum of solid substance with distinctly smaller particulate dimension that might have escaped being captured during the very first filtration step. At this specific critical stage the sintered-glass crucible will now be partially clogged by the precipitate already captured; and, therefore, a second filtration usually caters to capture certain extent of the very small amount of the residual solid particulate matter.

   (b) Solid. precipitate shall invariably exhibit a definite solubility, irrespective of its being two small. Importantly, the mother liquor should be well saturated, whereby its usage shall always predominantly check and prevent:

   • re-solubilization of any of the precipitate present in the **'precipitation flask',** and

   • re-solubilization of the precipitate present in the sintered-glass crucible.

6. **Use of a Policeman:** To dislodge the sticky, stubborn, and difficult-to-detach **solid particulate matters** from the inside of the precipitation flask/vessel may be affected by the help of a **'glass rod with a rubber sleeve at the end'** (known as **'Policeman'**). The **policeman** along with the dislodged (recovered) precipitate finally washed with the **'mother liquor'** to meticulously transfer even the last bit of the solid material which may be clinging on to the rod itself. One may, of course repeat the aforesaid process 4-5 times so as to recover even the **last-remains of the solid particulate material.**

7. **Ceramic Crucibles:** The crucible is usually made up of a high quality ceramic material so as to withstand heating in an electric oven conveniently. The oven is invariably pre-set at 90–95°C in order to allow the moisture (water) to escape out almost completely; however, one may even opt for higher temperature provided the **'precipitate'** is stable thermally. In case, the solid **particulate matter** has a tendency to get decomposed at a lower temperature, then it is always advisable to use even a temperature much 'lower' than the prevailing one evidently, in which case, the ceramic crucible should be heated for a longer duration of time. Soon after this heating process the crucible must be transferred to a desiccator to attain the room temperature over a certain stretch of time. The crucible plus the precipitate is now weighed carefully using a **four-figure electric balance** taking great care that it has fully attained the room temperature. In a situation, when the **'final weight'** drops, the whole heating-cooling-weighing exercise has got to be repeated till such time one arrives at the **consecutive concordant results.** Thus, the actual **'final mass'** of the precipitate may be duly calculated.

5.3.5 Washing

In a particular instance when the coagulated particles are subjected to filtration, they invariably retain the **'adsorbed' primary and secondary ion layers** together with the solvent (water). In fact, **washing** the coagulated particles with water enhances the degree of solvent (water) molecules very much existing between the layers. This ultimately renders the **'secondary layers'** to remain bound loosely, and thus the coagulated particles ultimately revert to the **'colloidal state'.** This particular phenomenon is usually known as **'peptization'.** Interestingly, at this point in time if one incorporates an appropriate **'electrolyte'** it may give rise to a **closer secondary layer,** besides it would distinctly promote and augment the phenomenon of coagulation.

Enhanced Coagulation

The coagulation may be enhanced further by the following *two* manners, namely:

(*a*) **Heating** aids to reduce the process of adsorption and the desired effective change in the prevailing **'adsorbed layers'** specifically which in turn would be helping **coagulation** predominantly, and

(*b*) Constant vigorous mechanical stirring either on a **'Magnetic Stirrer' or** by a **'Laboratory-Variable Speed Stirrer'.**

Removal of Coprecipitated Impurities: It is quite feasible to get rid of the **coprecipitated impurities** by affecting thorough **'washing'** of the precipitate soon after **filtration.** However, the resulting precipitate would be **'wet'** with the **mother liquor** and this may also be removed carefully by washing.

Note: There are several precipitates that cannot be washed even with pure water due to the obvious fact 'peptization' may come into play.

Removal of Foreign Ions

Washing the **coagulated particulate material** with pure water will not only dilute and remove the **'foreign ions',** but also the **'counter-ion'** shall occupy a larger volume having more solvent molecules existing between its and the ensuing primary layer. Ultimately, the overall net result is that the so called **'repulsive forces'** existing between the **solid particles** usually become strong again; and, hence, the said **solid particles** do revert to the **colloidal state partially** and thus easily pass *via* the filter. However, it may be prevented altogether effectively by the addition of an appropriate **'electrolyte'** in the wash liquid.

Example: Addition of either ammonium nitrate [NH_4NO_3] or nitric acid [NHO_3] for the precipitation of silver chloride [$AgCl$], but certainly not potassium nitrate [KNO_3] which being nonvolatile in nature.

Specific Criteria of the Electrolyte: These are as follows:

(*i*) Electrolyte must be volatile at the particular temperature at which either the **'drying'** or **'ignition'** takes place; besides, it should not dissolve the **'precipitate'** under investigation at all.

(*ii*) To determine exactly when the **'washing'** is to be completed. However, it may be accomplished by testing the filtrate periodically for the presence of an **ion of the precipitating reagent.** Subsequently, after several **washing** with relatively small quantum of the **'wash liquid'**, a few drops of the filtrate are duly collected in a separate test tube for performing the **'specific test'**.

5.3.6 Ignition [Incineration or Drying]

The carefully. collected **colloidal precipitate** should be heated to *first* get rid of **'water'**, and *secondly* to remove the **wash liquid.** In usual practice the **ignition** (or **incineration** or **drying**) may be accomplished effectively by heating at 110° – 120°C for a duration of 1 to 2 hours. However, one may perform the **ignition** at a much higher temperature provided the required precipitate should be converted to a more suitable and stable form for final weighing.

Examples: A few typical examples are cited below to elaborate the aforesaid statement of facts:

1. **Magnesium ammonium phosphate [$MgNH_4PO_4$]:** In is usually decomposed to the more suitable and stable form *viz,* **magnesium pyrophosphate** [$Mg_2P_2O_7$] by ignition at 900°C in a muffle furnace.

2. **Hydrous Ferrous Oxide [$Fe_2O_3x\ H_2O$]:** It is ignited to the corresponding **anhydrous ferric oxide** [Fe_2O_3].

5.3.7 Weighing to Constant Weight

The quartz/ceramic crucible after the process of **ignition** should be cooled to the ambient temperature in a desiccator for sometime. The exact weight of the crucible is taken on a pre-calibrated/standardized single pan electric balance upto the fourth place of the decimal. The crucible is again heated/cooled/weighed at least 3 to 4 times till one gets **three** constant and concordant readings. This indeed gives a fairly accurate and precise result.

5.4 SOLUBILITY PRODUCTS

The **solubility product [K_{sp}]** has been duly discussed in chapter 4 under Section 4.4.

5.5 THE COLLOIDAL STATE

The terminology **'colloid'** has been duly derived from the *Greek* word for *glue*, was applied in 1850 by Thomas Grahham—a British chemist to such substances as:

polypeptides: albumin, gelatin,

vegetable gums: acacia, starch, dextrin, and

. **inorganic compounds:** metal hydroxides *viz*, $Al(OH)_3$, $Fe(OH)_3$, $Cr(OH)_3$ etc.

All these compounds failed to crystallize, and diffuse very slowly when either dissolved or dispersed in water. Everett (1988)* observed that **colloidal substances** may be duly segregated from the ordinary solutes *e.g.*, sugar, salts, invariably termed as **'crystalloids'.** Importantly, these **crystalloids** get adequately diffused *via* the very fine pores of the dialysis membrane (usually made from the **'animal gut'**) that critically retained the colloidal particles en-block. However, the **'crystalloids'** get rapidly crystallized from the resulting solution.

Colloidality

Von Weimarn was pioneer in the proper identification of **colloidality** as a particular designated condition of the critical subdivisions of matter instead of a category of substances. It has been duly proved and established that Graham's colloids *viz*, **proteins** have already been crystallized; besides, Von Weimarn succeeded in the preparation of most of the **'crystalloids'** earlier discovered in the *colloidal state.*

Condensation Method: Virtually resulted from **high degree of relative supersaturation,** that ultimately gave rise to the formation of a good number of small nuclei.**

Examples:

(*a*) **Preparation of clear and transparent solidified jellies:** (Aqueous Solution) One may prepare such typical jellies by careful cooling the aqueous solutions of various salts *viz*, $Al_2(SO_4)_3$, $Ba(SCN)_2$, and $CaCl_2$.

(*b*) **Preparation of clear and transparent solidified jellies (Aqueous-Alcoholic Solutions):** The particular type of jellies may be prepared by cooling aqueous-alcoholic solutions of a variety of such salts as: NH_4Cl, NH_4NO_3, NaBr, NaCl, and KSCN.

It has been duly observed that the intensive and extensive research carried out over the years amply enlightened the relevance of the **colloid** and **surface chemistry** *vis-a-vis* with an appreciable and exceptionally broad spectrum of **industrial and biological systems.** However, it may be logistically exploited as a wonderful newer domain of **adhesives, catalysts, detergents, latexes for paints, lubricants, plastics, rubbers, and soaps.** Besides, its judicious applications may also be adequately extended to **aqueous humors, blood, cigarrete smoke, clays, cell membranes, ink, liquid crystals,** and **mucous membranes.**

In general, the colloidal particles are invariably very small in size ranging between 1–100 μm; and therefore, do exhibit a comparatively a very huge **surface-to-mass ratio,** that predominantly promotes **surface adsorption.**

Colloidal Dispersions: In reality, the colloidal dispersions essentially comprise of *two* absolutely discrete phases, namely:

(*a*) **Internal phases** – Consisting of one or more disperse phases, and

---

* Everett DH: **Basic Principles of Colloid Science,** Royal Soc., Chem. London, 1988.

** Alexander AE and Johnson P: **Colloid Science,** Oxford Univ., Press, Oxford (UKI), 1949.

(b) **External phase (or Dispersion medium or vehicle)** – Consisting of a continuous phase.

Colloidal Dispersions *Vs* Coarse Dispersions: The major points of difference between **colloidal dispersions** and **coarse dispersions** are as follows:

(i) Particle size of the disperse-phase.

(ii) Systems in the **colloidal state** essentially contain either one or more substances which do have the following *two* critical features, such as:

(a) At least one dimension falling within the range of 10–100 Å* at the **lower end,** and

(b) A few micrometers (mm)** at the **upper end.**

Examples: Various typical examples are as given below:

(i) Blood, milk, rubber latex, cell membranes, thinner nerve fibers, and the thick foam head of beer do represent the colloidal systems squarely.

(ii) Certain specific type of materials, such as: several emulsion types, oral-suspensions of quite a few drugs (insoluble ones) are evidently found to be **coarser than the true colloidal systems,** but eventually display almost identical behavioural pattern. We may come across, certain known product as: **serum albumin, polyvinylpovidone (PVP),** and **acacia** that specifically give rise to either the molecular solutions in water or true solution, whereby the actual size of the prevailing individual solute molecules strategically places these solutions in the colloidal range (particle size of which is greater than 10 Å or 1 nm.***

Colloidal Dispersion Vs Coarse Suspensions

The distinct points of difference between the **colloidal dispersions** and the **coarse suspension** are as enumerated under:

1. Colloidal dispersion particles are invariably too fine to be perfectly visible in a common **Light Microscope** by virtue of the fact that at least one dimension measures either 1 mm of even less.

2. **Colloidal dispersions** are often clearly visible under an **Ultramicroscope**, and always under an **Electron Microscope.**

3. **Coarse suspensions** are abundantly visible even with a naked eye, and always under a **Light Microscope.**

4. **Colloidal suspension particles** as usually opposed to the **coarse suspension particles,** found to pass through ordinary filter paper but are largely retained by either **ultra filtration membranes** or **dialysis.**

5. **Colloidal dispersions** due to their inherent small size virtually undergo no **creaming** or **sedimentation**. However, the ensuing **Brownian Motion** critically maintains the very disperse particles in **suspension form.**

---

* **1 Angstrom Unit** = 10^{-8} cm = 10^{-10} m or $1 - 10$ nm (1 manometer = 10^{-9} m)

** **1 Micrometer** = 10^4 = Å = 10^{-6} m.

*** Hunter RJ: **Foundations of Colloidal Science,** Vol 1, Claremdon Press, Oxford (UK), 1987;

Shaw DJ: **Introduction to Colloid and Surface Chemistry,** Butterworth-Heinemann, Oxford (UK), 1992.

Salient Features of Colloidal Particles

The various **salient features** of the **colloidal particles** are as stated under:

1. Due to the inherent small size of the **colloidal particles** a significant fraction of their respective atoms or ions or molecules are found to be strategically located in the **'boundary layer'** between:

   (*a*) particle and air (surface), and/or

   (*b*) particle and liquid or solid (interface).

2. **Ions** that are critically present in the surface of a **NaCl-crystal** and water molecules very much within the surface of a **'natural rain drop'** are duly exposed to obvious **unbalanced forces of attraction;** and the remaining materials are adequately surrounded by **identical ions** or molecules located on all the sides, having predominantly the so called **'balanced force fields'**. Interestingly, at this stage the skilful incorporation of a **surface free energy component** right into **total free energy of the colloidal particles,** that eventually turns out to be definitely more vital and important because the particles do become distinctly smaller in size *viz*, larger segments of their respective **ions, atoms** or **molecules** are duly positioned in either their **surface** or **interfacial zone.**

Conclusively, the overall solubility of the vapour pressure of extremely **tiny liquid droplets** and extremely fine **solid particles** are invariably observed to be relatively **'bigger'** in comparison to the corresponding values of **large drops** or **coarse particles** of the same substances respectively.

5.6 COPRECIPITATION AND FACTORS AFFECTING COPRECIPITATION

It has been duly proved and established that the **precipitation** obtained in the course of an analysis also take along with them various impurities that are found to be usually quite soluble by themselves.

Example: Sulphuric acid [H_2SO_4] on being incorporated gradually to a specific solution comprising of a mixture of **barium chloride [$BaCl_2$}** and **ferric chloride [$FeCl_3$],** one may commonly expect only **barium sulphate [$BaSO_4$]** to be duly precipitated. However, this is not the exact realistic status of the situation *i.e.,* the other salt **ferric sulphate [$Fe_2(SO)_3$]*** is water-soluble. In actual practice, however, this salt is also precipitated partially. Therefore, one may distinctly observe that when the ensuing precipitate is duly filtered/washed/ignited, the resulting precipitate is not absolutely white in appearance (*i.e.,* the original colour of $BaSO_4$) but would look more or less brownish on account of **ferric oxide [Fe_2O_3],** that is eventually formed by the actual decomposition of ferric sulphate [$Fe_2(SO_4)_3$] upon ignition, as given below:

$$Fe_2(SO_4)_3 \longrightarrow Fe_2O_3 + 3SO_3\uparrow$$

$$\text{Ferric sulphate} \qquad \text{Ferric oxide} \qquad \text{Sulphur trioxide}$$
$$\text{(Red)} \qquad \text{(Escapes)}$$

Thus, **coprecipitation** may be defined as **'the precipitation of any extraneous substances, that are not usually precipitated under the given conditions by the precipitant used'.**

Coprecipitation *Vs* **Chemical (ordinary) Precipitation:** Coprecipitation is easily distinguished from the **chemical (ordinary) precipitation** of the **'sparingly soluble impurities'** along with the major component, when their **solubility products [K_{sp}]** are adequately exceeded upon the careful incorporation of the precipitant.

---

* **Ferric sulphate** may be generated almost simultaneously.

Example: **Precipitation of Al^{3+} ion by NH_4OH in the presence of Fe^{3+} ion:** In true sense, Al^{3+} ion gets precipitated from a solution comprising of Fe^{3+} ion also by the help of NH_4OH solution; and, therefore, one may critically observe that $Fe(OH)_3$ should always be precipitated together with $Al(OH)_3$ due to the fact that its solubility product $[K_{sp}]$ gets exceeded predominantly.

Obviously, this particular effect may not be considered as coprecipitation of $Fe(OH)_3$ by virtue of the fact that the said product would have been duly precipitated by NH_4OH even in the **'absolute absence'** of Al^{3+} **ions.**

Importance

Coprecipitation reposes enormous importance in the ever-expanding field and **'analytical chemistry'**, which may be summarized as under:

1. It usually gives to the most vital and important **'sources of error'** in the **gravimetric analysis** due to the fact that a certain precipitate (in weighed state) essentially comprising of the so called **coprecipitated impurities.** Categorically fails to represent an absolutely **pure substance** having a known, definite, and perfect **chemical formula.***

> **Note:** Hence, analytical chemists or pharmaceutical analysists must take adequate measures to minimize the degree of coprecipitation of impurities to the bare minimum level and also the precipitant itself.

2. Coprecipitation's most positive role in the analytical practice may be visualized when the actual concentration of a specific substance in solution is low which cannot be ordinarily precipitated in the usual routine manner. Logically, therefore, the effective coprecipitation of this type of a **microcomponent**** with the aid of an appropriate **collector*** may be induced in such instances.

Example: **Determination of Pb^{2+} in potable water analysis:** In actual practice, the **microcomponents** (*e.g.,* Pb^{2+}) may be duly concentrated rather quickly and in simplified manner by careful and effective coprecipitation with appropriated **collectors** one may make use of **calcium carbonate ($CaCO_3$)** as the **collector** and the precipitate generated by the incorporation of **sodium carbonate [Na_2CO_3]** solution to the water sample. In this manner, virtually all the Pb^{2+} **ions** duly present in water sample are more or less completely precipitated along with $CaCO_3$. In a situation, whereby the small quantum of precipitate is filtered off and adequately dissolved in the **minimum possible quantum** of either acetic acid [CH_3COOH] or hydrochloric acid [HCl] a solution is obtained wherein the **concentration of Pb^{2+} ions** is almost thousands or even tens of the thousands times greater than the **'original water sample.'**

> **Note:** Assay of Pb^{2+} ion this type of 'sample' poses no problems at all.

Factors affecting coprecipitation: In actual practice, there are in all **five** cardinal factors which may eventually affect the phenomenon of **coprecipitation,** namely:

---

* Unless and until one comes to know about the **'exact chemical formula'** of the investigative precipitate it is quite impossible to calculate the precise quantum of the element being assayed.

** **Microcomponent:** Component that is present in a very low concentration.

*** **Collector:** It means carrier.

(*i*) Effect of the Adsorbent Area,

(*ii*) Effect of Concentration,

(*iii*) Effect of Temperature,

(*iv*) Effect of Nature of Adsorbed Ions, and

(*v*) Effect of Precipitation Conditions.

Each of the aforesaid factors will be treated individually in the sections that follows:

5.6.1 Effect of the Adsorbent Area

As we know that the analytes or ions or materials (under investigation) are duly adsorbed upon the **surface of the adsorbent**, the exact quantum of a substance adsorbed by a given adsorbent is found to be **directly proportional** to the availability of the **total surface area of the adsorbent.** Therefore, one may safely conclude that the phenomenon of **adsorption** actually renders most significant and important in the **pharmaceutical analysis** when one happens to deal with **specific amorphous precipitates**. This is also due to the fact that the particles in such precipitates are actually generated by the process of **'aggregation'** of a plethora of **small primary particles** thereby giving rise to an exceptionally **huge surface areas.**

5.6.2 Effect of Concentration

In reality, the adsorption of various analytes or ions enhances with an increase of their respective concentrations in solution. Nevertheless, the apparent increase is not directly proportional to the concentration but is observed to be slower as depicted in Figure 5.2.

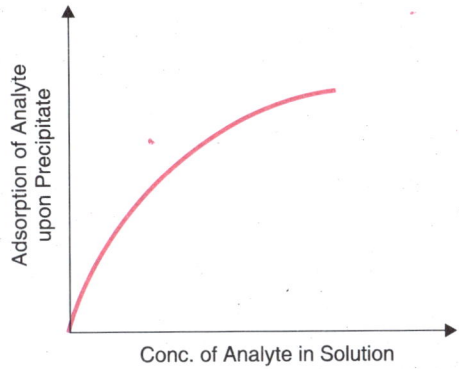

Fig. 5.2 Adsorption Variant of an Analyte with Concentration.

5.6.3 Effect of Temperature.

It is an universal truth that **'adsorption'** happens to be an **exothermic phenomenon**: and therefore, it must be duly supported as well as favoured by an appropriate decrease of temperature. On the contrary, a definite rise of temperature will always favour **'desorption'**, so that the precise quantum of the analyte adsorbed gets decreased substantially.

5.6.4 Effect of Nature of Adsorbed Ions

It has been observed that the phenomenon of **adsorption** is invariably characterized by a **high degree of selectivity.** Thus, a specific adsorbent usually absorbs certain **analytes** or **ions** very much in preference to others under the identical experimental parameters. Following is the guiding rule that is observed critically in most of the typical cases:

'**Adsorbents with ionic crystal lattices are found to absorb ions preferentially that generate either weakly dissociated or sparingly soluble compound having oppositely charged ions strategically located in the lattice; in particular, ions common with the precipitate.**'

Example: Following are some glaring examples:

(*a*) **Barium sulphate [BaSO$_4$]** precipitate preferentially adsorbs very much its own common ions *viz*, Ba^{2+} and SO_4^{2-}, that exclusively depends which of the two said ion is duly present in the solution in abundance. However, amongst the **extraneous ions**, the nitrate ions [NO_3^-] are invariably adsorbed more predominantly in comparison to the corresponding **chloride ions** [**Cl$^-$**] due to fact that the salt **barium nitrate [Ba(NO$_3$)$_2$]** is distinctly less soluble in comparison to **barium chloride [BaCl$_2$].**

(*b*) Likewise, the precipitate of **silver iodide [AgI]** very much adsorbs preferentially the Ag^+ and I^- ions.

(*c*) **Gegenions or Counter-Ions:** It has been amply proved and established as well that the adsorption of any ions by a specific precipitate adequately confers upon the corresponding electric charge upon the particles of the said precipitate; and therefore, each and every particle critically attracts the **oppositely charged ions** usually termed as the **Gegenions** or the **Counter-Ions.**

Example: **Adsorption of Ag^- and NO_3^- ions, by AgCl precipitate as Crystals:**

In a situation when an AgI precipitate to be in contact with silver nitrate [AgNO$_3$] solution the particles of the precipitate gets positively charged by the adsorption of **Ag^+ ions** and adequate attraction of the **NO_3^- ions** as the **counter-ions** or **Gegenions.** Thus, one may also pronounce that AgI precipitate gets overwhelmingly contaminated with the adsorbed AgNO$_3$.

In short, there exists prominently *two* distinct types of **adsorption,** namely:

(*a*) **Primary Adsorption:** In this particular instance the ensuing precipitate categorically adsorbs either its **own ions** or **ions** that may duly replace them **isomorphously.*** Here, the absorbed ions usually forms a single layer upon the surface of the precipitate particles, and ultimately confer either a +ve or –ve charge upon them, as shown in Figure 5.3.

(*b*) **Secondary Absorption:** As a consequence of the **primary adsorption,** the **secondary adsorption** of ions bearing the opposite ions *i.e.,* **counter-ions** or **Gegenions** by the respective particles. Ultimately, these ions do remain in solution and give rise to the **prominent diffuse layer** (Fig. 5.3) in the vicinity of the particle surfaces. Besides, it emphatically enhances at a tremendous speed with **increased charge of the adsorbed ions** together with the **reduced solubility** of the **adsorption compound generated.**

---

* Substances are said to be '**isomorphous**' in case they may crystallize with the formation of a joint crystal lattice *i.e,* mixed crystals.

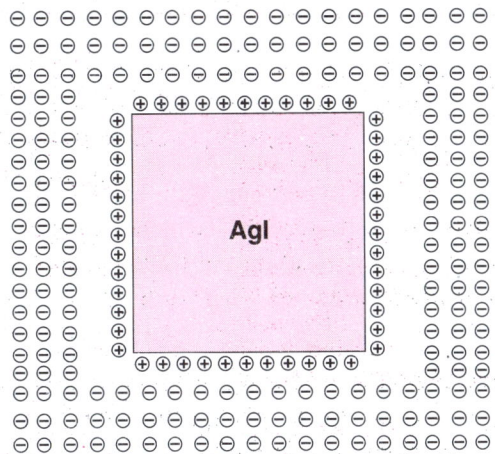

Fig. 5.3 Adsorption of Na$^+$ and NO$_3^-$ ions by Crystals of AgI Precipitate.

5.6.5 Effect of Precipitation Conditions

In actual practice one may observe that **adsorption** gets overwhelmingly influenced by the various **experimental parameters.**

Examples: Various befitting examples are as cited below:

(a) **Concentration of reacting solutions** play a significant role, whereby it is rather easier and more convenient to obtain the precipitate of **amorphous materials** *viz,* aluminium hydroxide [Al(OH)$_3$], ferric hydroxide [Fe(OH)$_3$]. These substances are usually obtained from relatively concentrated solutions based on the fact rather **denser precipitates of smaller surface area are formed** and, hence, they do **adsorb much lesser extraneous ions.** Contrarily, it is always preferred to precipitate the crystalline materials from the corresponding diluted solutions because relatively larger crystals are duly generated having a **smaller specific surface** *vis-a-vis* the **same weight of small size crystals.**

(b) **Ageing of crystalline precipitates** involves essentially an enhancement of the actual particle size; besides, the effective crystallization of the particles prominently with formation of rather highly perfect crystals. In a broader perspective the **'ageing of crystalline precipitates'** must give rise to definite partial removal of the particular adsorbed impurities from the ultimate precipitates.

5.7 POST-PRECIPITATION

Post precipitation usually refers to **'the explicitly deposition of an impurity from solution in a situation when the solution and the precipitate are duly left in contact with each other for a certain duration.'**

It may be further expatiated by the help of the following beautiful **examples:**

(a) **Separation of Group IV and Group III cations by Hydrogen Sulphide [H$_2$S] in an Acidic Medium:** Evidently, the precipitate formed initially is absolutely from **zinc sulphide [ZnS];**

however, if the filtration is performed after a certain lapse of time from **precipitation,** the precipitate is duly contaminated with ZnS by virtue of **post-precipitation** during the usual standing operation.

Causation of Post-precipitation: The precise reasons to cause **post-precipitation of ZnS** is due to the particular adsorption of the **sulphide ions [S^{2-}]** from the solution by the respective particles of the Group IV sulphide precipitates, in order that the concentration of these ions more or less becomes reasonably higher on the particle surfaces than the corresponding particles present in the solution. Interestingly, as the **rate of precipitation** solely depends upon it may not be quite out of place to expect and predict the actual separation of **ZnS precipitate** from the ensuing **supersaturated solution** very easily upon the precipitated particles of other sulphides.

(b) **Post-precipitation of Magnesium Oxalate [MgC_2O_4]:** When the calcium oxalate [CaC_2O_4] precipitate is allowed to remain in contact with a mother liquor comprising of **Mg^{2+} ions,** one may observe that the **magnesium oxalate [MgC_2O_4]** gets duly **postprecipitated** by virtue of the presence of adsorbed **oxalate ions [$C_2O_4^{2-}$]** strategically upon the particles of the prevailing **calcium oxalate [CaC_2O_4] precipitate.**

5.8 PRECIPITATION FROM HOMOGENEOUS SOLUTION

Gordon *et at* (1959)* critically observed that the **precipitation from a homogeneous solution** is invariably used to prevent and check the phenomenon of **supersaturation**. In reality, the **'precipitating agent'** is predominantly generated very much within the solution by the aid of a **homogeneous reaction,** whose rate is quite similar to that essentially required for the precipitation of the **specific species.**

5.9 CHOICE OF PRECIPITANTS [or PRECIPITATING REAGENTS]

In usual practice, the wide-spectrum of the **gravimetric precipitants** are invariably accomplished using a plethora of specific **organic reagents.** Although there are certain well recognized and profusely documented classical examples using particularly the **'inorganic reagents'**, for instance:

(a) Determination of Pb^{2+} as **Chromate, and**

(b) Determination of Ba^{2+} as **Sulphate**

However, the use of **'organic reagents'** predominantly outnumber the corresponding **inorganic reagents** based on the fact that the former not only possess the expected advantage of generating compounds that are **sparingly soluble besides being invariably coloured,** but also exhibit **high relative molecular masses** that will produce critically a corresponding huge amount of the precipitate from a small amount of the **available ions** being usually measured.

5.9.1 Ideal Organic Precipitants

In reality, the **ideal organic precipitants** should have the following characteristic features:

1. It must be **highly specific in character** *viz.,* it should give rise to a definite precipitate with **only one particular ion**. However, in usual practice the aforesaid ideology is hardly achievable,

---

* Gordon L *et al.*: **Precipitation from Homogeneous Solution,** John Wiley New York, 1959.

instead one would observe the **organic reagent(s)** to react with '**group of ions**' rather than an individual one. Importantly, by the meticulous rigorous control of the ensuing experimental parameters it is now quite feasible and possible to precipitate only one of the ions of the group.

2. Many a times the '**precipitated compound**' can be weighed directly after drying at a **suitable temperature**; whereas, in other particular instances the composition is not quite definite, and ultimately the desired compound is adequately converted by '**ignition**' to the corresponding **oxide of the metal**.

3. The '**titrimetric procedure**' is invariably used in certain particular instances that makes use of the **precipitated organic complex quantitatively**.

Guide to the Application of Organic Reagents: As an acceptable and a recognizable **guide to the acceptability of organic reagents** for various analytical procedures may be duly accomplished by adopting the following means, namely:

(*a*) An elaborative investigative study of the actual formation constant of the respective coordination compound*,

(*b*) The effect of the inherent nature of the '**metallic ion**' and of the '**ligand**' upon the **stability of complexes**, and

(*c*) The stability of the corresponding '**precipitation equilibria**' duly involved, specifically in the ultimate production of '**unchanged chelates**'.

5.9.2 Organic Reagents for Chelate Formation in Metal Analysis

Chelate may be defined as a – '**complex that is formed by the combination of a polyvalent metal ion with a molecule which essentially contains two or more groups that can donate electrons**'.

The following **organic reagents** represent typical of such those employed most frequently for the particular '**chelate formation**' in the **metal analysis:**

1. **Cupferron [$C_6H_9N_3O_2$; Mol. Wt.: 155.15]:**

N-Hydroxy-N-nitrosobenzenamine ammonium salt.

Cupferron helps to precipitate ferric [Fe^{3+}], vanadium [V^{5+}], titanium [Ti^{3+}], ziroconium [Zr^{4+}], cerium [Ce^{4+}], niobium [Nb^{5+}], tantalum [Ta^{5+}], tungsten [W^{6+}], gallium [Ga^{3+}], and tin [Sn^{4+}] — thereby segregating these elements from aluminium [Al^{3+}], beryllium [Be^{2+}], chromium [Cr^{3+}], manganese [Mn^{2+}], nickel [Ni^{2+}], cobalt [CO^{2+}], zinc [Zn^{2+}], uranium [U^{6+}], calcium [Ca^{2+}], strontium [Sr^{2+}], and barium [Ba^{2+}] in both **weakly and strongly acidic solutions**.

---

* It represents a measure of its stability.

2. **Dimethylglyoxime** [*Syn*: **Chugaev's Reagent**] [$C_4H_8N_2O_2$; Mol. Wt.: 116.12]:

$$\begin{array}{c} H_3C \\ C = N - OH \\ | \\ C = N - OH \\ H_3C \end{array}$$

2, 3—Butanedione dioxime.

Dimethylglyoxime produces a distinct **bright red precipitate** with **nickel salt solution** (*i.e.*, complex chelate as given below:

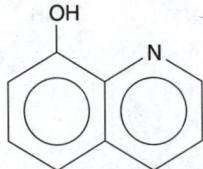

Nickel – Dimethylglyoxime Chelate [Ni(C$_4$H$_7$O$_2$N$_2$)$_2$]

In reality, the brick-red nickel-dimethylglyoxime chelate is duly precipitate in either an ammoniacal solution or a buffer solution comprising of **ammonium ethonate** and **ethanoic acid**. Besides, **Palladium (II) salt solution** produce a distinct and characteristic **yellow precipitate** in either diluted HCl or H_2SO_4 solution.

However, the exact composition of the palladium-dimethylglyoxime complex [Pd (C$_4$H$_7$O$_2$N$_2$)$_2$] is usually found to be very much akin to the aforesaid **nickel-complex**.

3. **8-Hydroxyquinoline** [*Syn*: **8-Quinolinol; Oxychinolin; Oxine;**] [C_9H_7NO; Mol. Wt.: 145.16]:

8-Hydroxyquinoline

Importantly, 8-hydroxyquinoline gives rise to sparingly soluble structural analogues (derivatives) with the metalic ions, that do have the following composition(s), such as:

M (C$_9$H$_6$ON)$_2$:   when the coordination number of the metal stands at 4 *viz.*, Mg; Zn, Cu, Cd, Pb, In.

M (C$_9$H$_6$ON)$_3$:   when the coordination number of the metal stands at 6 *viz.*, Al, Fe, Bi, Ga.

M (C$_9$H$_6$ON)$_4$:   when the coordination number of the metal stands at 8 *viz.*, Th, Zr.

Metal Oxide Oxinates

Exceptions : $TiO (C_9H_6OH)_2$ — Titanium Oxide – Oxine

$MnO_2 (C_9H_6ON)_2$ – Manganese dioxide – oxine

$UO_2 (C_9H_6ON)_2$ – Uranium Oxide – Oxine

$WO_2 (C_9H_9ON)_2$ – Tungston Oxide – Oxine

Table 5.1 records the various pH required essentially for the precipitation and the pH range for the complete precipitation of a series of **metal oxinates:**

S. No.	Metal	Initial Precipitation	Complete Precipitation
Table 5.1 Required pH for Initial Precipitation and pH Range for Complete Precipitation of Various Metal Oxinates			
1	Bismuth	3.7	5.2—9.4
2	Calcium	6.8	9.2—12.7
3	Copper	3.0	> 3.3
4	Lead	4.8	8.4—12.3
5	Magnesium	7.0	> 8.7
6	Molybdenum	2.0	3.6—7.3
7	Thorium	3.9	4.4—8.8
8	Tungsten	3.5	5.0—5.7
9	Vanadium	1.4	2.7—6.1
10	Zinc	3.3	> 4.4

5.10 REQUIREMENTS FOR THE PRECIPITATED FORM

Based upon the copious volume of research and documented evidences it may be concluded that there are *three* cardinal **requirements for the precipitated form**, namely:

1. **Low Solubility: Low solubility** offers a prime requirement without which virtually the complete precipitation either of the given element or the ion is almost impossible. However, the particular solubility of a sparingly soluble electrolyte is duly characterized by its actual **solubility product** (K_{sp})*. It has been critically observed that in the specific instance of the '**binary electrolytes**'** the precipitation gets completed in all respects as long as the **solubility product** of the precipitate fails to exceed 1×10^{-8}. Hence, such compounds whose solubility product is greater than 10^{-8} are invariably not employed as the '**precipitated forms**' in normal **gravimetric analysis**.

2. **Structure of the Precipitate:** In reality, the structure of the precipitate must be such so that the process of **filtration** and **washing** becomes quite rapid and fast. Importantly, the precipitates

---

* Alexeyev V: **Qualitative Analysis**, Sec . 24, Goskhimizdat, 1960.

** Such compounds the molecules of which usually get dissociated into pairs of ions *e.g.*, AgCl, $BaSO_4$.

comprising of relatively large crystals are found to be much more convenient by virtue of the following *two* vital and important plus points:

(*a*) Clogging of the pores in the filter paper are not usually noticeable, and

(*b*) Specific surface is not so extensive which categorically prevents the rapid adsorption of impurities from the solution; and are washed most conveniently free from the latter (*i.e.*, impurities)*.

> **Note: 1. Precipitates usually comprising of very small crystal *e.g.*, calcium oxalate [Ca(C₂O₄)₂];**
> **barium sulphate [BaSO₄] are definitely much less convenient in this particular aspect.**
>
> **2. Improper precipitation may obviously lead to such products that would rapidly gain an access *via* the filter pores.**
>
> **3. Ultimately, the 'precipitated form' should be easily and fairly convertible into the respective 'weighed form' completely, in order to obtain a precise and accurate reproducible result.**

5.11 AMOUNT OF PRECIPITATION REAGENTS [PRECIPITANT] REQUIRED

Precipitation reagents or **precipitants** are referred to as–'**the substances which essentially augment the phenomenon of precipitation**'.

Evidently, in the domain of '**qualitative analysis**' the solution of a specific sparingly-soluble electrolyte turns out to be saturated when the product of the activities (*viz.*, concentrations) of its ions attains a certain value and also remain constant at a given stipulated temperature, commonly termed as the **solubility product [K_{sp}]**.

Example: The above statement of facts may be further expatiated by the following typical examples of '**Lead Sulphate**'.

Therefore, for a lead sulphate [PbSO₄] solution saturated duly at 25°C, we may have the following expression:

$$[Pb^{2+}] [SO_4^{2-}] = SP_{PbSO_4} = 2.2 \times 10^{-8}$$

Now, let us assume that:

$$[Pb^{2+}] [SO_4^{2-}] < 2.2 \times 10^{-8}$$

thus, the resulting solution is **not** completely saturated, and hence certain more quantum of PbSO₄ may be dissolved into the said solution.

In case, one may consider that the **solubility product** gets adequately exceeded at a given temperature 20°C, one would have the following expression:

$$[Pb^{2+}] [SO_4^{2-}] > 2.2 \times 10^{-8}$$

thus, the resulting solution becomes **supersaturated**, and thereby a certain quantum of PbSO₄ should get precipitated automatically.

---

* The entrainmᵉⁿ (withheld) of **impurities** from solution by the precipitates consequent to adsorption is minimized appreciably.

Thus, according to the guiding rule of the solubility product—'**a precipitate is duly obtained only when the product of the activities of the corresponding ions distinctly exceeds the solubility product of the precipitated compound at a given temperature**'.

Explanations

When equal volumes of 0.0001 M **lead nitrate [Pb(NO$_3$)$_2$]** and **sodium sulphate [Na$_2$SO$_4$]** are duly mixed then lead sulphate [PbSO$_4$] is not precipitated. However, when equal volumes of these solutions are adequately mixed the **respective activities** of each of the *two* components (substances) gets simply halved, and ultimately comes out to be 0.0005 M or 5×10^{-5} M. As we know that the '**salts**' are usually **strong electrolytes**; and, therefore, get dissociated practically to completeness in an aqueous medium. In such a situation, each molecule of these salts undergoes dissociation to produce one **Pb^{2+} ion** or one **SO$_4{}^{2-}$ ion**, thereby the activities of these *two* aforesaid ions becomes almost **equal**:

Thus, we may have:

$$[Pb^{2+}] = [SO_4{}^{2-}] = 5 \times 10^{-5} \text{ g. ion. L}^{-1}$$

Therefore, the **ionic product*** in this particular instance, is given by the following expression:

$$[Pb^{2+}] \, [SO_4{}^{2-}] = 5 \times 10^{-5} \times 5 \times 10^{-5}$$

or
$$= 25 \times 10^{-10}$$

or
$$= \mathbf{2.5 \times 10^{-9} \text{ g. ion. L}^{-1}}.$$

Obviously, the **ionic product** of PbSO$_4$ *i.e.*, 2.5×10^{-9} is much less than the **solubility product** of PbSO$_4$ *i.e.*, 2.2×10^{-8}, whereby the resulting solution remains **unsaturated** with regard to PbSO$_4$ itself; and, therfore, this particular salt [PbSO$_4$] never gets precipitated.

Eventually, when the **ionic product** [Pb^{2+}] [SO$_4{}^{2-}$] predominantly **exceeds 2.2 $\times$ 10^{-8}**, the solution evidently gets supersaturated with regard to PbSO$_4$, which finally is duly precipitated. It is, however, pertinent to state here that as the above phenomenon of precipitation comes into being progressively, the activities (*i.e.*, concentrations) of the respective, ions present in the solution slowly undergoes reduction. Thus, as soon as their ionic product almost equalizes to the solubility product for the desired precipitate, the establishment of a **dynamic equilibrium** duly commences between the **two entities**, namely: **precipitate** and **solution**, thereby further precipitation practically comes to a hault.

Nevertheless, the complete precipitation of a specific ion it is obviously required to take a sufficient quantum of the **precipitating reagent** (*i.e.*, **precipitant**). The exact quantity involved may be calculated approximately based upon the reaction involved.

Example: To assay lead (Pb^{2+}) present in lead acetate [Pb(CH$_3$COO)$_2$.3H$_2$O] by the precipitation Pb^{2+} ions with H$_2$SO$_4$.

The following equation takes place:

$$\underset{\text{Lead Acetate Trihydrate}}{Pb(CH_3COO)_2.3H_2O} + \underset{\substack{\text{Sulphuric} \\ \text{acid}}}{H_2SO_4} \longrightarrow \underset{\substack{\text{Lead} \\ \text{sulphate}}}{PbSO_4 \downarrow} + \underset{\text{Acetic Acid}}{2CH_3COOH} + 3H_2O$$

---

* **Ionic Product:** It is the product of the concentration of the ions in solution.

Assuming, that the actual weight of lead acetate trihydrate [Pb(CH$_3$COO)$_2$.3H$_2$O] taken for the assay is 0.6525 g, we may write as follows:

1 mole of [Pb(CH$_3$COO)$_2$.3H$_2$O][equals 1 mole of H$_2$SO$_4$ or 0.6525 g of [Pb(CH$_3$COO)$_2$.3H$_2$O] equals 'x'g of H$_2$SO$_4$.

Rounding off the Quantities

As the above calculations particularly make use of mere approximations, hence a high degree of precision and accuracy is hardly needed. Therefore, the actual quantities in the said calculations may be **rounded off** conveniently. Finally, one may virtually round off the weight of Pb(CH$_2$COO)$_2$. 3H$_2$O to **0.7** g and its corresponding molecular weight to **380**, and that of H$_2$SO$_4$ to **98**. Now, we may rewrite the above cited expressions as follows:

$$380 \text{ g of Pb(CH}_3\text{COO)}_2.3\text{H}_2\text{O equals 98 g of H}_2\text{SO}_4$$

or $\quad$ 0.7 g of Pb(CH$_3$COO)$_2$.3H$_2$O equals 'x' g of H$_2$SO$_4$

Therefore, $$x = \frac{98 \times 0.7}{380} = 0.180 = \textbf{0.2 g}$$

Evidently, the **precipitating reagent (precipitant)** is invariably employed as a solution having a **definite known activity** thereby actually converting the **weight of sulphuric acid** into the corresponding **volume of solution**. In actual practice, however, the **solution activities** are normally expressed in terms of **percentages** *viz.*, (*a*) **moles** (or **molar solutions**), and (*b*) **gram-equivalents** (or **normal solutions**).

Percentage Concentration

The **percentage concentration** of a specific solution refers to the number of grammes of substance present in **100** g (*i.e.*, **percentage weight**) or in **100 mL** (*i.e.*, **percentage volume**) of the solution.

Molar Concentration: The **molar concentration** designates the actual number of **moles** (*i.e.*, **gram molecules**), and the **normal concentration** (*i.e.*, **the number of gramme equivalents. L^{-1} of solution**).

Example: A solution comprising of 15% (by volume) of sulphuric acid (H$_2$SO$_4$) is employed for the precipitation of Pb^{2+} ions. Here, the required volume may be determined by the simple terms of proportionality as given under:

100 mL of solutions contains H$_2$SO$_4$ = 10 g

or $\quad$ x mL of solution contains H$_2$SO$_4$ = 0.2 g

Hence, $$x = \frac{0.2 \times 100}{15} = 1.33 \text{ mL}$$

or $$x = \textbf{1.33 mL}$$

5.12 SALT EFFECT

It has been duly observed and substantiated that the particular solubility product relationship usually holds goods with enough accuracy and precision in order to achieve the cardinal objective of '**quantitative analysis**' solely to the ensuing saturated solutions of slightly soluble electrolytes, along with the presence of relatively small incorporations of some other salts. Therefore, in the very presence of the **moderate concentrations** of the 'salts' one would expect the apparent increase in the 'ionic strength' of the solution. In a broader perspective, this phenomenon will lower the activity coefficients of the **two ions**; and, therefore, there is a definite increase in the overall ionic concentrations so as to maintain a constant **solubility product**. In fact, this specific effect is usually termed as the **salt effect**.

In other words, **the various strong electrolytes that are mostly present in solution invariably enhance the solubilities of such precipitates that intimately remain in contact with them.**

The phenomenon of 'salt effect' may be expatiated with the help of the following **typical example**:

Solubility of Lead Sulphate [PbSO₄]

It has been duly seen that the **solubility of lead sulphate [PbSO₄]** is remarkably and distinguishably much more in the presence of such electrolytic inorganic salts as: potassium nitrate [KNO₃] and sodium nitrate [NaNO₃]; and eventually the recorded increases is much more marked and pronounced with perceptively higher total activities of such salts *i.e.*, the 'salt effect.'

In actual practice, the **product of the ion activities** is more or less **constant** in a saturated solution. The **activity** represents–'**the effective or apparent concentration of an ion, in accordance with which it interacts in a chemical reaction.**

Example: The realistic activities of both H^+ ion and Cl^- ion in a 0.1 M solution of HCl* are found to be **0.1 g-ion. L^{-1}.** Nevertheless, these two ions invariably play their respective roles in a variety of chemical reactions as if their real concentrations stands at **0.0814 g-ion . L^{-1}.**

Thus, we may express the above relationships as under

$$a_{H^+} = a_{Cl^-} = 0.0814 \text{ g-ion. } L^{-1}.$$

where,
$$a = \text{activity}.$$

Activity Coefficient [f_a]**: The **activity coefficient [f_a]** represents the ratio of the activity, '*a*' to the actual concentration, '**C**' of a specific ion. Therefore, in the above cited instance, we may have:

$$f_{H^+} = f_{Cl^-} = \frac{0.0814}{0.1} = 0.814$$

In a generalized manner, we may express above as:

$$f_a = \frac{a}{C} \qquad \qquad ...(i)$$

From Eqn. (*i*) with rearrangement we may have:

$$a = f_a C \qquad \qquad ...(ii)$$

From Eqn. (*ii*) we may duly infer that—

'**the activity of an ion is the product of the concentration and the activity coefficient.**'

---

* In modern concept one believes that HCl is completely dissociated in an aqueous solution.

** Activity coefficient [f_a] is also designated as '*f*' with a subscript showing the formula of the ion.

Let us take another fresh look at the 'salt effect' once more. In doing so one should first and foremost take note that the **solubility product $[K_{sp}]$ rule** in true sense indicates that it does not represent the **product of the ionic concentrations**, but instead the **product of the ionic activities** which remains constant in a **saturated solution**.

Example: **Lead Sulphate $[PbSO_4]$:** In the particular instance of **lead sulphate** the solubility product is given by:

$$a_{Pb^{2+}} \cdot a_{SO_4^{2-}} = SP_{PbSO_4} = CONSTANT \qquad \qquad ...(iii)$$

But, according to Eqn. (*ii*) *i.e.*, $a = f_a C$, we have:

$$a_{Pb^{2+}} = [Pb^{2+}] \, f_{Pb^{2+}}, \text{ and } a_{SO_4^{2-}} = [SO_4^{2-}] \, f_{SO_4^{2-}}$$

Therefore, we may have the following expression:

$$[Pb^{2+}] \, [SO_4^{2-}] \, f_{Pb^{2+}} \, f_{SO_4^{2-}} = SP_{Pb\,SO_4}$$

Hence, the ultimate product of the ensuing ionic concentrations in a saturated $PbSO_4$ solution is given by the following expression:

$$[Pb^{2+}] \, [SO_4^{2-}] = \frac{SP_{Pb\,SO_4}}{f_{Pb^{2+}} \cdot f_{SO_4^{-2}}} \qquad \qquad ...(iv)$$

From Eqn. (*iv*), the actual value of $SP_{Pb\,SO_4}$ is strictly constant at any given temperature. Evidently, the 'activity coefficients' get reduced with enhancement of the ionic strength of the solution. Therefore, any strong electrolyte *viz.*, KNO_3, $NaNO_3$ must lower the values of $f_{Pb^{2+}}$ and $f_{SO_4^{-2}}$, when it is duly incorporated into the solution.

5.13 FACTORS AFFECTING COMPLETENESS OF PRECIPITATION

The **completeness of precipitation** is usually governed by *two* major factors, namely:

(*a*) Effect of temperature upon completness of precipitation, and

(*b*) Effect of pH (H^+ ion concentration) upon completeness of precipitation.

These *two* aforesaid aspects will be treated individually in the section that follows:

5.13.1 Effect of Temperature upon Completeness of Precipitation

It has been well established that the prevalent degree of precipitation is basically established and estimated by the 'actual value of the solubility product' of the given precipitate. In actual practice, however, this product practically remains constant only if the **temperature remains unchanged**. In other words, if the temperature changes the solubility product of the ensuing precipitate also alters accordingly.

The precipitate of potassium tartarate $[KHC_6H_4O_6]$ usually obtained in the cold gets **redissolved on warming**, thereby suggesting profusely that the 'temperature' certainly exerts a predominantly strong influence upon the **completeness of the precipitation**.

Nevertheless, the prevailing effect of temperature upon the precise solubility of precipitates frequently has to be considered even in such instances where the precipitates seldomnly get dissolved completely upon exposure to heat (*i.e.*, heating).

Examples: **Solubility of Silver Chloride [AgCl] at Different Temperature:** In a typical example one may observe the drastic variance in the solubility of AgCl at:

10°C : Solubility as 1,

100°C : Solubility as **25 folds**.

Another suitable example is that of barium sulphate [BaSO$_4$] where the solubility definitely varies with rise in temperature, but not to the high extent at all:

10°C : Solubility as 1,

100°C : Solubility as **2 folds** only.

Factors that affect the **completeness of precipitation** due to heating are namely:

(*a*) **Heat Effect upon Dissolution:** In reality, the alteration of solubility with the temperature is entirely linked to the **heat effect upon dissolution**. In a rather simple but critical observation it is noticed amply that a plethora of salts usually undergo dissolution by rendering the solutions **colder** *viz.*, **heat gets absorbed** (**endothermic phenomenon**). Thus according to the **Le Chatlier Principle**, the observed solubilities of these type of salts must ordinarily rise with temperature. Contrarily, in case **heat is duly liberated** (**exothermic phenomenon**) on the dissolution of a salt, its ultimate **solubility gets reduced** with the **rise in temperature**.

(*b*) **Alteration in Crystal Lattice of Salt:** The **alteration in crystal lattice of salt** *viz*, a *crystalline hydrate*, takes place when it is converted from one form to the other due to the **application of heat**. From this one may safely conclude that the 'hydrate variants' almost react in an altogether different manner with regard to the rise of temperature, and hence the solubility will definitely undergo a 'change' accordingly.

Examples:

(*i*) **Calcium sulphate [CaSO$_4$]:** The aqueous solution of calcium sulphate [CaSO$_4$] at the ambient temperature is found to be in equilibrium with the **precipitate** of its corresponding hydrated salt *i.e.*, **CaSO$_4$.2H$_2$O,** the solubility of which enhances with the rise in temperature. Importantly, at a critical temperature of 60°C, the said hydrate sheds a portion of its inherent '**water of crystallization,** and ultimately gets converted duly into the 'partial hydrate as CaSO$_4$.1/2 H$_2$O. Conclusively, the partial hydrate of CaSO$_4$ *i.e.*, CaSO$_4$.1/2 H$_2$O is observed to be much less soluble at higher temperature in comparison to CaSO$_4$ distinctly shows a maxima at 60°C.

(*ii*) **Magnesium ammonium phosphate [MgNH$_4$PO$_4$], Lead sulphate [PbSO$_4$], and Calcium oxalate [CaC$_2$O$_4$]:** In the specific instance of such precipitates which do exhibit a **solubility** that usually gets enhanced significantly with the temperature, one should cool down the solution first completely before the commencement of '**filtration**' *e.g.,* MgNH$_4$PO$_4$, PbSO$_4$, CaC$_2$O$_4$.

Contrarily, in such cases where the solubility of a precipitate happens to be '**quite low**', and gets altered negligibly with rise in temperature, it is always preferred to filter the precipitate while the solution is still hot (*viz.,* hot liquids usually undergo filtration must faster than the cold ones).

Example: **Ferric hydroxide [Fe(OH)$_3$]**

5.13.2 Effect of pH (H⁺ Ion Concentration) Upon Completeness of Precipitation

The most vital and important factor that actually influence the degree of completeness of precipitation remains the **pH** *i.e.,* the H^+ ion concentration of the solution*. In actual practice, one may come across three highly specific cases that are influenced squarely by pH, namely:

   (*i*) Precipitation of Sparingly Soluble Metal Hydroxides,

   (*ii*) Precipitation of Sparingly Soluble Salts of Weak Acids, and

   (*iii*) Precipitation of Sparingly Soluble Salts of Strong Acids.

   All these *three* aboresaid cases shall now be treated individually as under:

5.13.2.1 Precipitation of Sparingly Soluble Metal Hydroxides

In this particular instance the hydroxide ion $[OH^-]$ serves as the **precipitating ion**. However, its concentration is intimately related to the corresponding H^+ ion concentration as given below:

i.e., $$[H^+]\,[OH^-] = K_{H_2O} = 10^{-14} \text{ at } 22°C \qquad\qquad ...(a)$$

Eqn. (*a*) evidently reveals that the OH^- ion concentration gets reduced drastically with an increase of the H^+ ion concentration *i.e.,* by lowering the pH of the solution. Nevertheless, the ensuing OH^- ion concentration predominantly establishes the legitimate precipitation of a given hydroxide, and the degree of its actual precipitation. From the above statement of facts one may conclude evidently that the 'solubility product of the hydroxide' is directly proportional to the **OH^- ion concentration**' essentially needed for the completeness of the precipitation.

   Therefore, one may easily calculate the pH essentially required for the complete precipitation of a hydroxide from its **solubility product (SP)**.

   Example: **Magnesium Hydroxide [Mg(OH)₂]:** In this case, we may have:

$$[Mg^{2+}]\,[OH^-]^2 = SP_{Mg(OH)_2} = 5 \times 10^{-12}$$

i.e., $$[OH^-] = \sqrt{\frac{SP_{Mg(OH)_2}}{[Mg^{2+}]}} \qquad\qquad ...(b)$$

Assumption: A reasonably good analytical balance (*i.e.,* single-pan electric balance) weights upto **10^{-4} g**, and the average **gramme-molecular weight** of different types of precipitates may be taken as **100 g**. Thus, the precipitation of a substance (**analyte**) is almost complete in case its molar concentration (in solution) at the end of the precipitation virtually stands at 10^{-4}: 100 or **10^{-6} M**. Therefore, the **Mg^{2+} ions** should have this specific concentration at the **completeness of precipitation**.

   From Eqn. (*b*), we may have:

$$[OH^-] = \sqrt{\frac{5 \times 10^{-12}}{10^{-6}}} \simeq 2 \times 10^{-3} \text{ g-ion. } L^{-1}$$

Hence, $$pOH = -\log 2 \times 10^{-3} = -(0.3 - 3) = \mathbf{2.7}$$

i.e., $$pH = 14 - pOH = 14 - 2.7 = \mathbf{11.3}$$

---

* The H^+ ion exponent pH is designated by the logarithms of the H^+ ion concentration with a –ve sign: $pH = -\log [H^+]$.

Based on the ultimate observations of the above cited example it may be infered that the **Mg^{2+} ion** is more or less completely precipitated as its hydroxide [*i.e.,* $Mg(OH)_2$] at **pH = 11.3**. In a situation whereby the **pH is duly enhanced beyond 11.3,** the overall precipitation is even more complete than before, due to the fact that the **Mg^{2+} ion** concentration renders less than **10^{-6} g-ion. L^{-1}**. Interestingly, at a **pH less than 11.3** either the precipitation does not commence at all or it becomes absolutely 'incomplete'.

5.13.2.2 Precipitation of Sparingly Soluble Salts of Weak Acids

It is amply proved that pH dominantly exerts its noticeable influence in the **precipitation of sparingly soluble salts of weak acids**. A few typical examples of such anions are: carbonate [CO_3^{2-}], oxalate [$C_2O_4^{2-}$], phosphate [PO_4^{3-}], and sulphide [S^{2-}]. Interestingly, the aforesaid **anions** do come in close contact with the **H^+ ions** in a solution, and should duly combine to form *two* different types of products at *two* stages, namely:

(*a*) **Stage-1: Formation of still weaker anions** *e.g.*

$$CO_3^{2-} \longrightarrow HCO_3^{-} ; \qquad PO_4^{3-} \longrightarrow HPO_4^{2-} \text{ and } H_2PO_4^{-} ;$$
$$C_2O_4^{2-} \longrightarrow HC_2O_4^{-} ; \qquad S^{2-} \longrightarrow HS^{-} ;$$

i.e., **'weaker anions'** are generated from the parent bivalent/trivalent anions, and undergoes dissociation very slowly.

(*b*) **Stage-2: Formation of undissociated moleculess from anions;** *e.g.,*

$$CO_3^{2-} \longrightarrow H_2CO_3 ; PO_4^{3-} \longrightarrow H_3PO_4 ;$$
$$C_2O_4^{2-} \longrightarrow H_2C_2O_4 ; S^{2-} \longrightarrow H_2S ;$$

i.e., corresponding carbonic acid from CO_3^{2-} (being highly unstable, oxalic acid from $C_2O_4^{2-}$, phosphoric acid from PO_4^{3-}, and hydrogen sulphide from S^{2-} are duly produced, and they usually have a low tendency to undergo dissociation.

Importantly, if both possibilities in (*a*) and (*b*) above are in existence we must determine the pH of the solution accurately so as to establish whether such salts are actually precipitated, and if so, to what extent the precipitation really takes place.

Therefore, according to the stagewise [(*a*) and (*b*) above] observed dissociation of these acids, the recombination of their **anions** with the **hydrogen ion [H^+ ion]** also takes place genuinely in stages, as given under:

(*i*) $HCO_3^{2-} + H^+ \rightleftharpoons HCO_3^{-} [K_2 = 5.6 \times 10^{-11}]$

(*ii*) $HCO_3^{-} + H^+ \rightleftharpoons H_2CO_3 [K_1 = 4.3 \times 10^{-7}]$

From (*i*) above, it is quite evident that **K_2** *i.e.,* the dissociation constant for HCO_3^{-} is significantly lesser in value in comparison to that of the acid (H_2CO_3) having **K_1** (high value). Therefore, a greater proportion of the carbonate [CO_3^{2-}] ion duly added with the excess reagent gets converted into the corresponding bicarbonate [HCO_3^{-}] ions. In other words, a small relative proportion of HCO_3^{-} ion gets further converted into the undissociated H_2CO_3 moles. Realistically, the said proportion may be determined from the following equation:

$$K_1 = \frac{[H^+][HCO_3^{-}]}{[H_2CO_3]}$$

or
$$\frac{K_1}{[H^+]} = \frac{[HCO_3^-]}{[H_2CO_3]} \qquad \qquad ...(p)$$

Eqn. (*p*) obviously signifies that when K_1 is more than $[H^+]$ the HCO_3^- ion concentration should be appreciably higher in comparison to the corresponding concentration of the undissociated carbonic acid $[H_2CO_3]$ molecules. Of course, in such a critical situation one may completely ignore and disregard the actual generation of H_2CO_3 molecules without meeting any significant error. Thus, it may be assumed that:

$$[CO_3^{2-}] + [HCO_3^-] \simeq C$$

where, C = Total concentration of precipitant in the solution at the completeness of precipitation.

5.13.2.3 Precipitation of Sparingly Soluble Salts of Strong Acids

Various supportive and well defined experimental evidences established that the sparingly soluble salts of certain strong monobasic acids *viz.*, AgCl, AgBr, AgI, are adequately precipitated by the respective corresponding anions, such as: chloride $[Cl^-]$ ion, bromide $[Br^-]$ ion, and iodide $[I^-]$ ion. Obviously, these particular **anions** never display any tendency to combine with the available hydrogen $[H^+]$ ions by virtue of the fact that HCl, HBr, and HI are the '**strong acids**' ; and hence are practically dissociated completely in aqueous solution. Perhaps, this could offer the most plausible and acceptable explanation that the extent of precipitation of the '**sparingly soluble salts of these acids**' is found to be absolutely independent of the pH of the existing solution.

Influence of Excess Acid in Solution

One must take into consideration the observed influence of excess acid in solution in some instances due to the underlying fact that the '**salt effect**' gets a boost in the presence of excess acid; besides, in some cases some **complexes**' are duly obtained both from the **acid anions** and the **salt cations** *e.g.*,

$$AgCl + HCl \longrightarrow H [AgCl_2]$$

and this ultimately enhances the solubility of the desired precipitate of AgCl.

Precipitation of Sparingly Soluble Sulphates [SO_4^{2-}]

The analogy is distinctly different in carrying out the precipitation of the '**sparingly soluble sulphates**', because the ensuing dissociation of sulphuric acid $[H_2SO_4]$ is practically complete at the very first stage itself, as given below:

Stage - 1 : $H_2SO_4 \longrightarrow H^+ + HSO_4^-$

Stage - 2 : $HSO_4^- \longrightarrow H^+ + SO_4^{2-}$

Importantly, the **second stage** actually gets through across in a very large extent, since K_2 possesses an extremely high value almost equal to 1.2×10^{-2} ; however, it fails to achieve total completeness of precipitation.

Special Points

These are as stated below:

  1. In a situation, when the **solubility product (SP)** of the ensuing **precipitate** *viz.*, $BaSO_4$, is not too small, and the **H^+ ion concentration** is fairly high, the resulting ions do have a marked

tendency to combine favourably with the available SO_4^{2-} **ions** to yield the **bisulphate [HSO$_4^-$] anions**. Therefore, it evidently shows that the pH of the prevailing solution must not be overlooked or ignored at all in the phenomenon of precipitation of the **sulphates**.

2. The overall actual precipitation of the sparingly soluble sulphates must be less complete in '**acidic solutions**' in comparison to the '**neutral**' or '**alkaline solutions**'. However, this particular effect is more clearly noticeable with the more soluble sulphates, for instance:

Calcium Sulphate [$CaSO_4$] : SP = 6.1×10^{-5} ;

Strontium Sulphate [$SrSO_4$] : SP = 2.8×10^{-7} ;

Lead Sulphate [$PbSO_4$]   : SP = 2.2×10^{-8} ;

Barium Sulphate [$BaSO_4$]   : SP = 1.1×10^{-10} ;

Inspite of the least soluble barium sulphate, it gets precipitated from the **acidic solutions**, since it usually gives rise to the formation of relatively bigger crystals in the precipitate.

Therefore, one may actually arrest the '**increased solubility**'* at the fag-end of the process of precipitation by the careful incorporation of **excess precipitant (or precipitating reagent)**.

5.14 THERMAL DEGRADATIONS AND THERMOGRAVIMETRIC ANALYSES [TGA]

In the traditional or conventional '**gravimetric analysis**' one may critically observe that how '**heat**' may be used skilfully in '**drying a precipitate**'. In this particular context it is extremely vital and important that the '**analyte**' is duly weighed in a **thermal equilibrium** very much within its immediate surroundings. It is, however, pertinent to mention here that the **thermal gravimetric analysis [TGA]** specifically makes use of the '**temperature**' as an extremely critical and vital experimental variable. However, the intensive and extensive **thermal gravimetric investigative studies** are found to be equally meaningful and useful for determining the optimal temperature parameters for drying samples very much within the domain of the so called **conventional gravimetric assays**.

TGA essentially involve the meticulous monitoring of the weight of an '**analyte**' as the temperature is enhanced in a **linear fashion along with time**.

Thermograms: The resulting profiles duly obtained from the mass-temperature observations are commonly termed as **thermograms**.

Principle: A plethora of chemical substances (**analytes**) usually get decomposed on being exposed to thermal (heat) treatment. It is this idea of heating a sample to observe **weight changes** marks the fundamental principle of **thermogravimetric analysis (TGA)**. In fact, **TGA** may be further classified into *two* heads, namely:

5.14.1. Static Thermogravimetric Analysis

In this particular instance the sample under analysis is duly maintained at a constant temperature for a certain specified duration within which any changes in weight are observed carefully.

---

* On account of the presence of acid.

5.14.2 Dynamic Thermogravimetric Analysis

In **dynamic thermogravimetric analysis** an 'analyte' is duly subjected to conditions of predetermined, carefully modulated, continuous increase in temperature which is invariably found to be linear with respect to time.

Instrumentation: The vital and important requirements for an instrument designed for TGA are shown in Figure 5.4, which essentially comprises of the following components, namely:

(*a*) A high-precision balance,

(*b*) A furnace meticulously programmed for a 'linear rise' of temperature with time, and

(*c*) A sensitive recorder.

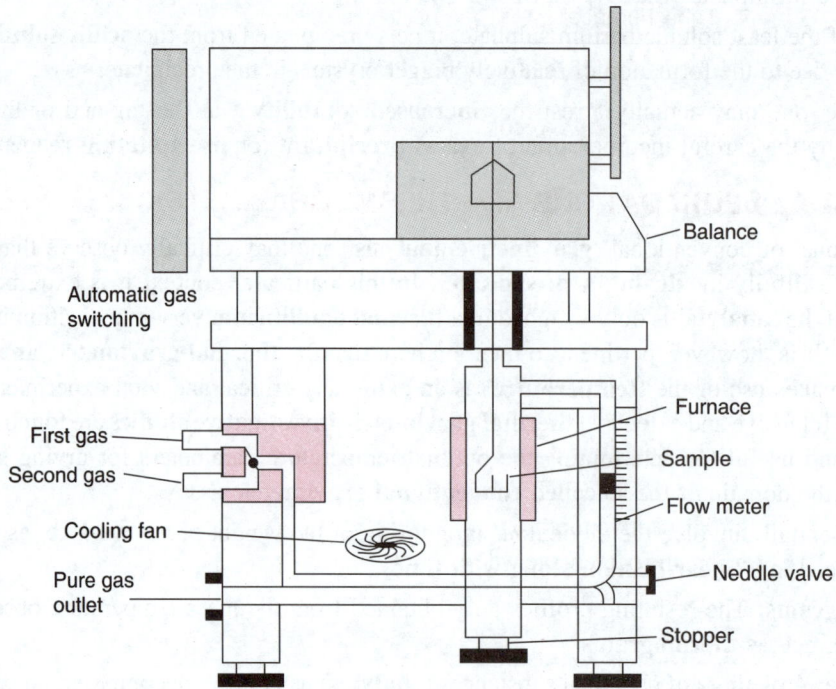

Fig. 5.4 A Thermobalance for Thermogravimetric Analysis in a Controlled Atmosphere upto 1000°C.

Balances: The high-precision **balances** are of *two* types, namely:

(*i*) **Null-Point Type** — It uses a suitable sensing-element that quickly detects any slightest deviation of the balance beam and duly provides the application of a '**restoring force**' directly proportional to the '**variation in weight**', thereby returning the '**beam**' to the original **null-point**. The resulting '**restoring force**' is recorded either by direct means or with the help of a '**transducer**'.

(*ii*) **Deflection Type** — It makes use basically of either an **usual analytical balance** components as – helical spring, cantilever beam, and strain gauze, or a **torsion analytical balance** using the conversion of deviations directly into a record of the observed weight change.

Furnace: The furnace is designed meticulously to incorporate a suitable smooth input to maintain either fixed temperature or a **predetermined linear–heating programme** (*viz.*, from 10° to 600°C per hour).

Temperature control of the furnace is accomplished satisfactorily through a thermocouple strategically mounted in the vicinity of the furnace–winding. However, one may obtain **maximal operational temperature** by employing various thermocouples judiciously as given below:

S.No.	Specifications	Max. Temp. (°C)
1	Nickel-Chrome (Nichrome)	1100
2	Platinum-Rhodium	1450
3	Graphite-Tube Furnace*	> 1500

*Control and measurement of temperatures are not only critical but also problematic in nature.

Recorder: The ideal and effective recorder should be such so as to:

(*i*) record both temperature and weight continuously, and

(*ii*) make a definite periodic record of the time.

Methodology

The 'thermogram' for **calcium oxalate mono hydrate [CaC$_2$O$_4$.H$_2$O]** is illustrated duly in Figure 1.1. (Chapter – 1)

From this figure it is quite obvious that in a '**multicomponent system**' where in more than one component shows weight variations, and that too at different temperature zones, the composition of the original compound may be determined accurately.

However, in a particular instance whereby an '**inert material**' is very much in existence along with a pure analyte, from the respective thermogram the precise composition of the '**original mixture**' may be adequately derived from the percentage weight variation that critically occurs relative to the percentage weight variation as observed with the '**pure analyte**' by using the following expression:

$$\text{Pure Analyte (wt. \%)} = \frac{\% \text{ wt. change for mixture}}{\% \text{ wt. change for pure analyte}}$$

5.15 PHARMACEUTICAL APPLICATIONS OF GRAVIMETRIC TECHNIQUES

In **pharmaceutical analysis** the various techniques of '**gravimetric analysis**' are carried out meticulously in the assay of following substances, namely:

(*i*) Sulphate [SO$_4^{2-}$] — as Barium Sulphate [BaSO$_4$],

(*ii*) Aluminium [Al^{3+}] — as Aluminium Oxide [Al$_2$O$_3$],

(*iii*) Calcium [Ca^{2+}] — as Calcium Oxalate [CaC$_2$O$_4$], and

(*iv*) Magnesium [Mg^{2+}] — as Magnesium Pyrophosphate [Mg$_2$O$_7$P$_2$].

5.15.1 Sulphate [SO$_4^{2-}$] as Barium Sulphate [BaSO$_4$]

The assay of **sulphate [SO$_4^{2-}$] as barium sulphate [BaSO$_4$]** may be accomplished by the gradual incorporation of a diluted solution of barium chloride [$BaCl_2$] into a perceptively hot solution of the 'sulphate' slightly acidified with hydrochloric acid [HCl]. Thus, we have:

$$Ba^{2+} + SO_4^{2-} \longrightarrow BaSO_4 \downarrow$$

The precipitate of barium sulphate [$BaSO_4$] is duly filtered off, thoroughly washed with water (DW), ignited carefully at a red heat, and ultimately weighed as barium sulphate. It is indeed an usual practice to prevent and check the possible formation of the respective barium salts of such anions as: **chromate** [CrO_4^{2-}], **carbonate** [CO_3^{2-}], and **phosphate** [PO_4^{3-}], that are invariably found to be quite insoluble in 'neutral solution'. Besides, the desired precipitate thus obtained usually comprises of relatively bigger crystals ; and, therefore, can be filtered more conveniently.

Salient Features

The **salient features** for the assay of **sulphate ions** are as enumerated under:

1. Importantly, the precipitation should be carried out preferably at the **boiling temperature**, because the extent of **relative supersaturation** is remarkably quite less at **higher temperatures**.

2. Concentration of Cl is very much restricted as well as limited by the observed solubility of **barium sulphate** [$BaSO_4$]; however, at a concentration of **0.05 M** it becomes almost **negligible**.

3. Washing of the ultimate desired precipitate with **cold water (DW)**. Thus, one may grossly ignore or neglect the incurred losses by virtue of the ensuing **solubility influences**, except for the most accurate analytical assays.

4. **Barium Sulphate** [$BaSO_4$] most frequently displays a marked and pronounced tendency to **carry down** other **salts** as well prominently. Thus, the ultimate results would be either **high** or **low** shall solely rest upon the prevailing nature of the final **co-precipitated salt**. In this way, the *two* salts, namely: **barium nitrate** [$Ba(NO_3)_2$] and **barium chloride** [$BaCl_2$] get usually precipitated rapidly.

5. **Highly-erroneous results:** In fact, highly erroneous results would be obtained due to the undue addition of these two salts [$Ba(NO_3)_2$ and $BaCl_2$] into the 'true weight' of desired **barium sulphate** [$BaSO_4$]; besides, the **nitrate** shall yield '**barium oxide**', and the **chloride** remains almost **unchanged** upon ignition.

   (*a*) **Removal of Nitrate Ion [NO_3^-]:** The **nitrate ion** may not be avoided that easily ; and hence, it should always be removed by subjecting it to evaporation along with an excess of HCl before commencing precipitation.

   (*b*) **Removal of Chloride Ion [Cl^-]:** The removal of the Cl^- ion may be substantially afforded by the extremely slow and careful addition of hot diluted $BaCl_2$ solution into the hot sulphate solution.

6. **Pure Barium Sulphate:** It has been duly observed that **pure barium sulphate** fails to undergo decomposition on being heated in absolutely '**dry air**'; however, at a temperature nearly 1400°C it gets decomposed as given below into one mole each of **barium oxide** [BaO] and **Sulphur trioxide** [SO_3]:

$$BaSO_4 \xrightarrow{\text{1400°C}} BaO + SO_3 \uparrow$$

7. **Conversion of BaSO$_4$ to BaS:** The barium sulphate precipitate gets easily converted into its corresponding **barium sulphide** at a prevalent temperature more than 600°C in the presence of **carbon** derived from the filter paper, as stated below:

$$BaSO_4 + 4C \xrightarrow{\text{600°C}} BaS + 4CO \uparrow$$

The aforesaid reduction may be safely circumvented (overcome) by first allowing the charring of the filter paper carefully **without inflaming,** and subsequently burning off the '**carbon**' gradually at a **low temperature** but in an atmosphere of free air.

5.15.2 Aluminium [Al^{3+}] as Aluminium Oxide [Al$_2$O$_3$]

Aluminium [Al^{3+}] may be assayed by complete precipitation with ammonia and subsequent conversion of aluminium hydroxide [Al(OH)$_3$] precipitate to alumina [Al$_2$O$_3$] by direct ignition in a muffle-furnace.

Methodology

The various steps involved are as follows:

1. The requisite amount of the '**analyte**' is first converted into its hydroxide *i.e.*, (Al(OH)$_3$, which being an **amphoteric hydroxide** gets solubilized significantly in an excess of NH$_4$OH. Hence, it is an absolute necessity to allow the complete precipitation of Al^{3+} by adjusting pH of the ensuing solution most carefully*.

2. The gelatinous precipitate of aluminium hydroxide [Al(OH)$_3$] is rather difficult to filter off, and also to wash out the undesired absorbed impurities duly embeded in the precipitate.

3. Aluminium oxide [Al$_2$O$_3$] obtained after careful ignition to red hot and subsequent cooling to the ambient temperature in a desiccator, happens to be an extremely **hygroscopic product** that essentially needs extra precautionary measures to weigh ultimately to the constant weight.

4. Finally, the presence of ammonium hydroxide [NH$_4$OH] is really problematic in the sense that several other **cations** *viz.*, Cu^{2+}, CO^{2+}, Ni^{2+}, Zn^{2+} etc., that **are not** usually prone to precipitation by NH$_4$OH of their own also get predominantly **coprecipitated** together with Al(OH)$_3$; and, therefore, are profusely retained so much so that it is indeed next to impossible to obtain an almost completely pure precipitate of Al(OH)$_3$ even after several reprecipitation procedures.

> **Note: Keeping in view the enormous disadvantages associated with Al$_2$O$_3$ method, it is most preferentially assayed by the precise and accurate precipitation of Al^{3+} with 8-hydroxyquinoline *i.e.*, an organic analytical reagent.**

5.15.3 Calcium [Ca^{2+}] – as Calcium Oxalate [CaC$_2$O$_4$]

The assay of Ca^{2+} is accomplished by its complete precipitation in the form of **calcium oxalate** [CaC$_2$O$_4$]. The latter is duly obtained by the interaction of ammonium oxalate [(NH$_4$)$_2$C$_2$O$_4$] and calcium chloride [CaCl$_2$] as given below:

---

* The solution should be perfectly neutral *i.e.*, pH =- 7, which may be accomplished by carrying out the precipitation in the presence of **Phenol Red** indicator, that has an **orange colour** at this pH.

$$CaCl_2 \;+\; (NH_4)_2\,C_2O_4 \;+\; H_2O \longrightarrow CaC_2O_4 \cdot H_2O \downarrow \;+\; 2NH_4Cl$$

Calcium   Ammonium   Calcium oxalate
chloride   oxalate   monohydrate (I)

Microcrystalline Precipitate of Calcium Oxalate (I)

There is an obvious tendency to obtain the **microcrystalline** form of the precipitate that would most conveniently pass through the filtration medium, thereby rendering the entire procedure unnecessarily complicated and hence cumbersome. Hence, it is extremely important and vital to obtain rather **'sufficiently coarse–grained precipitates of calcium oxalate'**; and this may be achieved quite effectively either from a **slightly super saturated solution** or from an **acid solution** rather than a neutral solution.

Explanation: The oxalic acid $[H_2C_2O_4]$ undergoes dissociation as stated under in *two* different **states:**

Stage-1 : $H_2C_2O_4 \rightleftharpoons H^+ + HC_2O_4^-$

Stage-2 : $HC_2O_4^- \rightleftharpoons H^+ + C_2O_4^{2-}$

The corresponding **dissociation constants** for **stage-1** (*i.e.,* K_1), and that of **stage-2** (*i.e.,* K_2) are as given below:

$$K_1 = \frac{[H^+][HC_2O_4^-]}{[H_2C_2O_4]} = 5.9 \times 10^{-2}$$

$$K_2 = \frac{[H^+][C_2O_4^{2-}]}{[HC_2O_4^-]} = 6.4 \times 10^{-5}$$

Obviously, the **second dissociation stage** gives rise to the formation of the **oxalate $[C_2O_4^{2-}]$ ions** having a value of K_2 which is astonishingly quite negligible *i.e.,* 6.4×10^{-5}. Hence, it may be concluded that when the solution is duly acidified, major proportion of the oxalate $[C_2O_4^{2-}]$ ions duly incorporated into the reaction medium as ammonium oxalate $[(NH_4)_2C_2O_4]$ are adequately combined first as $HC_2O_4^-$ **ions** and subsequently as **free oxalic acid $(H_2C_2O_4)$** as indicated below:

$$C_2O_4^{2-} + H^+ \longrightarrow HC_2O_4^-$$
$$HC_2O_4^- + H^+ \longrightarrow H_2C_2O_4$$

From the above *two* reactions one may safely draw a conclusion that the concentration of the **oxalate $[C_2O_4^{2-}]$ ions** get reduced progressively as the quantum of **H$^+$ ions** are carefully added into the solution. Importantly, one may critically observe that at a considerably higher acidity of the ensuing solution the corresponding concentration of the **solubility product (SP)** of **calcium oxalate $[CaC_2O_4]$** becomes practically not achievable ; and hence absolutely no precipitate is duly generated *i.e.,*

$$SP_{CaC_2O_4} \longrightarrow [Ca^{2+}]\,[C_2O_4^{2-}] = 2.6 \times 10^{-9}$$

At this juncture, if dropwise incorporation of **ammonium hydroxide $[NH_4OH]$** is maintained right into the acidic solution, the **distinct fall in the H$^+$ ion concentration** occurs, whereas the **concentration of the oxalate $[C_2O_4^{2-}]$ ion gains a positive increment.**

Cardinal Points: The various **cardinal points** in the **assay of Ca^{2+} – as calcium oxalate** are as described under:

1. As the product of the *two* concentrations *viz.*, [Ca^{2+}] and [Ca$_2$O$_4$$^{2-}$] becomes **significantly more** than the **solubility product (SP)** of the **desired precipitate**, the latter starts to form gradually.*

2. Precipitation of Ca^{2+} ions is invariably rendered to enhanced completion with corresponding lowering in the H$^+$ ion concentration in solution.

3. At a pH $\geq$ 3.3 the complete precipitation is duly accomplished.

4. In order to precisely detect the critical point at which the pH of the solution attains 4 the ensuing process of precipitation must be carried out using **methyl orange** as **indicator**, that particularly alters its initial colour from **pink** to **yellow** (at the said pH 4).

5. Calcium oxalate [CaC$_2$O$_4$] precipitate is generously water soluble; and, therefore, washing it with water may actually cause an appreciable loss. Hence, it is absolutely necessary to incorporate **oxalate ions** into the '**washing liquid**' so as to minimize the solubility of the desired precipitate.

6. To achieve better results it is always advisable to remove the **chloride [Cl$^-$] ions** by thorough washing, because the effective losses are prevented on account of the inadvertent formation of the **volatile calcium chloride [CaCl$_2$]** in the course of '**ignition**' of the final precipitate.

7. In actual practice, the **ultimate weighed product** in this particular assay is **calcium oxide [CaO]**, that is eventually formed from the **calcium oxalate monohydrate** [CaC$_2$O.H$_2$O] between 900 to 1200°C by the aid of the following reaction:

$$CaC_2O_4 . H_2O \rightleftharpoons CaO + CO_2 \uparrow + CO \uparrow + H_2O \uparrow$$

8. **Disadvantage of Calcium Oxide [CaO]:** The major critical disadvantage of calcium oxide **[CaO]** is due to the fact that it is highly hygroscopic in nature, and hence very much prone to **adsorb carbon dioxide [CO$_2$]** from the atmosphere; and, therefore, appropriate precautionary measures must be taken in the **final weighing procedure**. Besides, the actual percentage content of **calcium [Ca^{2+}]** duly present in **CaO**** is quite high and hence detrimental in nature.

Remedial Measures: The following **remedial measure** may be adopted and adhered to strictly:

It is quite often preferred to convert **CaC$_2$O$_4$.H$_2$O** first into **calcium carbonate [CaCO$_3$]** by careful **ignition** at nearly 500°C or alternatively into **calcium sulphate** [CaSO$_4$] by subsequent treatment with sulphuric acid [H$_2$SO$_4$] solution, and ultimate removal of the excess of acid by careful evaporation, and **final ignition** of the dried residue.

5.15.4 Magnesium [Mg^{2+}] – as Magnesium Pyrophosphate [Mg$_2$O$_7$P$_2$]

The assay to **magnesium [Mg^{2+}]** as the **magnesium pyrophosphate [Mg$_2$O$_7$P$_2$]** may be accomplished with utmost accuracy and precision by **gravimetric analysis**.

---

* Since, NH$_4$OH is being incorporated dropwise, the C$_2$O$_4$$^{2-}$ ion concentration rises in a gradual manner. Hence, the actual precipitation usually starts from a solution very negligibly supersaturated with calcium oxalate, and the crystals do grow adequately.

** That is, the prevailing **conversion factor** is also high.

In this specific instance the **phosphate [PO$_4^{3-}$] ions** essentially needed to **precipitate magnesium [Mg^{2+}] ions** are judiciously incorporated in the form of **disodium hydrogen phosphate** [Na$_2$HPO$_4$] (which being basic in nature), and the requisite **ammonium** [NH$_4^+$ ions are duly loaded with NH$_4$OH. The chemical reaction taking place may be expressed as under:

$$MgSO_4 + Na_2HPO_4 + NH_4OH \longrightarrow MgNH_4PO_4 \downarrow + Na_2SO_4 + H_2O$$

Importantly, when the precipitate of **magnesium ammonium phosphate [MgNH$_4$PO$_4$]** is carefully ignited it apparently loses a mole each of **ammonia [NH$_3$]** and **water [H$_2$O]**, which ultimately represents the weighed form: Thus, we may have the following expression:

$$2\ MgNH_4PO_4 \longrightarrow Mg_2O_7P_2 + NH_3 \uparrow + H_2O \uparrow$$

Ammonia gets partially dissociated in an aqueous medium as given below:

$$NH_4OH \rightleftharpoons NH_4^+ + OH^-$$

However, the actual dissociation constant of NH$_4$OH is quite small, namely:

$$K = \frac{[NH_4^+][OH^-]}{[NH_4OH]} = 1.79 \times 10^{-5}$$

It is, however, pertinent to state here that the **hydroxyl [OH$^-$]** concentration by virtue of the presence of ammonia is quite enough for the **ionic product [Mg^{2+}] [OH$^-$]^2** to supersede the **solubility product (SP)** of Mg(OH)$_2$, that stands at 25°C to be 5×10^{-12}. Therefore, it suggests vehemently that **magnesium hydroxide [Mg(OH)$_2$]** may get precipitated along with desired compound **magnesium pyrophosphate [Mg$_2$O$_7$P$_2$]**; and hence, the ultimate result would be grossly erroneous (wrong). Therefore, in order to prevent, check, and minimize the '**gross error**' it is advisable to incorporate **ammonium chloride [NH$_4$Cl]** in the course of the entire process of precipitation. However, the NH$_4$Cl shall exert the '**common-ion effect**' predominantly along with NH$_4$OH, which overwhelmingly suppresses the undesired dissociation of the latter.

Crystalline Precipitate of Magnesium Pyrophosphate [Mg$_2$O$_7$P$_2$]

In order to arrive at a reasonably good quality crystalline precipitate of **magnesium pyrophosphate [Mg$_2$O$_7$P$_2$]**, it is meticulously precipitated from **HCl solutions** essentially comprising of **disodium hydrogen phosphate [Na$_2$HPO$_4$]** and **ammonium chloride [NH$_4$Cl]** by incorporating a diluted solution of NH$_4$OH gradually. In this manner, the acid *i.e.*, HCl, gets neutralized primarily, and subsequently the precipitated of Mg$_2$O$_7$P$_2$ is formed adequately.

5.16 APPLICATIONS OF GRAVIMETRIC ANALYSIS IN ASSAY OF DRUGS

There are several assays mentioned in the '**Official Compendia**' *viz.*, USP, BP, IP, Int.P., Eur. P; that may be carried out by adopting the method of '**gravimetric analysis**'. A few typical examples shall now be discussed briefly in the sections that follows:

5.16.1 Assay of Papaverine Hydrochloride Tablets

The underlying principle for the assay of **papaverine hydrochloride tablets** is very simple, wherein the alkaloidal base (*viz.*, **papaverine**) is adequately extracted with at least three to four successive times with chloroform. The combined chloroform layer is thoroughly washed with DW, aqueous washings again extracted with $CHCl_3$, and mixed with the main-bulk of chloroform layer. The excessive quantum of the solvent is carefully removed (distilled off) under vacuum till it gets reduced to a '**small volume**'. About 2-3 mL of absolute ethanol is now added and then evaporated to complete dryness, and the residue (mainly **papaverine**) is carefully dried to constant weight at 105°C.

Calculations:

$$C_{20}H_{21}NO_4.HCl \equiv C_{20}H_{21}NO_4$$

or $374.45g\ C_{20}H_{21}NO_4.HCl \equiv 339.0\ g\ C_{20}H_{21}NO_4$

or $1.105g\ C_{20}H_{21}NO_4.HCl \equiv 1g\ of\ C_{20}H_{21}NO_4$

i.e., 1 g of dried residue (papaverine) is equivalent to 1.105 g of $C_{20}H_{21}NO_4.HCl$.

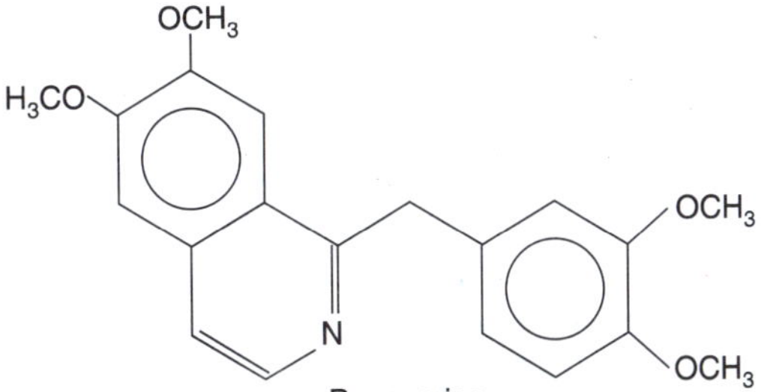

Papaverine
[$C_{20}H_{21}NO_4$; M.wt : 339]

5.16.2 Assay of Amodiaquine Hydrochloride

Theory: Amodiaquine hydrochloride essentially possesses 2 moles of inherent water of crystallization; and, therefore, the percentage base (*viz.*, **amodiaquine**) is precisely calculated with reference to the dried substance over phosphorus pentoxide [P_2O_5] at a pressure not exceeding 5 mn Hg. In usual practice, the assay is carried out on one segment of the '**analyte**', whereas the drying on an altogether separate portion.

Nevertheless, the entire process is based upon the precipitation of **amodiaquine base** which is produced quantitatively as a precipitate when the salt is duly decomposed in an aqueous medium with dilute ammonia [NH_4OH].

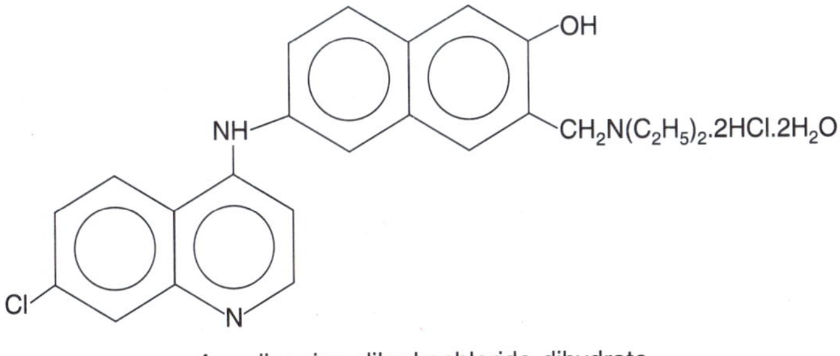

Amodiaquine dihydrochloride dihydrate
[$C_{20}H_{22}ON_3Cl.2HCl.2H_2O$; M.Wt. 464.35]

Calculations

$$464.35g\ C_{20}H_{22}ON_3Cl.2HCl.2H_2O \equiv 355.4\ g\ C_{20}H_{22}ON_3$$

or 1.306 g $C_{20}H_{22}ON_3Cl. 2HCl . 2H_2O \equiv 1$ g of $C_{20}H_{22}ON_3$

i.e., 1 g of dried residue (amodiaquine) is equivalent to 1.306 g of $C_{20}H_{22}ON_3$.

RECOMMENDED READINGS

Day RA (Jr.) and Underwood AL: **Quantitative Analysis**, Prentice-Hall of India Pvt Ltd., New Delhi, 1993.

Erdey L: **Gravimetric Analysis, International Series of Monographs in Analytical Chemistry**, Vol . 7, Pergamon Press, London (UK), 1965.

Everett DH: **Basic Principles of Colloid Science,** Royal Society of Chemistry, London (UK), 1988.

Hawkins MD: **Calculations in Volumetric and Gravimetric Analysis**, Butterworth, London (UK), 1970.

Higson SPJ: **Analytical Chemistry**, Oxford University Press, New Delhi, 2005.

Laitinen HH and Harris WE: **Chemical Analysis**, McGraw-Hill, New York, 2nd edn, 1975.

Mendham J *et al.:* **Classical Methods of Chemical Analysis**, A COL-Wiley, Chichester (UK), Vol. II, 1987.

Nielson AE: **Precipitates: Formation, Coprecipitation, and Aging**, In: **Treatise on Analytical Chemistry**, Kolthoff LM and Elving PJ (eds.), Interscience Publishers, New York, Vol. 3, 2nd.edn., 1983.

Paulik F: **Special Trends in Thermal Analysis**, John Wiley, Chichester (UK), 1995.

Smith WF: **Analytical Chemistry of Complex Matrices**, John Wiley, Chichester (UK), 1996.

Tyson J: **Analysis**, Royal Society of Chemistry, London, 1994.

Wineforder JD *et al.*: **Treatise on Analytical Chemistry**, 2nd. edn. Vol.13, Part1, **Thermal Methods**, John Wiley, Chichester (UK), 1998.

PROBABLE QUESTIONS

1. (*a*) What do you understand by the **Gravimetric** (or **Mass-Based) Analysis**? What are its specific advantages.

    (*b*) Discuss the theoretical aspects of **Gravimetric Analysis.**

2. Explain the various **Precipitation Techniques** in termes of the following procedural aspects:

    (*i*) Solution Preparation   (*ii*) Precipitaion

    (*iii*) Digestion or Ostwald Ripening   (*iv*) Filtration

    (*v*) Washing   (*vi*) Ignition

    (*vii*) Weighing to constant weight.

3. What is the importance of 'Colloidal State' in the domain of **Gravimetric Analysis**? Explain explicitly.

4. What do we mean by the term 'Coprecipitation'? Enumerate the various vital factors affecting the phenomenon of **Coprecipitation**. Explain with suitable examples.

5. Discuss the 'Choice of Precipitants' in the exclusive **Gravimetric Analysis**. Give examples.

6. What are the cardinal requirements for the 'Precipitated form' in **Gravimetric Analysis**? Support your answer with typical examples.

7. Give a detailed account with regard to the **Amount of Precipitation Reagents** required to accomplish the **Gravimetric Analysis** effectively.

8. What is the importance of **Salt Effect** in **Gravimetric Analysis**? Explain with appropriate examples wherever necessary.

9. Describe the effect of:

    (*a*) Temperative; and (*b*) pH

    upon the 'Completeness of Precipitation' in carrying out the **Gravimetric Analysis.** Give examples.

10. Write a **detailed account** on:
    (*a*) Thermal Degradations,
    (*b*) Thermogravimetric Analyses (TGA)

11. Discuss the **Pharmaceutical Applications** of Gravimetric Analysis in the **Assay** of drugs:
    (*a*) Papaverine Hydrochloride Tablets
    (*b*) Amodiaquine Hydrochloride

12. Applications of **Gravimetric Techniques** in the **quantitative determination** of:
    (*i*) Sulphate Ion $[SO_4^{2-}]$ – as Barium Sulphate
    (*ii*) Aluminium Ion $[Al^{3+}]$– as Aluminium Oxide
    (*iii*) Calcium Ion $[Ca^{2+}]$ – as Calcium Oxalate
    (*iv*) Magnesium Ion $[Mg^{2+}]$ – as Magnesium Pyrophosphate

    Discuss the above with reactions and salient features.

Appendix I
International Atomic Masses*

Name	Symbol	Atomic Number	Atomic Mass
Actinium	Ac	89	[227]
Aluminium	Al	13	26.981538 (2)
Americium	Am	95	[243]
Antimony	Sb	51	121.760(1)
Argon	Ar	18	39.948(1)
Arsenic	As	33	74.92160(2)
Astatine	At	85	[210]
Barium	Ba	56	137.327(7)
Berkelium	Bk	97	[247]
Berylium	Be	4	9.012182(3)
Bismuth	Bi	83	208.98038(2)
Boron	B	5	10.811(7)
Bromine	br	35	79.904(1)
Cadmium	Cd	48	112.411(8)
Calcium	Ca	20	40.078(4)
Californium	Cf	98	[251]
Carbon	C	6	12.0107(8)
Cerium	Ce	58	140.116(1)
Cesium	Cs	55	132.90545(2)
Chlorine	Cl	17	35.4527(9)
Chromium	Cr	24	51.9961(6)
Cobalt	Co	27	58.933200(9)
Copper	Cu	29	63.546(3)
Curium	Cm	96	[247]
Dysprosium	Dy	66	162.50(3)
Einsteinium	Es	99	[252]
Erbium	Er	68	167.26(3)
Europium	Eu	63	151.964(1)

Name	Symbol	Atomic Number	Atomic Mass
Fermium	Fm	100	[257]
Fluorine	F	9	18.9984032(5)
Francium	Fr	87	[223]
Gadolinium	Gd	64	157.25(3)
Gallium	Ga	31	69.723(1)
Germanium	Ge	32	72.61(2)
Gold	Au	79	196.96655(2)
Hafnium	Hf	72	178.49(2)
Helium	He	2	4.002602(2)
Holmium	Ho	67	164.93032(2)
Hydrogen	H	1	1.00794(7)
Indulim	In	49	114.818(3)
Iodine	I	53	126.90447(3)
Iridium	Ir	77	192.217(3)
Iron	Fe	26	55.845(2)
Krypton	Kr	36	83.80(1)
Lanthanum	La	57	138.9055(2)
Lawrencium	Lr	103	[262]
Lead	Pb	82	207.2(1)
Lithium	Li	3	6.941(2)
Lutetium	Lu	71	174.967(1)
Magnesium	Mg	12	24.3050(6)
Manganese	Mn	25	54.938049(9)
Mendelevium	Md	101	[258]
Mercury	Hg	80	200.59(2)
Molybdenum	Mo	42	95.94(1)
Neodymium	Nd	60	144.24(3)
Neon	Ne	10	20.1797(6)
Neptunium	Np	93	[237]
Nickel	Ni	28	58.6934(2)
Niobium	Nb	41	92.90638(2)
Nitrogen	N	7	14.00674(7)
Nobelium	No	102	[259]
Osmium	Os	76	190.23(3)
Oxygen	O	8	15.9994(3)
Palladium	Pd	46	106.42(1)
Phosphorus	P	15	30.973761(2)
Platinum	Pt	78	195.078(2)
Plutonium	Pu	94	[244]

Name	Symbol	Atomic Number	Atomic Mass
Polonium	Po	84	[209]
Potassium	K	19	39.0983(1)
Praseodymium	Pr	59	140.90765(2)
Promethium	Pm	61	[145]
Protactinium	Pa	91	231.03588(2)
Radium	Ra	88	[226]
Radon	Rn	86	[222]
Rhenium	Re	75	186.207(1)
Rhodium	Rh	45	102.90550(2)
Rubidium	Rb	37	85.4678(3)
Ruthenium	Ru	44	101.07(2)
Samarium	Sm	62	150.36(3)
Scandium	Sc	21	44.955910(8)
Selenium	Se	34	78.96(3)
Silicon	Si	14	28.0855(3)
Silver	Ag	47	107.8682(2)
Sodium	Na	11	22.989770(2)
Strontium	Sr	38	87.62(1)
Sulfur	S	16	32.0066(6)
Tantalum	Ta	73	180.9479(1)
Technetium	Tc	43	[98]
Tellurium	Te	52	127.60(3)
Terbium	Tb	65	158.92534(2)
Thallium	Tl	81	204.3833(2)
Thorium	Th	90	232.0381(1)
Thulium	Tm	69	168.93421(2)
Tin	Sn	50	118.710(7)
Titanium	Ti	22	47.867(1)
Tungsten	W	74	183.84(1)
Uranium	U	92	238.0289(1)
Vanadium	V	23	50.9415(1)
Unnilennium	Une	109	[266]
Unnilhexium	Unh	106	[263]
Unniloctium	Uno	108	[265]
Unnilpentium	Unp	105	[262]
Unnulquadium	Unq	104	[261]
Unnilseptium	Uns	107	[262]
Ununnilium	Uun	110	[269]
Unununium	Uuu	111	[272]

Xenon	Xe	54	131.29(2)
Ytterbium	Yb	70	173.04(3)
Yttrium	Y	39	88.90585(2)
Zinc	Zn	30	65.39(2)
Zirconium	Zr	40	91.224(2)

*The 1995 values from the IUPAC World Wide Web page at http:// www. chem.qmw.ac.uk/iupac/AtWt/ Numbers in parentheses indicate the uncertainty in the last digit of the atomic masses. Values enclosed in brackets for example [209], indicate the mass number of the longest-lived isotope of the element. Three such elements (Th, Pa and U) do have a characteristic terrestrial isotopic composition, and for these elements, an atomic mass is tabulated. For a detailed discussion of the values in this table, see *Pure Appl. Chem.*, **1996**, 68, 23339.

Appendix II
Formula Weights

AgBr	187.77	$CuSO_4$		159.61
AgCl	143.32	$Fe\ (NH_4)_2\ (SO_4)_2.\ 6H_2O$		392.14
AgI	234.77	FeO		71.85
$AgNO_3$	169.87	$FeSO_4$		151.91
AgSCN	165.95	Fe_2O_3		159.69
$Al\ (C_9H_6NO)_3$		$Fe_2(SO_4)_3$		399.88
(Al quinolinate)	459.44	Fe_3O_4		231.54
$AlCl_3$	133.34	HCl		36.46
$Al(NO_3)_3$	213.00	$HClO_4$		100.46
$Al(OH)_3$	78.00	HNO_3		63.01
Al_2O_3	101.97	$(HOCH_2)_3\ CNH_2$ (THAM)		121.14
As_2O_3	197.84	$HONH_3Cl$		69.49
$BaCl_2$	208.24	$(HO_2C)_2$ (oxalic acid)		90.04
$BaCl_2.2H_2O$	244.27	$(HO_2C)_2.2H_2O$		
$BaCrO_4$	253.32	(oxalic acid)		126.07
BaS	169.40	HO_2CH (formic acid)		46.03
$BaSO_4$	233.39	HO_2CCH_3 (acetic acid)		60.05
$Ba_3(PO_4)_2$	601.93	HO_2CCHCl_2		
C_2H_5OH	46.07	(dichloroacetic acid)		128.49
$C_9H_{12}O_6$ (glucose)	180.16	$(HO_2CCH_2)_2\ C(OH)$		
$CO(NH_2)_2$ (urea)	60.06	CO_2H (citric acid)		192.13
CO_2	44.01	HO_3SNH_2 (sulphamic acid)		97.09
$CaCO_3$	100.09	H_2O		18.02
CaC_2O_4	128.10	H_2O_2		34.01
$CaC_2O_4.H_2O$	146.11	H_2SO_4		98.08
$CaCl_2$	110.98	H_3BO_3		61.83
CaO	56.08	H_3PO_4		98.00
$CaSO_4$	136.14	$HgCl_2$		271.50
$CuCl_2$	134.45	Hg_2Cl_2		472.90
CuO	79.55	KBr		119.00

KCN	65.12	NaH_2PO_4	119.98
KCL	74.55	$NaNO_2$	69.00
$KHC_8H_4O_4$ (KHPhthalate)	204.22	NaOCl	74.44
$KH(IO_3)_2$	389.91	NaOH	40.00
KH_2PO_4	136.09	NaO_2CCH_3	
KI	166.00	(sodium acetate)	82.03
KIO_3	214.00	$Na_2B_4O_7$	201.22
$KMnO_4$	158.03	$Na_2B_4O_7$ $10H_2O$	381.87
KNO_3	101.10	Na_2CO_3	105.99
KOH	56.11	$Na_2C_2O_4$	134.00
KSCN	97.18	Na_2HPO_4	141.96
$K_2Cr_2O_7$	294.18	$Na_2H_2Y.2H_2O$	
K_2HPO_4	174.18	(Y = EDTA)	372.24
Li_2SO_4	109.95	Na_2SO_3	126.04
$MgCO_3$	84.31	Na_2SO_4	142.04
$Mg(C_9H_6NO)_3$		$Na_2S_2O_4$	158.11
(Mg quinolinate)	456.76	$Na_2S_2O_3.$ $5H_2O$	248.19
$MgCl_2$	95.21	Na_3PO_4	163.94
$MgSO_4$	120.37	$Pb(NO_3)_2$	331.21
$Mg_2P_2O_2$	222.55	$PbSO_4$	303.26
MnO_2	86.94	SO_2	64.06
NH_3	17.03	SO_3	80.06
NH_4HF_2	57.04	Sb_2S_3	339.70
NH_4Cl	53.49	$SnCl_2$	189.62
NH_4NO_3	80.04	SnO_2	150.71
$(NH_4)_2C_2O_4.2H_2O$	160.13	$Th(IO_3)_4$	931.65
$(NH_4)_2Ce(NO_3)_6$	548.23	ThO_2	264.04
$(NH_4)_2SO_4$	132.14	TiO_2	79.88
N_2H_2	32.05	Tl_2CiO_4	524.76
NaBr	102.89	U_3O_8	842.08
NaCN	49.01	V_2O_5	181.88
NaCl	58.44	$ZnCO_3$	125.40
NaF	41.99	$Zn_2P_2O_7$	304.72
$NaHCO_3$	84.01	$Zr (HPO_4)_2$	283.18
		ZrP_2O_7	265.17

Appendix III
Compounds for Preparing Standard Solutions

Element	Compound	Formula weight (g)	1000 ppm* (g/L)	Sol. Net	Comments
Aluminium	Al metal	26.982	1.0000	Hot, dil.HCl	b
Antimony	KSbOC$_4$ H$_4$O$_6$.H$_2$O	333.92	2.7427	Water	e
Arsenic	As$_2$O$_3$	197.84	2.6406	Dil.HCl	a, i
Barium	BaCO$_3$	197.35	1.4369	Dil.HCl	
Bismuth	Bi$_2$O$_3$	465.96	1.1148	HNO$_3$	
Boron	H$_3$BO$_3$	61.833	5.7200	Water	f
Bromine	KBr	119.00	1.4894	Water	b
Cadmium	CdO	128.40	1.1423	HNO$_3$	
Calcium	CaCO$_3$	100.09	2.4972	Dil. HCl	a
Cerium	(NH$_4$)$_2$Ce(NO$_3$)$_6$	548.23	3.9126	Water	
Chromium	K$_2$Cr$_2$O$_7$	294.18	2.8290	Water	a
Cobalt	Co metal	58.933	1.0000	HNO$_3$	b
Copper	Cu metal	63.546	1.0000	Dil.HNO$_3$	b
	CuO	79.545	1.2517	Hot HCl	b
Fluorine	NaF	41.988	2.2101	Water	c
Germanium	GeO$_2$	104.60	1.4410	Hot 1M NaOH	
Gold	Au metal	196.97	1.0000	Hot Aqua Regia	b
Iodine	KIO$_3$	214.00	1.6863	Water	a
Iron	Fe metal	55.847	1.0000	Hot HCl	b
Lanthanum	La$_2$O$_3$	325.82	1.1728	Hot HCl	
Lead	Pb (NO$_3$)$_2$	331.21	1.5985	Water	b
Lithium	Li$_2$CO$_3$	73.890	5.3243	HCl	b
Magnesium	MgO	40.304	1.6583	HCl	
Manganese	MnSO$_4$H$_2$O	169.01	3.0764	Water	g
Mercury	HgCl$_2$	271.50	1.3535	Water	
Molybdenum	MoO$_3$	143.94	1.5003	1 M NaOH	
Nickel	Ni metal	58.69	1.0000	Hot HNO$_3$	b
Palladium	Pd metal	106.42	1.0000	Hot HNO$_3$	

Element	Compound	Formula weight (g)	1000 ppm* (g/L)	Sol. Net	Comments
Phosphorus	KH_2PO_4	136.09	4.3937	Water	
Platinum	K_2PrCl_4	415.12	2.1278	Water	
Potassium	KCl	74.551	1.9065	Water	b
	$KHC_8H_4O_4$	204.22	5.2228	Water	a. i
	$K_2Cr_2O_7$	294.18	3.7618	Water	a. i
Scandium	Sc_2O_3	137.91	1.5339	Hot HCl	
Selenium	Se metal	78.96	1.0000	Hot HNO_3	
Silicon	Si metal	28.086	1.0000	Conc. NaOH	
	SiO_2	60.085	2.1391	HF	
Silver	$AgNO_3$	169.87	1.5748	Water	b d
Sodium	NaCl	58.442	2.5428	Water	a
	$Na_2C_2O_4$	134.00	2.9146	Water	a. i
Strontium	$SrCO_3$	147.63	1.6849	HCl	b
Sulphur	K_2SO_4	174.27	5.4351	Water	b
Thallium	Ti_2CO_3	468.75	1.1468	Water	
Tin	Sn metal	118.71	1.0000	HCl	
	SnO	134.71	1.1348	HCl	
Titanium	Ti metal	47.88	1.0000	9M H_2SO_4	b
Tungsten	$Na_2WO_42H_2O$	329.86	1.7942	Water	h
Uranium	UO_2	270.03	1.1344	HNO_3	
	U_3O_6	842.08	1.1792	HNO_3	a. i
Vanadium	V_2O_5	181.88	1.7852	Hot HCl	
Zinc	ZnO	81.39	1.2448	HCl	b

Weight of substance per liter to give an element concentration of 1000 ppm.

a : Primary standard.

b : These compounds conform very well to the criteria and approach primary standard quality.

c : Sodiumn fluoride solutions will etch glass and should be freshly prepared.

d : When kept dry. silver nitrate crystals are not affected by light solutions of silver nitrates should be stored in brown bottles?

e : Antimony potassium tartrate loses the H_2O with drying at 110° C. After drying f.e.w. 324.92, 1000 ppm-2. 6687. The water is not rapidly regained, but the compound should be kept in a dessicator after drying and should be weighed quickly once it is removed. The edried compound is water soluble.

f : Boric acid may be weighed accurately directly from the bottle. It will lose one H_2O_2 molecule at 100°C and a second H_2O_2 molelcule at approximately 130-140°C and is different to dry to a constant weight.

g : $MnSO_4$. H_2O may be dried at 110°C without losing the water of hydration.

h : Sodium tungstate loses both water molecules at 110°C. After drying f. w. = 293.83 1000 ppm = 1.5982 g. The weight is not rapidly regained but the compound should be kept in a desiccator after drying and should be weighed quickly once it is removed.

i : These compounds are sold as primary standards by the National Bureau of Standards Office of Standards Reformer Materials.

Appendix IV
Acronyms and Abbreviations of Significance in Pharmaceutical Analysis

Acronym or Abbreviation	Name
AED	Atomic Emission Detector
AES	Atomic Emission Spectroscopy
AES	Auger Electron Spectroscopy
AFM	Atomic Force Microscopy
AFS	Atomic Fluorescence Spectroscopy
ALU	Arithmetic Logic Unit
amu	Atomic Mass Unit
AOAC	Association of Official Analytical Chemists
AOTF	Acousto-Optic Tunable Filter
ASCII	American Standard Code for Information Interchange (computers)
ASTM	American Society for Testing Materials
ASV	Anodic Stripping Voltammetry
ATR	Attenuated Total Reflectance
BCD	Binary-Coded Decimal
BJT	Bipolar Junction Transistor
BUN	Blood Urea Nitrogen
CARS	Coherent Anti-Stokes Raman Spectroscopy
CCD	Charge-Coupled Device
CE	Capillary Electrophoresis
CGE	Capillary Gel Electrophoresis
CHC	Chlorinated Hydro Carbons
CI	Chemical Ionization source
CID	Charge-Injection Device
CIEF	Capillary Iso Electric Focusing electrophoresis
CITP	Capillary Iso TachoPhoresis
CL	Chemi Luminescence

Acronym or Abbreviation	Name
CL	Confidence Level
CL	Confidence Limit
CMC	Critical Micelle Concentration
CMRR	Common Mode Rejection Ratio
CPU	Central Processing Unit
CRT	Cathode Ray Tube
CSP	Chiral Stationary Phase partition chromatography
CT	Computerized Tomography
CTD	Charge Transfer Detector
CV	Cyclic Voltammetry
CVD	Chemical Vapour Deposition
CW	Continuous Wave (laser)
CZE	Capillary Zone Electrophoresis
DAC	Digital-to-Analog Converter
DBR	Distributed Bragg Reflector
DCP	Direct Current Plasma
DCPMS	Direct Current Plasma Mass Spectrometry
DCU	Decade Counting Unit
DMCS	Di Methyl Chloro Silane
DME	Dropping Mercury Electrode
DMM	Digital Multi-Meter
DNA	Deoxyribo Nucleic Acid
DPV	Differential Pulse Voltammetry
DRIFTS	Diffuse Reflectance Infrared Fourier Transform Spectroscopy
DSC	Differential Scanning Calorimetry
DTA	Differential Thermal Analysis
DVM	Digital Volt-Meter
EAAS	Electrothermal Atomic Absorption Spectrometry
EAROM	Electrically Alternable Read Only Memory
EC	ElectroChromatography
ECD	Electron Capture Detector
EDL	Electrodeless Discharge Lamp
EDTA	Ethylene Diamine Tetraacetic Acid
EDXFS	Energy Dispersive X-ray Fluorescence Spectroscopy
EI	Electron Impact, as in EI MS
ELSD	Evaporative Light Scattering Detector
EMI	Electro Magnetic Induction

Acronym or Abbreviation	Name
EMR	Electro Magnetic Radiation
EOF	Electro Osmotic Flow
EPA	Environmental Protection Agency
EPROM	Electronically Programmable Read Only Memory
ERT	Electrical Resistance Tomography
ESCA	Electron Spectroscopy for Chemical Analysis; same as XPS
ESI	Electro Spray Ionization mass spectrometry
ESR	Electron Spin Resonance Spectroscopy
ETAAS	Electro Thermal Atomic Absorption Spectroscopy
ETAFS	Electro Thermal Atomic Fluorescence Spectroscopy
ETV	Electro Thermal Vaporization
FAAS	Flame Atomic Absorption Spectroscopy
FAB	Fast Atom Bombardment (MS)
FD	Field Desorption
FDA	Food and Drug Administration
FDJ	Free Diffusion Junction
FES	Flame Emission Spectroscopy
FET	Field Effect Transistor
FFP	Fiberoptic Fabry-Perot interferometer
FI	Field Ionization (MS)
FIA	Flow Injection Analysis
FID	Flame Ionization Detector
FID	Free Induction Decay
FL	Fluorescence
FPD	Flame Photometric Detector
FSOT	Fused Silica Open Tubular column
FT	Fourier Transform
FTIR	Fourier Transform Infrared Spectroscopy
FT/NMR	Fourier Transform Nuclear Magnetic Resonance
FTIR-PAS	Fourier Transform InfraRed Photo Acoustic Spectroscopy
FTMS	Fourier Transfrom Mass Spectrometry
FTNMR	Fourier Transform Nuclear Magnetic Resonance
FWHM	Full Width at Half Maximum
FY	Fiscal Year
GC	Gas Chromatography
GC/FTIR	Gas Chromatography/Fourier Transform Infra Red spectrometry
GC/IR	Gas Chromatography/InfraRed spectroscopy

Acronym or Abbreviation	Name
GC/MS	Gas Chromatography/Mass Spectroscopy
GD	Glow Discharge
GDAAS	Glow Discharge Atomic Absorption Spectroscopy
GDAES	Glow Discharge Atomic Emission Spectroscopy
GDMS	Glow Discharge Mass Spectroscopy
GLC	Gas-Liquid Chromatography
GSC	Gas-Solid Chromatography
HCL	Hollow Cathode Lamp
HDME	Hanging Drop Mercury Electrode
HETP	Height Equivalent to a Theoretical Plate
HPLC	High-Performance Liquid Chromatography
IC	Ion Chromatography
ICP	Inductively Coupled Plasma
ICP-AES	Inductively Coupled Plasma-Atomic Emission Spectroscopy
ICPMS	Inductively Coupled Plasma-Mass Spectroscopy
IEC	Ion Exchange Chromatography
IEF	Iso Electric Focusing
IMA	Immuno Assay
IR	InfraRed
ISE	Ion Selective Electrode
ISFET	Ion-Selective Field Effect Transistor
ITD	Ion Trap Detector
ITMS	Ion Trap Mass Spectrometry
IUPAC	International Union of Pure and Applied Chemistry
LA	Laser Ablation
LAN	Local Area Network
LASS	Laser Spark Spectrometry
LC	Liquid Chromatography
LC/MS	Liquid Chromatography/Mass Spectroscopy
LCD	Liquid Crystal Display
LCEC	Liquid Chromatography with Electrochemical Detection
LD	Laser Desorption source
LED	Light Emitting Diode
LIBS	Laser-Induced Breakdown Spectroscopy
LIF	Laser-Induced Fluorescence
LIFI	Laser-Induced Fluorescence Imaging
LIMS	Laboratory Information Management Systems

Acronym or Abbreviation	Name
LIMS/DM	Laboratory Information Management Systems/Data Management
LIMS/SM	Laboratory Information Management Systems/Sample Management
LLL	Lawrence Livermore Lab
LMMS	Laser Microprobe Mass Spectrometry
LOD	Limit of Detection
LOGS	Laser Opto Galvanic Spectroscopy
LOL	Limit of Linearity
LOQ	Limit of Quantitation
LOW	Liquid Observation Well
LSB	Least Significant Bit
LSER	Linear Solvation Energy Relationships
MALDI	Matrix-Assisted Laser Desorption/Ionization
MDMI	Monodisperse Dried Microparticulate Injector
MECC	Micellar Electrokinetic Capillary Chromatography
MIP	Microwave-Induced Plasma Source
MIPMS	Microwave-Induced Plasma Soruce, Mass Spectrometry
MOSFET	Metal Oxide Semiconductor Field Effect Transistor
MRI	Magnetic Resonance Imaging
MS	Mass Spectrometry
MS/MS	Mass Spectrometry/Mass Spectrometry
MSB	Most Significant Bit
MSD	Mass Selective Detector (now called simply MS)
NAA	Neutron Activation Analysis
NAPL	Non-Aqueous Phase Liquid
NBS	National Bureau of Standards (the predecessor to **NIST**)
NIH	National Institutes of Health
NIR	Near InfraRed spectroscopy
NIST	National Institute of Standards and Technology
NMR	Nuclear Magnetic Resonance
NRL	Naval Research Lab
NSF	National Science Foundation
NSOM	Near-field Scanning Optical Microscopy
OA	Operational Amplifier
ODS	Octo Decyl Silane
ONR	Office of Naval Research
op amp	Operational Amplifier
OSHA	Occupational Safety and Health Administration

Acronym or Abbreviation	Name
OT	Open Tubular
PAGE	Poly Acrylamide Gel Electrophoresis
PAH	Polynuclear Aromatic Hydrocarbons
PAS	Photo Acoustic Spectrometry
PAWS	Portable Acoustic Wave Sensor
PC	Paired-ion Chromatography
PC	Paper Chromatography
PCE	Per Chloro Ethylene
PCF	Plasma Centrifugal Furnace
PD	Plasma Desorption
PDA	Photo Diode Array
PI	Principal Investigator
PID	Photo Ionization Detector
PITTCON	Pittsburgh Conference on Analytical Chemistry and Applied Spectroscopy
PLOT	**Porous Layer Open Tubular Column**
PLS	Partial Least Squares
PM	Photo Multiplier tube
PMT	Photo Multiplier Tube
PNA	Poly Nuclear Aromatics
ppm	Parts Per Million
PROM	Program Read Only Memory
QCM	Quartz Crystal Microbalance
R&D	Research and Development
RAM	Random Access Memory
RID	Refractive Index Detector
ROM	Read Only Memory
RPC	Reverse Phase Chromatography
RRS	Resonance Raman Spectroscopy
RSD	Relative Standard Deviation
RTR	Real-Time Radiography
SAW	Surface Acoustic Wave
SCD	Sulfur Chemiluminescence Detector
SCE	Saturated Calomel Electrode
SCF	Super Critical Fluid
SCOT	Support Coated Open Tubular
SCP	Scanning Probe microscopy
SDS	Sodium Dodecyl Sulfate

Acronym or Abbreviation	Name
SEAC	Society for Electro Analytical Chemistry
SEC	Size Exclusion Chromatrography
SEM	Scanning Electron Microscope
SERS	Surface Enhanced Raman Spectroscopy
SFC	Supercritical Fluid Chromatography
SFE	Supercritical Fluid Extraction
SGE	Slab Gel Electrophoresis
SHE	Standard Hydrogen Electrode
SIMS	Secondary Ion Mass Spectrometry
SNR (or S/N)	Signal-to-Noise Ratio
SPE	Solid Phase Extraction
SPM	Scanning Probe Microscopy
SSMS	Spark Source Mass Spectrometry
STM	Scanning Tunneling Microscope (or Microscopy)
STNG	Sealed-Tube Neutron Generator
STP	Standard Temperature and Pressure
TA	Thermal Analysis
TCD	Thermal Conductivity Detector
TCE	Tri Chloro Ethylene
TDGC/MS	Time Domain Gas Chromatography/Mass Spectrometry
TDR	Time Domain Reflectometry
TFR	Thin Film Resonators
TG	Thermo Gravimetry
TGA	Thermo Gravimetric Analysis
TID	Thermlonic Detector
TIMS	Thermal Ionization Mass Spectrometry
TIRS	Transient InfraRed Spectroscopy
TISAB	Total Ionic Strength Adjusting Buffer
TLC	Thin-Layer Chromatography
TMA	Thermo Mechanical Analysis
TMS	Tetra Methyl Silane
TOF	Time-Of-Flight mass spectroscopy
TS	Thermospray Source
UPS	Ultraviolet Photoelectron Spectroscopy
USDA	United States Department of Agriculture
USGS	United States Geological Survey
UV	Ultra Violet

VOC	Volatile Organic Compound
VOST	Volatile Organic Sampling Train
VTVM	Vaccum Tube Volt Meter
WCOT	Wall Coated Open Tubular column
XES	X-Ray Emission Spectrometry
XFS	X-Ray Fluorescence Spectroscopy
XPS	X-Ray Photoelectron Spectroscopy
XRF	X-Ray Fluorescence
YAG	Yttrium Aluminium Garnet
ZDV	Zero Dead Volume

Index